THE CLASH

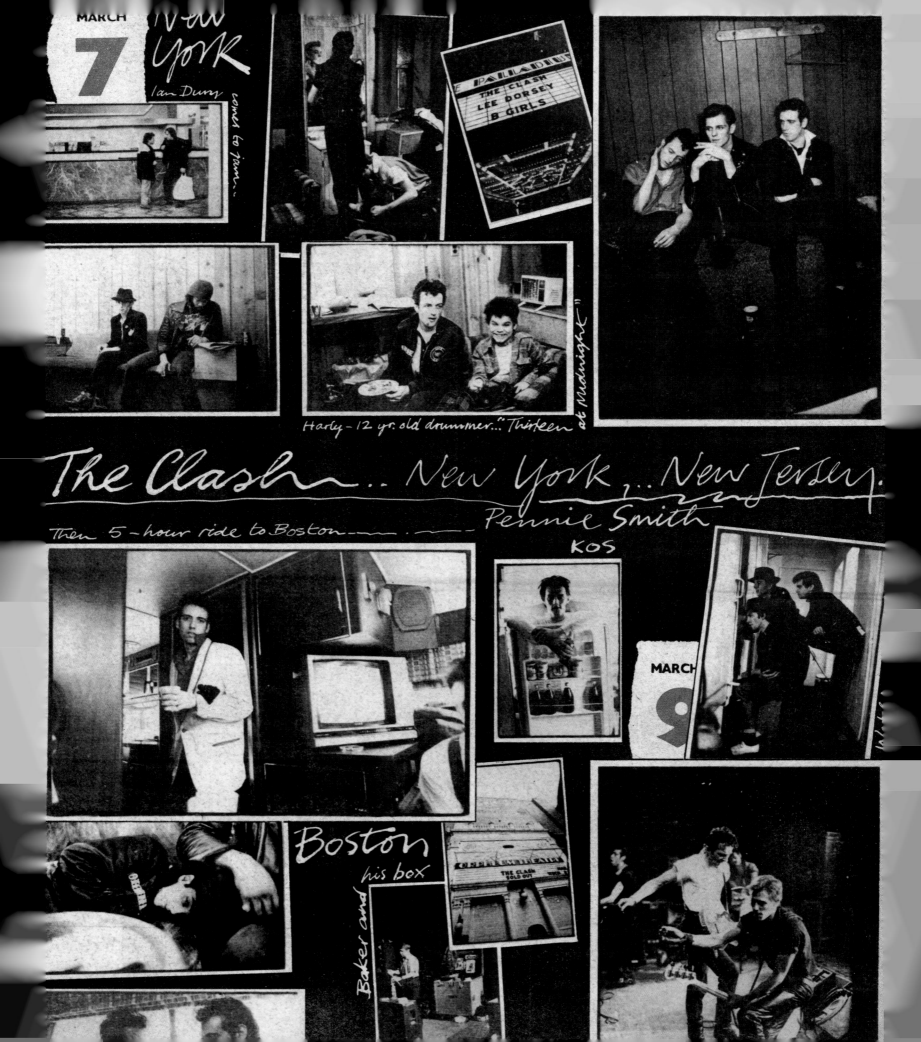

MARCH 7 New York
Ian Dury comes to town...

THE PALLADIUM
THE CLASH
LEE DORSEY
B GIRLS

Harley — 12 yr. old drummer... "Thirteen at Midnight"

The Clash... New York,.. New Jersey.
Pennie Smith
Then 5-hour ride to Boston——.

KOS

MARCH 9

Boston
his box

Baker and

THE CLASH

STRUMMER | JONES | SIMONON | HEADON

GRAND CENTRAL
PUBLISHING

New York   Boston

Grand Central Publishing
Hachette Book Group USA
237 Park Avenue
New York, NY 10017

Visit our Web site at
www.HachetteBookGroupUSA.com.

First Edition: November 2008

10 9 8 7 6 5 4 3 2 1

Executive Producer: Tricia Ronane
www.theclash.com

Produced for Grand Central Publishing
by Essential Works Ltd
www.essentialworks.co.uk

All interviews conducted by Mal Peachey.

Editor: Mal Peachey
Design: Kate Ward
Picture research: Nikki Lloyd

Grand Central Publishing is a division
of Hachette Book Group USA, Inc.

The Grand Central Publishing name and logo is
a trademark of Hachette Book Group USA, Inc.

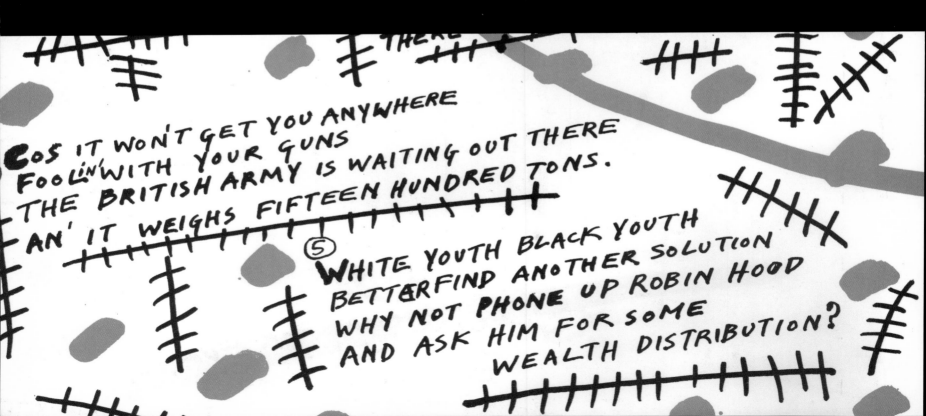

Introduction

by the Editors

In 1976, not long after Joe Strummer and Mick Jones had begun to write songs together for their band The Clash, they came up with 1977. The lyrics take us through the years from 1977 to 1984, demanding a world without Elvis, the Beatles and the Rolling Stones. It was the perfect punk song; iconoclastic, fast, angry, catchy as hell, and oddly prophetic. As Mick Jones comments in his interviews for this book, The Clash as we knew them – with the line-up of Strummer, Jones, Simonon and Headon – truly began in 1977. And by 1984 they were finished.

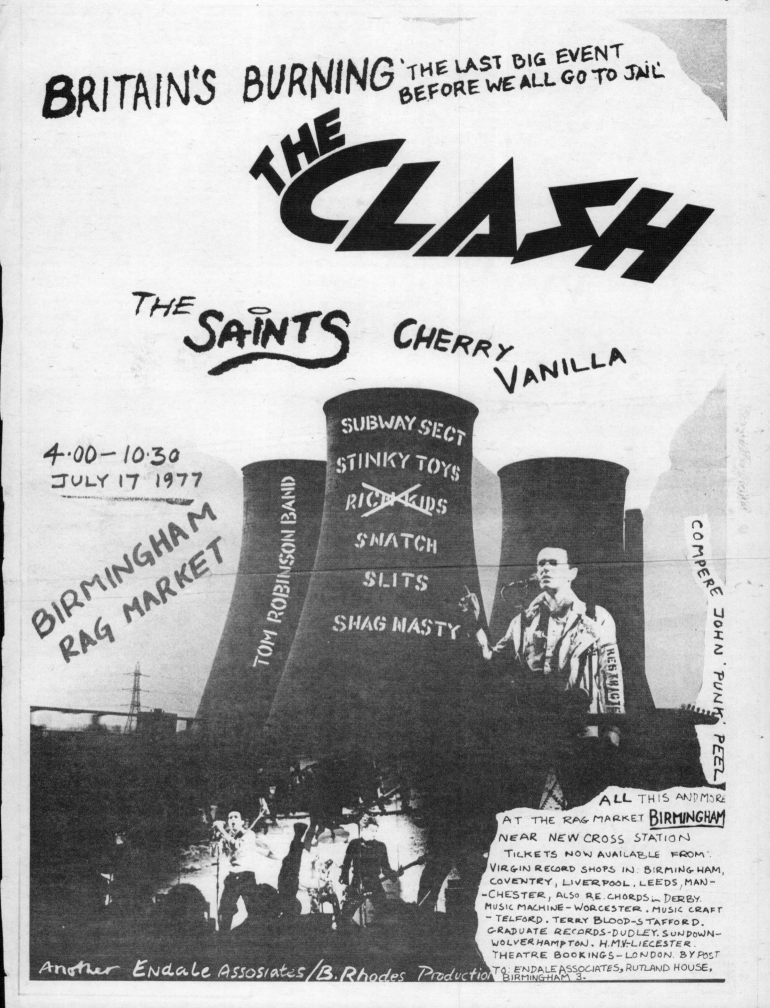

The beginning of the end was the sacking of Topper in 1982. Mick leaving a year later saw the final dissolution of the legendary Clash line-up. While Joe and Paul did go on to recruit three new members to replace Topper and Mick in 1984, Joe says firmly in his interviews for this book that the end of The Clash began with that loss of Topper.

Before the drummer joined them, The Clash had presented themselves pretty much as a trio, despite playing their first few gigs in summer 1976 as a five-piece which included a third guitarist, Keith Levene, and drummer Terry Chimes. The latter was credited on their debut album as 'Tory Crimes', as much for his stated desire to own an expensive sports car in complete contrast to the punk ideals held by the rest of the band, as for the fact that by the time it was released, he'd left. Before Topper joined, The Clash were only interviewed and photographed as a trio. As soon as the drummer had said yes to joining them in April 1977 though, The Clash became a quartet.

They remained that perfect foursome for only five years, but between Topper joining and being sacked they released sixteen sides of long playing records and seventeen singles (many of which were not included on album releases at the time). They toured the world almost non-stop, and made their own short movie, *Hell W10*, written and directed by Joe, starring Mick and Paul. They always made themselves available for interviews, always allowed fans backstage to meet and talk, and never stopped questioning the status quo not only of the music business, but of the political states of the world — both in song and interview. The Clash were uniquely political, truly anti-authoritarian and yet, as Topper observed, twenty five years later everyone's forgotten the politics, but the music stands up well.

Each member brought to the group his unique musical and political per-spectives, but they all shared the same desire to be in a band that played great music. Drawing on their influences, whether it be Jamaican, American, English or Latin American, The Clash were always British, but worldly with it.

The way that they looked was always of concern to The Clash. From the beginning Paul was the style and design director and he produced their original look using paint, stencils and slogans. As the band evolved and their music changed so, too, did their look. Each album release saw a change in stage gear and backdrops on Clash tours. *London Calling*, for instance, reflected both their interest in and love for 1950s-era clothes, music and typography. The subsequent 16 Tons Tour, named after the Tennessee Ernie Ford hit single from 1955 which would be played just before the band took to the stage, saw the front men splendidly outfitted in either black, white or red shirts and black suits. Often the band changed their look and sound before their original fans were 'ready' for it.

Because they came of age during the first wave of UK punk, at home they suffered for a long while from the parochial prejudices of their peers. The UK music press in general was unappreciative of The Clash spreading their sphere of influence around the world. But The Clash always had global plans. They may not always have been as well structured as they'd have liked, but they didn't want to play American stadiums simply to be 'famous'; they had a message to put across to as many people as possible. That they played I'm So Bored With The USA and Career Opportunities in front of 70,000 fans at Shea Stadium and even more at the US Festival is proof of that. They could have just played 'the hits' and basked in adulation. Instead they played songs from their punk, debut album, which was released in slightly amended form in America (because the record company didn't think that it would sell).

The interviews that make up this book were largely conducted over five days, with each band member giving between ten and fifteen hours of his time to recall the story of how, what, why and when The Clash did what The Clash did, during the hectic seven years of their existence. A small part of the interviews went towards making the Grammy Award-winning documentary *Westway To The World*, directed by their old friend, Don Letts. There have also been new interviews conducted for this book, which presents for the first time ever, the story of The Clash by The Clash, in their own words.

Admittedly it's something that they had done before, but in much briefer form, telling their own story in first a press release given away to journalists at the launch of their second album, *Give 'Em Enough Rope* which was then updated for the specially-created programme that was sold on the London Calling Tour of 1980, *The Armagideon Times*.

Here is that version of the early days of The Clash, written by Joe and Mick in 1979:

Joe: 'If you want some information then this is where you'll get it.

In May 1976 a drummerless group began rehearsing in a small squat near Shepherds Bush Green in London. Paul Simonon was the bass player and he'd been playing for only six weeks. He was from the wilds of Brixton; his parents had split up and he'd lived mostly with his father before landing a free scholarship to a posh art school. Then a friend had said 'Why don't you join my group?' The guy who said this was Mick Jones, the lead guitarist, also from Brixton. Mick's dad was a cab driver, and Mick lived with his parents until they divorced when he was 8. His mum went to America and his dad left home so Mick went to live with his gran. When The Clash formed he was occasionally showing up at Hammersmith Art School. These two guys asked Joe Strummer to be the singer. At the time Joe was singing with a London bar band which he had formed in order to pass the time and pay the rent. Upon being asked, he quit his group immediately and joined the prototype Clash. Keith Levene, guitarist, was also a founder member but he left the group early on saying he had some urgent business to take care of in North London.

In August '76 this group was refurbishing an abandoned warehouse in Camden Town. When it was finished the rock began. Terry Chimes, a drummer, was enlisted and every day the warehouse shook with the sound of hard practice. At this time there was nowhere to play. For example, the Marquee Club, supposedly the home of rock & roll, told The Clash: 'Sorry,

Front and back of *The Armagideon Times*, produced for the London Calling Tour of 1979.

The Armagideon **TIMES**

mate. No punk rock in here.' So gigs were created by Bernie Rhodes the manager. One day during a particularly nasty gig when the bottles and cans were coming down like rain Terry Chimes quit after watching a wine bottle come flying over and smash into a million pieces on his high hat. Oh well. A drummerless group is a no-good group. So auditions were held every afternoon in Camden Town. 206 tried, and 205 failed. Nicky 'Topper' Headon out-drummed all candidates and won the hot seat. By this time, although the group were unaware, they had caused quite a reaction in the outside world.

For example CBS coughed up a load of money and signed the group. They got to use CBS number 3 Studios in London, and they made an LP in three weekend sessions using their sound man as producer. They went out as bottom of the bill opening act on the ill fated Anarchy tour of December '76.

They put together and headlined their own White Riot tour in early '77 taking along the Buzzcocks, the Slits, and the Subway Sect. No one had seen anything like it as the tour bus rolled further away from London. Journalists from *The Sunday Times* wrote detailed accounts as Roadent the roadie carved his arm up with Coke cans and cigarette ends.

The LP shocked the group by entering the charts at number 12. But luckily their singles, with a guaranteed lack of airplay, could not get past number 28.

Thus they were saved from Bay City Rollerdom on any scale, and just to make sure they refused to appear on *Top of the Pops*, considering it an old pop TV show left over from the 1960s, which requires performers to mime along as their record is played at a low volume somewhere in the distance.

For a long time now the new 'dub' and 'reggae' from Kingston, Jamaica, had been making itself felt to those prepared to listen in London. Police & Thieves was a summer reggae hit in the clubs but not on the radio. The Clash recorded a six-minute punk rock translation of this song and included it on their LP, although at the time most white musicians believed that attempting to play such music showed a lack of respect and an attitude of condescension. But luckily when they heard this they KNEW it was a good idea.

Lee Perry, or 'Scratch the Upsetter', was co-author and producer of the original Junior Murvin tune, and when he heard their version added a picture of The Clash to his 'Wall of Fame' at the Black Ark Studios in Jamaica. Theirs are the only white faces on this wall.

Scratch visited London in mid-'77 and found himself producing a new Clash song Complete Control. Mid-way through the session the Upsetter was moved to tell Mick Jones that he played guitar 'with an iron fist'. The song also donged the number 28 spot, but even this was not enough to stop the tour, which played in every major town and city where the group were not banned (with Richard Hell from America and the Lous from France completing the bill). After the smoke cleared there was nothing but a big pile of bills all addressed to The Clash. Since this time the group have found it a financial necessity to play unseated venues, the replacement rate for seats pegging around £20 a seat. This was also the heyday of spitting or 'gobbing' and I would like to thank Richard Hell and his Voidoids on behalf of The Clash for drawing more than his fair share of the fire.

The Clash rode aeroplanes all round Europe. Ceaselessly for more than a month they struggled with police and hoteliers in Munich, irate TV producers in Bremen, bomb threats and attacks from the Rageri in Sweden, beer and short change from the Rhineland bar keepers, threats on the Reparbahn. And when they got back home they found that everything was different. Many of their contemporary groups had splintered, their daily movements had become a subject of interest in the music press, some of the clubs were shut and generally a great depression had settled on the town.

Withstanding scathing and sneering attacks in the press The Clash learned that you got to take the rough with the smooth and decided not to break up.

During this time various members of the group were continually being arrested and fined for petty theft and vandalism culminating in an incident that took place on the top of the group's warehouse in Camden Town. A helicopter and armed police arrested two members of the group and they were charged with various gun offences and the shooting of some valuable racing pigeons. While the case was on remand The Clash released White Man in Hammersmith Palais b/w I Don't Wanna be the Prisoner and took on a Clash Out on Parole Tour with Suicide from New York and the Specials from Coventry.

To get back to music, it was time to make a second LP. In order to prevent arguments, producer Sandy Pearlman was hired for the job. He seemed keen to do it. The schedule was interrupted by the usual disasters. However no one quits easily around here…

The new LP was recorded in London before going out on tour. The tour was the best ever with Suicide taking and handling a violent assault from the rougher British Clash audience. After the tour the guitar solos were added at the Automat in San Francisco. Final mixing was done at the Record Plant NYC.

Give 'em Enough Rope was completed and released in November 1978 and shot straight to number 2 in the British charts the week of release. It also gave The Clash their first bonafide hit with Tommy Gun.

The Clash embarked on another British tour, the Sort it Out Tour, during which time they parted company with their former manager, Bernie Rhodes.

They did their first US tour in February, the Pearl Harbour Tour, taking along the legendary Bo Diddley as support. The Clash played in Vancouver, Toronto, San Francisco, Los Angeles, Boston, Cleveland and New York, sold out everywhere and devastated both critics and fans alike.

Alone with my own cold thoughts …………..The update is long overdue. It is something that should be done!

My memory does not serve me well – brief flashing images pass before me – things that had to be done, past achievements, places visited. They are all there in my memory, fragmented, timeless within me. I must extradite the facts from the mist around me. I must file them chronologically (up here and on paper) so that some sense is made of the story. How this is done or the

An original poster advertising the first two nights of the Radio Clash Tour in 1981.

actual circumstance of the task is far less important than who is chosen to do it. Certainly I was there and I have witnessed almost every breath The Clash have taken.

Mick: Joe Strummer started this (although I doubt if he wrote the last three paragraphs attributed to him) and now only a year later it has been handed to me to contribute (albeit a small piece of the whole) in the tradition of stories passed by hand or word of mouth with continual revisions and additions made *ad-infinitum*. Lots of great books were conceived and formed this way – many modern day scholars believe the Bible to be amongst them.

This of course is not the Bible and believe me I'm not trying to make any comparisons. It is simply just another story… 'Ere! What's all this stuff about the Bible then' sneers a flake white apparition of Topper Headon – The Clash's solid stixman. 'He's having delusions of Grand liquors!' a second like spirit interjects – the lean angled frame of bassman Paul Simonon – a playful presence hard to ignore (not that any would want to ignore him!)

'Oh we've got religion now have we' screamed the mass *en masse*.

'Not really – all it is, is a fanciful thought, nothing more! There is after all no telling what or whose writing will survive the next thousand years or so'. Here was Strummer walking into my waking dream – always in my estimation a fair man, I've said it before, a real 'salt of the earth' type. From a crud to King Solomon through to T.E. Lawrence. He's a noble Turk that Joe the Lion. Stop! Wrong 'em boyo – back to the story, back to the facts –

On their return to England from their first US tour The Clash rehearsed, wrote new material, worked on an as yet untitled film and recorded an extended-play record entitled *The Cost of Living EP* which was released on election day. We all know what happened on that day and it was no surprise when one critic exclaimed that the record sounded like 'left-wing paranoia' and that 'The Clash should relax and enjoy the ride like the rest of us.' The Clash, who claim no allegiance to either the left or the right, did not blindly dismiss that criticism but instead observed the so called 'ride' itself more carefully than ever.

The Cost of Living EP did well and charted in England at number 22. One song on the EP – The Clash's rendition of the classic Bobby Fuller Four/Sonny Curtis tune I Fought The Law was also released as The Clash's first single in the US. It received a fair amount of Radio Airplay (very unusual for The Clash, very, very important in the US) and this helped create more interest for the band's next tour there.

But at home 'the ride' was getting rougher and with the constant threat of authoritarian violence and crippling inflation many people were righteously fighting the law in reality. Following the Southall anti-fascist demos a Southall defence fund was set up by Rock Against Racism and two benefit concerts at a seatless Rainbow theatre were presented. The first night Pete Townsend, Misty (brutally attacked by the S.P.G. at Southall) and The Pop Group appeared. The second show saw the return of The Clash to the London

Mick and Topper in typically explosive live action, 1979.

stage. Sharing the bill that night were Aswad and The Members. Both shows were attended by capacity crowds and a good time was had by all with no trouble. All proceeds went to the before-mentioned defence fund.

After this event came more of what's commonly know by The Clash as the three 'R's' – Rehearse, 'Rite and Record. All the time closely observing what was going on around them, they could not help but notice that despite the short-lived Tory tax cuts (specifically designed to help the already rich – *not* the poor) The Bee Gees did not return to these shores.

The Clash went to Finland for the day and when they returned set about recording their third LP. For their sins they recalled their first ever producer, one Guy Stevens of Forest Hill (formerly of Swiss Cottage). A somewhat legendary figure of the swinging sixties, Guy's trademarks were energy, excitement, a true passion for Rock 'n' Roll and an ability to work fast. The group and the producer were made for each other. They were in fact so productive that it became clear after only a few days that the new Clash LP was going to be a double album. This in itself caused problems, with an eye to the current economic climate. The solution was found – the record would retail two for the price of one!

After a month's recording in Highbury the band embarked once more for the new world on The Clash Take The Fifth tour. Ignoring the energy crisis, the band along with busloads of family, friends and roadies scoured the land from Monterey to Minneapolis, from Texas to New York, from Toronto to Hollywood and back round again. Incidentally the group really did take the 'Fifth' and the 'Fifth' was the inclusion of Micky Gallagher of Ian Dury and the Blockheads on organ. He played on all the dates from Boston onwards.

Along the way the band had the good fortune to have such luminaries as Sam & Dave, Screamin' Jay Hawkins and Bo Diddley play with them as well as newer acts such as Joe Ely, David Johansen, The Cramps and The Rebels. Determined to make an impression The Clash found their sell-out shows generally well received with New York, Chicago, L.A. and the Texan performances standing out as the highlights of the excursion. After six weeks which felt like six days the tour ended almost abruptly in Vancouver. Then it was every man for himself back to Blighty.

The group drifted homeward to put the finishing touches to their new record which was to be titled *The New Testament* until someone said it had been done before and everybody else thought it too pretentious anyway. So instead the record was called *London Calling* which is the first cut on the LP.

These are disappointing times even for the most optimistic. The Clash however are as optimistic as ever.

You may thing this naivety!

You may think it stupidity!

But as the fourth man of the 'El Clash Combo' I can positively say we are not living for the future we're living day to day.

Now, in the present – we shall have to see what happens!' [1979]

Joe Strummer

B. 21/08/1952 D. 22/12/2002

'I called myself Joe Strummer because I can only play all six strings at once, or none at all.'

BIRTH, SCHOOL. . .

My father was at a very junior level in the Foreign Office and he only became a British citizen two years before I was born. He had been born in India and his father worked on the railways, but died when my dad was very young, so he grew up in orphanages in India. His father (my grandfather) was English but his mother was Indian; he studied hard at school and won scholarships and ended up in the Indian Army during World War II. When the war ended he came to London, passed his exams for the Civil Service, met my mum, joined the Foreign Office and was posted to Ankara – which is how I came to be born in Turkey.

After Turkey we were posted to Mexico City for a couple of years and I went to a kindergarten where they didn't speak English, which is why I can speak a bit of Spanish, though only in the present tense. It's a kind of pidgin-Spanish which I've never been able to improve. After Mexico we went to live in Bonn in what was then West Germany before I was sent to boarding school in England.

Boarding school in those days was very militaristic. There were uniforms for the boys and penalties for not wearing a cap – it was the worst for that type of thing. I ran away when I was nine with this other guy and we got about five miles away before teacher was sent out, and they found us. I remember being taken back to the school and the vice-headmaster coming out and shouting at us for not wearing our caps and I was thinking, 'You idiot, do you really think we're going to run away with our caps on?' I couldn't believe it.

In 1976, after leaving the 101'ers, Joe Strummer had his hair cut, borrowed some clothes and took fashion advice from new band-mates Mick and Paul. Emerging from the basement of the squat where his new band practised, Joe was photographed by former 101'er member Julian Yewdall in his new punk rock incarnation.

The school would only let you go home once a year, though they did make it twice a year before I left. I felt like it was dog eat dog there at times.

My brother went to the school as well and he was in the year above me, being older. It was a little strange for me because he was very shy, the complete opposite to me. I was this big-mouthed load of trouble, always up to no good. The running joke in the school was that he hadn't said a word all term, which was more or less true.

There was a lot of bullying and I was one of the principal bullies. It was either bully or be bullied and there was no protection from anyone or anything. You'd be beaten up for any reason, like eating a biscuit without permission. They said it was because there was a problem with mice and rats at the school, so no-one was allowed food. There was no-one to protect you and I quickly realized that you either became a power or you were crushed — so I formed a gang. I wasn't very pleasant, but it was self-preservation.

I was happy at that school really though, because I was a ringleader. I could control what was going on. I was a mouthy little git and I knew how to hide when they were dishing out chores, or they wanted to find someone to beat up. Yeah, I was happiest at school because I was in charge of my own world.

I would say that going to a school like that, in a place like that [the City of London Freemen's School in Ashtead, Surrey], meant that you became independent. You didn't expect anybody to do anything for you, and that was a big part of punk, because no-one was going to help.

Because of my upbringing, I felt that authority was something to be well avoided if possible. If you could get in and attack it and get away without being burnt, I would say yeah, do it. Questioning authority was high on the list of (my) priorities. I could see from an early age that authority was a system of control which didn't have any inherent wisdom . . . and was therefore non-applicable. It was just something to get around.

My relationship with my father was terrible, because I was a lousy student, always last in class. I began to dread seeing him because he'd pulled himself up by the bootstraps of his own intelligence. Can you imagine being an orphan in India in the 1920s? He pulled himself out of the misery by studying and getting scholarships to university and so he had a big 'study' ethos. He was more English than the English, in a way, and I had a horror of seeing him — even once a year — because my reports would be so terrible, the worst you could imagine — and then some! He'd blow a gasket when he saw them. I wouldn't have gone home at all in the holidays if I'd been given the choice, and often thought of legging it when it was time to go.

I often think about my parents and how I must have felt about being sent away to school at the age of nine and seeing them only once a year. It was rather weird. When you're a child, though, you just deal with it. It really changed my life because I realized that I had to forget about my parents, in order to keep my head above water. When you're a kid you go straight to the heart of the matter, no procrastination, you don't have the processes available to deal with the loss. I forgot about my parents and told myself, 'deal

In 1964, aged twelve, Joe heard the Rolling Stones' Not Fade Away in the common room of his public school in suburban England and had a revelation. Watching Mick Jagger prance around on the school's black and white television set one Saturday lunchtime inspired the young John Mellor to want to know much more about the world than he could find in school.

with this'. I feel bad now because I was a bad son to them when they eventually came back to live in England and never went to see them enough. I do feel bad about that now.

MUSIC LESSONS

My parents weren't musical at all and I think if I have got any musical tradition it comes from my mother's side. She was born on a farm fifty miles south of John O' Groats, in a town called Bonar Bridge. I think I must have inherited some musical feeling through her side of the family, which is very Highland and wild.

My parents had Can-Can records from the Folies Bergère and that was about it, maybe a few show tunes like *Oklahoma*, the kind of thing you'd expect in the late 1950s. I mostly remember hearing children's favourites like Ten Green Bottles on the BBC, but also all the Top Ten songs that the *Light Programme* would play, things like Tennessee Ernie Ford's Sixteen Tons.

The first record I bought was The Beatles' *I Wanna Hold Your Hand*, and then the early Stones singles. I remember when music really hit me though, and it was while I was at boarding school, aged eleven. I had to be tough there, it could be oppressive and if you didn't go in fighting people would kill you. I remember hearing Not Fade Away blasting out of this huge wooden radio in the day room – they always kept it on really loud – and I walked into the room as it started (Joe hums the opening bars) and thought, 'This is something else! This is the complete opposite of all this other stuff I'm having to suffer here.' And it felt like I'd found a gap in the clouds, a light shining. That's the moment I fell for music. I later discovered that it was Gene Pitney playing the maracas on that record, making it swing.

I made a subconscious decision then to follow music forever, that music would be the way that I'd live. Everyone at that school needed something like that. It was a place where people hung themselves.

In those days there were no music papers. The *NME* and *Melody Maker* were kind of jazz papers and not really read by teenagers, so we got into music through a TV show named *Thank Your Lucky Stars* that went out at 6.30 on Saturday night and was hosted by Brian Matthew or Pete Murray. That was where I first saw the Stones, way down the bill, on the dead-end slot, playing Come On, the Chuck Berry song. We just flipped when we saw it, the whole school was gathered in the day room to watch and we didn't need anyone to tell us that this was the new thing. Likewise with The Beatles. In fact, without the music, without the explosion of music going off in London with the Beatles, Stones, Kinks, Yardbirds, I can't imagine how we'd have got through being in that school. I can't imagine how, had it been ten years earlier, say, that I'd have been able to stand it. Hearing great new records got me through every weekend.

We younger boys weren't allowed out of the school gates of course, but the older ones would go out and bring back new records and play them every Saturday night in the main hall. They played them on an old radiogram. The hall had speakers everywhere and we'd all dance. It sounded great – maybe 'cos the hall had wooden walls.

It didn't take long before we had a school band, called the Burgher Masters. They were a kind of sub-Shadows outfit, all twanging guitars and that. Because it was made up of boarders like me – none of the day boys were around for the Saturday dances of course – I got to see how a band worked, up close. I remember the kid who owned the first electric guitar in the school snivelling because an older boy had nicked it off him in order to play at the school social. The drummer would practise with his brushes on newspapers spread on his desk. But it never occurred to me to join in on the playing because I was completely non-musical.

I wasn't in any choir and didn't learn an instrument, and I mean none. I couldn't have been more removed from music except that I was a fervent listener. It was only after I left school, though, that I began to think that I could actually play music. Yet it seemed like a mythical world to me, where only mythical beings could actually play, and I had a big problem getting over that. So when I managed to get some chords together I was chuffed. All I've ever wanted to do is play chords.

Jimi Hendrix said that if you can't play rhythm guitar then you can't play lead, and I think he's right. I never got to the lead guitar playing, but still, rhythm guitar playing is an art.

1968

In 1968 I took my 'O' levels and the whole world was exploding. There was Paris, Vietnam, Grosvenor Square, the counter-culture, and it seemed normal because we had no other frame of reference. We thought that '68 was the norm and that was the year I came of age. It was like riding a rocket but I didn't realize how lucky I was until later. Although by the time I reached London the whole hippie thing was over, regrettably, and I never got to see the Stones in the Park or the Kinks or the Yardbirds. But God knows it was a great year to have come of age, fantastic.

Street Fighting Man was a great song though I don't think we understood what it was saying, we just accepted it as normal, like all the other Stones songs. It seemed that everyone was running with the police in the streets and rioting and all that. But I was stuck in a bubble about 30 miles outside London, looking on, thinking, 'Let's get on with it'.

ART SCHOOL

In those days, if you were in the position I was then in there was only one answer to what you were going to do after school, and that was art school; the last resort of malingerers, bluffers and people who basically don't want to work. I applied to the Central School of Art [in London] and was amazed when I got in. When I turned up I realized that all the lecturers were lechers – they'd chosen twenty-nine girls and ten blokes to make up their quota. They had obviously chosen the twenty-nine most attractive female applicants and

Joe as a thirteen-year-old public schoolboy in the uniform of the City of London Freemen's School. Taken by Pablo LaBritain behind the school's Philip House in 1965, Joe is standing next to housemaster Johnny Lansdowne's beehive.

In March 1968 the
second of a series of
anti-American
involvement in Vietnam
demonstrations erupted
into a riot in London's
Grosvenor Square
(below). Present at the
beginning of the riot,
Mick Jagger returned to
his Chelsea home as the
real violence flared and
wrote the lyrics to
Street Fighting Man.

then spent the next year hitting on them. And that was art school.

I soon peeled off from that 'cos I realized that they weren't teaching us anything except how to make arty marks on a page. They weren't teaching us
how to draw an object, they were teaching us how to make a drawing that
looked as if we knew how to draw an object. It was a load of rubbish.

Then we got hold of acid (LSD), started to take it and the course looked
even more transparent. I don't think I even lasted six months there. I tried to
get into other art schools, but they told me to get lost, as I obviously had
a portfolio of nothing, just dripping noodles of paint in a festering spaghetti
of nonsense.

I remember bumming a train ride back from Norwich to London and got
caught, so was thrown off the train. I had a big cardboard portfolio of stuff

In 1974 Joe fronted the 101'ers and played at pubs local to the squats that they (mostly) lived in. Here he is photographed in the Elgin Arms at 96 Ladbroke Grove, W11, with Tymon Dogg on violin and 'Big John' Cassell on saxophone.

under my arm and I threw it in a skip, because I realized that art was going nowhere. I had to hitch back to London. There was no way I was carrying all this nonsense with me, so I dumped it. And that was it for me and art school. So it was either work for a living or play music.

BRAVE NEW WORLD

The first instrument I ever touched was a bass made in woodwork by Pablo LaBritain, the drummer of 999, which I've still got and it looks kinda like a Steinberger, you know those guitars with no headstock? I watched him make it and then I watched him learn how to play it, and that was the first time I thought, 'Wow, he's actually playing the blues on it.'

After I left school I bought a ukulele, 'cos I figured that had to be easier than a guitar, having only four strings. And that's how I got into playing, following a musician named Tymon Dogg around the London Underground and collecting money for him like a Mississippi blues apprentice. We went around Europe busking, bumming around Belgium and France. But we mainly stayed on the Underground in London.

Eventually I learned to play Chuck Berry songs on the ukulele and went out on my own. One day I was in the Underground, playing Sweet Little Sixteen on the uke when an American happened to walk past, and he stopped in front of me. 'I don't believe it, I can't believe it!' he said, and then started smacking his forehead, staggering around looking like he was gonna faint. So I stopped playing and he says, 'You're playing Chuck Berry on a ukulele!' I hadn't considered it to be odd at all and only began to think so after he'd pointed out the ridiculousness of it. So I got a guitar and learned to play it from Tymon who sort of tolerated me as a follower.

I became known as Woody because, after busking around Europe with Tymon and sleeping in hedges, being chased around Paris by the gendarmes and all that nonsense, I romanticized the whole thing into, 'Hey there were hobos out there in the Delta, too' and it became an affectation of mine. I decided to name myself after Woody Guthrie and I knew about the union-busting and the humanity of his music. That stuff was inspiring – it was a 'one day hopefully I'll be as good as him' nickname. But I don't think everyone who called me Woody had even heard of Woody Guthrie, they just thought it was a groovy name.

I ended up in Wales after serving my apprenticeship with Tymon as there didn't seem to be any way of making a living in London or even surviving. This was before I discovered squatting. I followed a girl to Cardiff Art School but she told me she didn't want to know and so I started to hitchhike back to London. The first place I landed was Newport, where I met up with some people I'd known at Central School of Art in London, and I crashed with them for a while. I got a job as a gravedigger and then crashed my way into Newport Art School. I got into the art school rock band and learned my chops there. We were called the Vultures. We weren't as good as the band who'd been there the year before (1971), who were called the Rip-Off Park Allstars and did a lot of rock 'n' roll revival stuff like Sha-Na-Na were doing. The Vultures were an R&B band which was more up my street.

We played gigs, but to a captive crowd 'cos it was the Newport Art School kids. We did get as far as Bristol for a gig once though, where they pelted us with beer glasses. I'd drawn a big cartoon saying how brilliant the band were and conned a poor booker in Bristol to book us into a big blues club. But we were crud, it was way past 11 o' clock and the audience weren't having it.

We also played some places in the Welsh valleys, where things were even worse. After one gig the announcer said, 'And next week we'll have some decent music for a change.' During the breaks, wags would detune our guitars while we were having a cigarette in the alley, so we'd come back on, put our guitars on, go '1-2-3-4 – kerrang!' and everyone in the club would fall about pissing themselves. When they'd had enough beer they'd lob their glasses at us until we left. That was a taste of real life.

We realized that we needed a bit of attitude just to get started at those places, not to mention getting paid and getting out of there alive. They didn't take any prisoners in Merthyr Tydfil, I'll say that for them.

But there were a couple of things to come out of my time in Newport that inspired me, that got me back to London by 1974. One was Mickey Foote, who was also at art school there and whom I got to know. The other was discovering reggae.

One day in Newport this guy who looked the spitting image of Jim Morrison came up to me, he was a student who used to hang out in Corporation Street with black guys and smoke weed. He said to me, 'Hey, there's this thing called Dub, come with me.' So we went to a joint called Silver Sands and that was the first time I heard any reggae that wasn't the Pioneers. It was the first time I ever saw something of a rebel nature going down, that roots rock scene, and I realized that I had to go back to London because if this was happening on the black scene in Newport, then I needed to get back to the capital somehow. The Vultures had finally crashed and I had to do something new...

A page from Joe's scrapbook, with the first interview he did with a music paper. It tells the story of how his band The 101'ers came to exist, their gig at the Charlie Pigdog Club which was raided by the police and how Joe got his guitar and amplifier. It was published in the *Melody Maker* music weekly paper in July 1975.

FOLLOWING PAGE: Paul, Mick and Joe at one of the first open-air gigs by The Jam, Soho Market, October 1976.

Pop from the beginning

Melody Maker. 26:7:75.

IT was sometime back in February that I first saw the 101'ers. They had a residency in the Charlie Pigdog Club in West London. It was the kind of place which held extraordinary promises of violence. You walked in, took one look around, and wished you were the hell out of there.

The general feeling was that something was going to happen, and whatever that something was, it was inevitably going to involve you. After ten minutes glancing into secluded corners half-expecting to see someone having their face decorated with a razor, the paranoia count was soaring.

The gig that particular evening ended in a near massacre. As the 101'ers screamed their way through a 20-minute interpretation of "Gloria" which sounded like the perfect soundtrack for the last apocalyptic days of the Third Reich, opposing factions of (I believe) Irish and gypsies attempted to carve each other out. Bottles were smashed over defenceless heads, blades flashed and howling dogs tore at one another's throats, splattering the walls with blood . . . No one, I was convinced, is going to crawl out of this one alive. . . .

The band tore on, with Joe Strummer thrashing away at his guitar like there was no tomorrow, completely oblivious of the surrounding carnage. The police finally arrived, flashing blue lights, sirens, the whole works. Strummer battled on. He was finally confronted by the imposing figure of the law, stopped in mid-flight, staggered to a halt and looked up. "Evening, officer," he said. . . .

The 101'ers no longer play at the Charlie Pigdog Club. "The builders moved in and started to wreck the f—— place," Strummer remarks caustically.

We find them now at the Elgin in Ladbroke Grove, where they have a Thursday residency, involved in a slight altercation with the manager. Jules, their newly appointed manager, and Mick Foote, their driver and unofficial publicist, are at the bar trying to placate a band called Lipstick who've turned up to play at the manager's request. The manager is under the impression that he's hired the 101'ers for Monday nights, and Lipstick for Thursday. Lipstick want to play.

"Look," says Foote, "what are you doing on Monday. Nothing? Right you play on f—— Monday, then."

The argument is resolved. The 101'ers will play. Lipstick can watch from the sidelines.

The band, according to Strummer (rhythm guitar and voice), was formed, "in a basement early last summer. We had a couple of guitars and a few Concord speakers and we thought we were the cat's knackers. . . . Hey, d'you want to know how I got my Telecaster? Well, I was working at the Royal Opera House carrying out the rubbish. A f—— great job. Only had to work two hours of the day. There was this hole in the basement, where I'd creep off to play guitar. Anyway, the manager found me and fired me. Gave me £120 to get out as soon as possible. So I went out and scored an AC 30."

I thought you were going to tell us about your guitar.

"Oh yeah, yeah. I was working in Hyde Park, and I met this South American chick who wanted to get married. To stay in the country, see? She paid me a hundred quid. So I quit the job, and got a Telecaster to go with the AC 30. . . . I'll get the divorce through in about two years."

The initial line-up of the band seems to have varied from rehearsal to rehearsal, but eventually a nucleus of musicians evolved around Strummer and they played their first gig at the Telegraph on Brixton Hill on September 7 last year.

"We had this f—— mad Chilean sax player, Alvaro. He got us a gig at a political benefit for Chilean refugees. We had live days to knock something together, we could only play six numbers. Then our f—— drummer went on holiday. That's when the Snakes joined for the first time."

Snake Hips Dudanski, former head boy at Salesan College and zoology student at Chelsea University, had never played drums before. "After a couple of days of frantic practice I thought I could handle it. It wasn't too difficult. I just bashed everything in sight. I still do. There's only one difficulty . . . playing with odd sticks. That, and having to buy them secondhand."

He's now permanently installed in the rhythm section alongside The Mole. Like Snake Hips, The Mole had never even looked at a musical instrument until he was invited to join the 101'ers when they were short of a bass player. For such a relatively immature musical combination, Snake Hips and The Mole lock together magnetically on stage, thrusting the 101'ers along with vicious energy.

. . . guitarist, Clive W. H. Timperlee, are the only members of the band with any substantial musical experience. Strummer once fronted a legendary outfit called Johnny & The Vultures back in 1973, an erratic but occasionally stunning formation that played a handful of gigs before sinking without trace. Timperlee, affectionately referred to as Evil by Strummer, has been playing for about ten years, starting in the mid-sixties with a band called Captain Rougely's Blues Band, which included Martin Lamble, the original drummer with Fairport Convention (unfortunately killed in a road accident in 1969). After that he worked his way through a succession of none too successful bands, arriving on the 101'ers' doorstep in January.

He's recently precipitated a minor crisis by threatening to leave the band. He's had a lucrative offer from some "lame-brained singer/songwriter," as Strummer describes him. "He'd be a f—— fool to leave us now. But we've advertised for a new guitarist. . . . We have to be careful. We want a guitarist for a beat group, we don't want any bloody acid casualties thinking they're going to join the Grateful Dead. We want someone who can whip their axe. I mean, if you go to see a rock group you want to see someone tearing their soul apart at 36 bars a second, not listen to some instrumental slush. Since '67, music has been chasing itself up a blind alley with all that s——."

As you might have gathered, the 101'ers are fairly uncompromising in their attitude towards most contemporary rock music. They are about energy: pure rock 'n' roll dynamics. They concentrate almost exclusively on standard rock material, but their greatest strength lies in Strummer's own compositions, like "Motor, Boys, Motor," and particularly "Steamgauge 99" and the stunning "Keys To Your Heart," and in his own ragged charisma. He's a naturally powerful performer, given to sudden explosions of passion.

"That's what it's all about. That energy. I mean, we usually have to do a two and a half hour set here. If we're on a bill with some other bands we cut it down to an hour and a half. Or play until they throw us off. Playing that long every night can kill you. Like, there's this line in 'Roll Over Beethoven' . . . 'Early in the morning, I'm giving you my warning/Don't you step on my blue suede shoes. . . .' And if you're a classy Chuck Berry kind of singer, you've got to do the whole line in one breath to keep the energy flowing.

"Straight after that line I usually faint. Everything goes white. If you haven't eaten for a few days, and you haven't had any sleep, you just keel over backwards. But I always get back on my feet for the next line. 'Hey diddle, diddle I'm playing my fiddle/I got nothing to lose. . . .' That's just such a great line, you've got to stay on your feet for that. "And we'll always be on our feet. We're gonna take this all the way"

ALLAN JONES

JOE STRUMMER: faints onstage

Mick Jones

B. 26/06/1955

'I decided that I'd go to art school in order to meet other musicians and get a grant so I could buy some equipment.'

BIRTH, SCHOOL. . .

I was born in Clapham, at the South London Hospital for Women, and brought up in Brixton. My parents split when I was about eight years old and my grandmother took over my upbringing. I lived with her in Brixton and then later with her, and her sister and step-sister in West London.

I think music became an escape for me to a certain extent as a child. Before they split up my parents used to fight a lot and my gran would take me down to the bomb shelter in the basement of the flats we lived in. They used to fight quite badly and it scared me. So Gran and I would wait for the raid to pass and then we'd go back upstairs.

Because of my parents' separation I was often on my own and I'd do lots of things alone. I filled my time with doing stuff that interested me, like collecting things and thinking about stuff. I guess I must have inhabited my own world really. It was like, I guess I was trying to fill a gap — though I wasn't aware of it. That's how I ended up like I am, I guess. It was definitely a kind of built-in self-preservation thing that I've got. It's inherent. To survive I created my own world.

When my parents split up my dad moved just up the road, so I'd see him sometimes, but my mum moved to America. My grandmother, to all intents and purposes, became my mother.

My mother had been a wild person. She fell in love with an American soldier in World War II and he took her on a boat to America with him — she was a stowaway — and she got as far as Texas before the authorities found

Mick Jones co-wrote some of the great rock songs of the late 1970s with Joe Strummer and The Clash.

out and called my grandparents. My grandfather had to go and bring her back.

But she loved America and married an American serviceman and went to live in Michigan after she split from my father. Then that marriage broke up and she met another guy there, married him and lived happily in Ironwood.

My mother did come back to visit me sometimes when I was young, and it really used to freak me out, knowing that she'd be going away again.

My nan (my mum's mum) and I were on the housing list for years and occasionally went to see flats, but it just never seemed to happen. I was living with three old ladies, which was pretty strange. They were really Jewish, too. I remember I once got a Snoopy and the Red Baron T-shirt and they freaked because it had an iron cross on it, so they confiscated it.

My nan's sister was head of the family, which was pretty big. There were seven sisters and two brothers on my nan's side and their parents had escaped from Russia, so my mum was the first English-born member of the family and the first to marry out of the faith. I wasn't bahmitzvahed though

Mott the Hoople were one of Mick's favourite bands. Lead singer Ian Hunter (centre) and guitarist Mick Ronson (right; he would also perform with David Bowie) welcomed fans into their dressing room and treated the teenagers almost as mates. This was something Mick never forgot, and carried on in The Clash.

my nan was religious. She nurtured me, rescued me from all the fighting and stuff when I was really young, and protected me as much as she could and never questioned it.

London was a very different place when I was growing up. We used to play on bomb sites around the corner from where I lived in Brixton. Now it's a garden square, but back then there was a bomb shelter with a corrugated metal shutter that had been prised off so we could get inside. It had this smell – of the War and of the dark inside it. We used to play 'hold the fort' on the hill where the shelter was, have mock battles against other kids, holding the high ground. In the winter we'd sleigh down that hill. There were bomb sites everywhere in those days.

Saturday mornings I'd go to the local flea pit cinema, the Classic in Brixton, which is now the Ritzy, and watch action films. There were a lot of Tartars in them I recall, Genghis Khan and Tartars on double-bills.

I sometimes used to get a 'rover' bus pass for the red double-deckers and ride around London, on the top deck. I'd go to St Pauls, the West End – to Carnaby Street in the early 1960s on the weekends and nick stuff, just little things. It was a pretty exciting time to grow up. There was music everywhere it seemed, coming out of shops, on the radio, it was like we had a soundtrack to our lives.

The first real records I bought with my own money were Jimi Hendrix's *Smash Hits* and *Disraeli Gears* by Cream. They cost about 33 shillings I think it was. I used to listen to them over and over again, Hendrix especially. I only had the one speaker in a radiogram and I used to just sit in front of it. I knew from a very early age that I wanted to do music. That's all I ever wanted to do.

My school work definitely suffered when I discovered music. When you're young there aren't too many outlets. There's football of course, and I was really into that for a while. I used to collect footballers' autographs. I knew all the hotels where they stayed and I'd fill these books called *Topical Times Football Books*, which had photographs of the players in them, with their autographs. I had all of the England 1966 World Cup-winning team in this book and was really pleased about it. But at some point I had to make a choice, it was football or music.

I'll always remember going into the office of the careers advice people at school and saying, 'I wanna be in a band', and they said, 'Well you can't be. If you're too useless you go into the Army or the services. Or there's the Civil Service.' There were no real choices, there wasn't a vegetarian option on the menu.

MUSIC LESSONS

There was a band at school and I was a year lower than them. I was kind of the little one but always curious about making music and I started off roadying for them. I was happy enough to lug the gear for a bit. Then I gradually built myself up to playing the guitar, though I played the drums, too. And the bass. The guitar came after that.

I wanted to play the guitar because I always imagined it was the coolest spot to be in. No-one was cooler than the guitar player. Provided you stay in tune you could just cruise.

I never had any lessons. My friend Robin Banks tuned the guitar for me before I knew how to. I almost took my first guitar back to the shop because it wasn't in tune. I thought there was something wrong with it!

I learned by playing along to records and spent a year in the bedroom just playing along, learning the solos and all the little nuances on Stones records.

Music was definitely the main thing for me, from the age of twelve or so. I was going to gigs at twelve.

At the time there were all-night concerts on Parliament Hill in North London and they had groups like Yes who were kind of hip at the time, about '69, and Soft Machine. The first gig I ever went to was a free concert in Hyde Park which had The Nice, Blossom Toes, The Pretty Things and The Action. They used to put on free gigs in the Park back then, not like today where they charge an arm and a leg for any old rubbish. That gig was put on by Blackhill Enterprises who later managed us for a time [as The Clash].

My mum used to send me *Cream* and *Rock Scene* magazines from America. They were a revelation to me because they had all this stuff about bands that no-one else had heard of. *Rock Scene* always had stuff about the New York Dolls in it, for instance.

The New York Dolls had a massive effect on me. They were incredible and blew my mind with the way they looked – their attitude was they didn't care about anything. They weren't that great sounding, but that didn't matter – the whole thing transcended the music.

And *Cream* magazine had Lester Bangs writing for it and covered bands like The Stooges and Embassy Five, the Dolls, bands whose records you could only get in this record shop in Praed Street run by a French guy. He sold Flamin' Groovies records too, long before punk happened.

I followed Rod Stewart and the Faces around the country when I was 16 or so. We used to bunk on trains to Newcastle and other places and try to jump off just as we came into the station, then climb over fences and hotfoot it off to the venue. Then we'd try to bunk in there, too, often by hiding in the toilets before the show. Sometimes we'd be frog-marched out by bouncers but we'd try to get back in again and that was all part of the fun.

I used to follow Mott The Hoople around as well. There was a whole bunch of us from school and we'd go to most of their gigs around London and the suburbs, though sometimes we'd travel further – I went to Liverpool to see them once. One of our lot would always jump on stage during the encore so the band got to know us and they'd sometimes let us in for nothing. They'd actually talk to us, too, which was quite different to other groups at the time.

ART SCHOOL

After leaving school I spent a year doing odd jobs like working at the labour exchange, but decided that I'd go to art school in order to meet other

L-R: Billy Watts, Mick, Paul, Alan Drake and Keith Levene, 1975.

musicians and get a grant so I could buy some equipment. And that's how I thought you got into bands, by going to art school.

At Hammersmith Art College I looked like Johnny Thunders. I had really long hair and used to totter around on platform shoes in really tight jeans that had been taken in specially. But it was half an art college and half a building college, so the guys who came in for bricklaying and painting had to queue in the canteen alongside us. I got a lot of flak for the way I looked, which was pretty wild back then, 'cos there weren't too many people who were into the New York Dolls or MC5 or the Stooges at the time.

There were only a few people who knew about the right stuff then, and it didn't matter to me that everyone would take the mickey out of me. That first day I made a grand entrance and from then on had aggro every day I went to college. I didn't care. I guess that's how Viv [Albertine, later of punk band The Slits] noticed me. Viv lived in a squat in Davis Road which was just up the road from Hammersmith Art College, with this guy Alan Drake. I'd go there a lot 'cos it was convenient. I met Keith Levene there, 'cos he was a friend of Alan's and he played a bit of guitar.

I'd also got to know Tony James [later of Generation X, Sigue Sigue Sputnik and Carbon Silicon] at art college. We hit it off immediately and became great friends. We spent most of our formative years together and used to drive everywhere in his car, which was one of those really little Fiats.

BRAVE NEW WORLD

Once I'd dropped out of art school I took a job at a Social Security office. It was on the first floor of a modern building across the road from Euston station and there were these old-fashioned benches around the wall for people to sit on. One day I saw this guy who'd been there all day, being given the run around. They used to employ the most unsympathetic people at the counters – to give short shrift to anyone making bogus claims. Anyway, after four hours of waiting this guy picked up one of the huge benches and pushed it through the window, out onto Praed Street, out of sheer frustration.

My job was to open packages in the back room of the office, and this was at a time when the IRA were very active in London. There was a letter bomb campaign being waged by them so it wasn't exactly a dream job. Hence the line in Career Opportunities.

There was a little café in Praed Street where I used to meet with Tony James. When we started a band we managed to get records that we wanted on the café jukebox and so we'd audition people for the band in there.

I met Bernie Rhodes in 1975, in a place in West Kensington called The Nashville Rooms. He had this cap on and he looked rock 'n' roll, sort of like Gene Vincent, so I went over to talk to him and said, 'Are you a piano player?' and he said, 'No I'm not, but you're wearing one of my t-shirts.' I was wearing a t-shirt that said 'You're Gonna Wake Up', which I'd bought from a place called Let It Rock on the King's Road, Chelsea [owned by Malcolm McLaren and Vivienne Westwood, it would later become Sex and then Seditionaries]. He was an interesting guy, Bernie. We got talking and soon after he started working with me and Tony on a band. He told us about the Sex Pistols who were just forming.

I met Chrissie Hynde through Bernie and for a while we were going to put a band together. We'd go up to my Nan's bedroom and play songs together as duets. That's where Every Little Bit Hurts came from. We never got the band together. She did cut my hair, though.

Mick photographed backstage at an early (1976) Clash gig, in one of Paul's spray-painted shirts.

FOLLOWING PAGE: Joe, Paul and Mick at Rehearsals Rehearsals, 1976.

Paul Simonon

B. 15/12/1955

'I wanted to be Pete Townshend, the bloke who throws his arms around and jumps up and down.'

BRIXTON 1962 – BOMBSITES & SKA. . .

Growing up in the slums of Brixton was a fantastic place for a child, it bristled with energy and the multicultural mix of people gave it a unique atmosphere. Bus conductors used to yell out 'United Nations' whenever their bus stopped outside Lambeth Town Hall. The area had an already strong West Indian Community which was expanding and as an English seven-year-old it was an exciting place to grow up.

Me and my younger brother Nick attended Effra Junior and Infants school just off the Railton Road. We were living in Shakespeare Road opposite the railway lines leading to Clapham Junction at the time. It was only a five-minute walk to school. Come the weekend I used to visit my school friends and we'd play in Somerleyton Road, which was littered with bombsites that made perfect play areas, as did the railway line.

The people that lived on this street were mostly from the Caribbean with a few Irish families, some Polish and a German who I think had been interned in Britain during the war.

Going into a West Indian home for the first time was quite an eye-opener for me. My friend Marcus invited me to his home where he lived with his mum. Walking up to the second floor of this crumbling Victorian house on its creaking staircase I entered a small room that was brought alive by coloured lights and a pink plastic flamingo in the corner. It felt a bit like Christmas every time I went there. Marcus introduced me to his mum, and it took me a while to understand what she was saying. She was a very busy woman so we

sat on the sofa while she took the lid off a giant pot and served us some food. The music from the record player bounced as we balanced a plate of chicken, rice 'n peas on our laps. Wow, what a taste. My mum never made this for me to eat. The music playing at Marcus' place was the type I sometimes heard booming from flats and basements around the area. I didn't know at the time it was called Ska.

BRIXTON 1962 – A FEW MEMORIES MORE

One early evening a police car and ambulance pulled away from the kerb by a house where there had been an argument and a knife fight between two West Indians in the top-floor flat. A small group dared each other to go visit the dead man's room. I volunteered to go, asking my younger brother to shadow me up the stairs for support. Slowly we crept up the narrowing staircase, our hearts beating like drums. We reached the top of the decrepit Victorian house to see that the door was ajar. I stole into the room, which was lit by a very weak bulb. In one corner there was an unmade bed and the window was half open, the ragged curtains flapping in the breeze. I saw that puddles of blood had already seeped into the patterned carpet. My eyes shot around the room and I was struck by immaculately pressed suits on coat hangers that had been hung upon nails along the wall or on the edge of the window frame. One suit shimmered in the breeze, the dim yellow bulb reflecting from its blue and green sheen. Another was a shiny black and gold. There was a dark purple suit and an orange one that glowed. They brought the dead man's room alive, and in a space of seconds I was ready to leave. I spied two half crown coins by the unmade bed and thought they would be proof that I had entered the room. I took them and fled the room. My sudden exit startled my brother who turned and ran. We both thundered down the stairs and out into the street to be met by the worried expressions on our friends' faces. I threw open my hand to show off the silver coins, and we went to celebrate our good fortune at 'Snooks' sweetshop

Nearly every Sunday morning the local West Indians would sit on a corner wall of Somerleyton Road recovering from the party the night before. They were still dressed in flashy suits and hats. I got to know some of them by the way they arranged their shapes against the wall or their walk, which was as if they were off to have a shoot out with Jack Palance. Sometimes, I'd run errands for them and buy them a packet of five cigarettes, or a single. They introduced me to their friends as their 'spa' [side kick].

I was a happy kid, until one day my father asked me into the front room and delivered the devastating news that he wouldn't be living with us anymore; no reasons or explanations as to why. The news completely crushed me and my outlook on life changed. Within a few days, maybe even a week, my new father arrived at our house, his name was Michael .

It was difficult for all of us. My younger brother didn't really understand what had happened, and I refused to adapt to the change and struggled with the new regime. Over the next few months my stepfather's belongings were

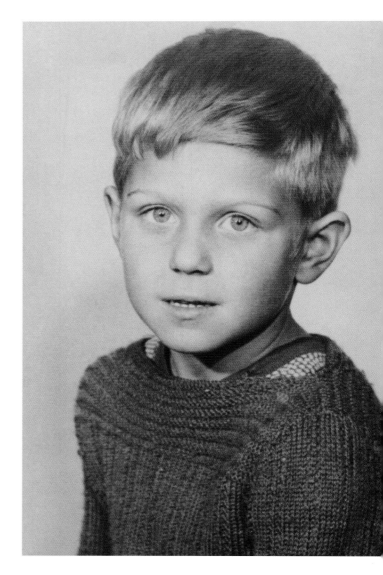

Paul in a 1961 school photograph.

moved in, among them his piano [he was a composer].

I spent even more time roaming the Brixton area, stealing from shops and generally causing trouble with a small gang of friends. Granville Arcade or Woolworth's were good for robbing.

Sometimes we'd go to the Empress Theatre on Brighton Terrace to see Mick McManus wrestling, but religiously we would attend The Brixton Astoria for Saturday morning pictures. I liked walking past Desmond's Hipcity record shop afterwards, where the speakers were placed outside and people use to dance to the latest hits from Jamaica.

By the evening, with no desire to go home, I would loiter with my friends till they were called indoors for bed or sometimes a blues party would be warming up and we'd sit outside watching people arrive. If it was my friend's house we would eat and listen to the records from Jamaica.

As it was getting late I would start to make my way home. It was hard to leave the excitement of the party and the early sounds of Rocksteady. Walking home alone was a good way to reflect on the day's events, with the music still humming in my head.

BRIXTON 1965 – BRIXTON TO SIENA

One early evening my mother and stepfather said they were going out to see a film and that we were to put ourselves to bed. At some point me and my brother ended up playing with a box of matches. Getting bored we got talking about the basement and the rats in it – as well as lots of discarded newspapers. I don't really remember what happened next but within a few minutes the cellar was a raging inferno and our neighbours were banging on the front door. We went outside and saw the black plumes of smoke pouring out of the gaps in the coal hole. The fire brigade arrived and used axes to get into a room. It was really exciting, but I knew I was for it. Me and my brother were taken to Brixton Police Station and spent a few hours playing with broken toys. Eventually our mum and stepfather turn up looking rather sheepish and we were taken home. Not a word was said about the fire.

By the autumn of 1965 me and my brother were told that our stepfather had won a scholarship to study music in Italy and we were all going to live there for a year. We accepted the news with excitement. I suppose we thought that meant the end of school forever.

In 1966 we left Brixton via Victoria Station for Siena. The train journey took ages and when we had a stop off in Florence we went and had pizza (my first ever) and I was allowed a glass of wine. We went back to the station sloshed. Siena was a different world: it was a paradise. It was sunny, they had grapes and melons, wine and spaghetti. We rented a top floor flat, ate pasta and listened to the drums of the local contrada parading their area in the build up to The Palio.

Italian school was discussed and I refused to go because the school uniform was a big blue smock with a big black bow in the front. Mum taught us herself in the evenings. During the day me and my brother roamed the

Paul playing at a bombsite in Brixton with US Cavalry hat from Woolworths, the first in a long line of hats...

streets just like we had in Brixton. The language was a big problem, but not for long. A group of Italian teenage girls adopted us, eager to improve their English. Because the Beatles were very popular and my name being Paul, I was treated like a little prince.

I had a very small transistor radio that I was given by my aunt for Christmas. In Italy the music on the radio was not always exciting, but every so often this strange distorted guitar instrumental would rip out of it. My Mum took me to see Spaghetti Westerns, which seemed more like action packed operas. The music was really exciting, some of which was the stuff I'd heard on my transistor radio. I really missed my dad, though.

By the end of December 1966, after living in Rome for five months we moved back to London and I had my tenth birthday on the ferry to Dover.

HERNE HILL 1967 – HERNE HILL TO LADBROKE GROVE

Back in London we went to live in Herne Hill, about a mile from Brixton, and I was sent to Bessemer Grange School for the rest of the year. It was hard to adjust to the school system but I soon made new friends and prepared for Secondary School, which was a place called William Penn Boys School. It had a very bad reputation and was a constant problem for the area. I didn't care much for school so I started taking time off, playing truant.

The skinhead movement was just beginning to take shape and was very appealing to budding misfits like me. The hippie movement held no such attraction, since I didn't care for the music or the look.

Aged twelve or thirteen years old you are too old for Saturday morning pictures and too young for clubs. But a friend told me about a place called the Streatham Locarno that put on Saturday morning dances. We all dressed up. I had a white Ben Sherman shirt, white Levi's, thin red braces and Dr Martens boots. My friend Clive Teagle had a two-tone suit (I was jealous of that suit and eventually bought it off him and wore it in the early days of The Clash).

The Locarno had a very rowdy crowd of boys and some girls. Once inside we listened to lots of Lee Perry instrumentals, which made a great soundtrack to the fights that broke out on the dance floor.

The Streatham Locarno was eventually closed because of fighting. So it was at a friend's home with a newly purchased Tighten Up album, or the sound system at Brockwell Park Funfair where I heard the current releases. Flash clothes, Jamaican music, fighting and football were our obsessions. Girls came later.

LADBROKE GROVE 1970 – A NEW LIFE ACROSS THE RIVER

As the sixties were coming to a close I'd become completely out of control. I hardly attended school and the relationship with my stepfather, though never good, was now on a knife edge. My mother needed help and made a phone call. A day or two later I was asked if I wanted to live with my father. I agreed immediately and packed.

My father lived just off the Portobello Road. When I arrived we sat down

Desmond Dekker (1941–2006) was one of the first reggae singers to score hit records in the UK pop charts. His Rude Boy songs made him a skinhead hero. The Israelites in 1968 gave him a UK number 1 hit single and it also cracked the US Billboard chart Top Ten – a first for a Jamaican singer. The Israelites was a big song for the skinhead movement, as was Long Shot Kick De Bucket.

and went through my belongings. He pulled out all my precious football programmes, ripped them in half and threw them into the bin and said, 'We are not having any of that rubbish in this house!'

My whole world took a dramatic turn. I felt imprisoned and struggled to adapt to the new order. I was sent to Isaac Newton Boys School just off the Golborne Road. Despite the strictness of home life, Isaac Newton School was complete freedom. It was just as rough as William Penn School and teachers came and went. I enjoyed the anarchy of the place though.

The area I was now living in was the West London equivalent of Brixton, the West Indian influence was strong and was very familiar to me.

I had a Saturday job in Portobello Market and felt very at home. Over the next few years my life became more relaxed and I was able to escape in the evenings and socialize with the boys from my school and catch up on the latest reggae tunes.

LADBROKE GROVE 1973 – PAINT & GUITARS

In 1973 I stayed on at Isaac Newton for a final year, but because the school didn't have enough teachers, the 6th form would have to continue our lessons in the local Ladbroke Girls School. At this time I set my sights on art college. The art teacher at Ladbroke Girls School took a shine to me and

The skinhead cult developed in England out of Mod culture. Originally often the younger brothers of Mods, but too young to afford the smart suits and expensive haircuts, skinheads adopted a uniform look of Sta-Prest jeans, Ben Sherman shirts, Crombie overcoats and shiny boots or brogues as casual wear, and two-tone shiny suits for dress. Paul was inspired by Jamaican Rude Boys who lived on the same street as he, and wore the two-tone suits which skinheads revered so much.

FOLLOWING PAGE: The Clash in full flight at the Coliseum, Harlesden, March 1977. In the audience, at the lower right corner, Roadent can just be seen. Standing (in red trousers) is Sebastian Conran, and crouched to his right is Arianna Forster (Ari-Up) of the Slits. The head just visible above the amplifier at the back is Tessa Pollitt, also of the Slits, who were the support act that night.

encouraged me to apply to The Byam Shaw School of Art in Notting Hill Gate where they accepted you on the quality of your portfolio. I was accepted and managed to convince The County Council that I was worthy of a scholarship.

After a year's foundation course my attention started to wander, though. The American Abstract movement of the Sixties was still strong in the minds of some of the teachers and the way I wanted to paint was too old-fashioned for them. I only wanted to learn how to draw and paint. I was told that I would have to redo my foundation course. So I got my grant and in a few months I'd vanished.

A month before I left, I went with a friend from art college to an audition as a drummer. I tagged along just to back him up. We got to Praed Street in Paddington and entered what looked like a dungeon. These three blokes with really long hair and guitars asked if I was a singer. 'No I'm a painter'. They ignored my answer, or maybe they couldn't hear cause of the long hair? Anyway, my friend bashed the drums and I was encouraged to have a go at singing songs I'd never heard of. It was a disaster.

On leaving the dungeon I saw this man sitting in the corner... 'Are you their manager or something?' I asked. 'No, why, what's it to you?' he replied. His name I later discovered was Bernard Rhodes.

A week or two later I ran into the guitarist from the audition, his hair was shorter. His name he told me was Mick Jones, and he was attending Hammersmith School of Art. We became chatty and met a few times in the local pubs. One night he asked if I played an instrument. 'No... but I'd like to.'

Mick and I met up at his home, which was in a tower block off the Harrow Road. He struggled to teach me a few chords on a guitar and we both got very frustrated. He said, 'Maybe you should try a bass guitar, it might be easier.' I wasn't excited about the idea because I thought the bass player in a rock 'n' roll group stood in the background.

I gave it a try though. We got hold of a bass and Mick told me that there was an exhibition of paintings at Camberwell Art College, by someone called Stuart Sutcliffe. He used to be in a group called The Beatles and he couldn't play bass either, explained Mick. So after Mick's musical history lesson I started to learn.

It was a struggle, but it was made easier by playing along to reggae records. I could hear the basslines and I knew the tunes only too well. Our friendship developed and I was introduced to another guitarist called Keith Levene. He was a spiky personality and we got on well. We rehearsed together for months trying out singers and drummers under the watchful eye of Bernard Rhodes who had been helping a new group called The Sex Pistols; he had found them a singer called John.

Over the next month we rehearsed on and off with a drummer called Terry Chimes and before long we found our singer – although he was in a group called the 101'ers. His name was Joe Strummer...

Topper Headon

B. 30/05/1955

'Drumming became my first addiction. I'd play for eight hours a day.'

BIRTH, SCHOOL

I was born in Bromley in 1955, my father and mother were both teachers and my father got his first headship (of a primary school) in Dover so we moved there when I was thirteen. I grew up in the Bromley, Dartford area and went to the primary school where my father was a teacher and I think in order to be accepted by the other kids there, I I used to play up a bit more than I had to

I became the class clown and have no bad memories of that time at all, it was lovely. Then I had one year at Dartford college which was also good.

My life became worse, though, when I moved to the grammar school in Dover, because everyone else in my year had been to local primary schools and knew each other, and they knew girls outside of school (it was an all-boys school). I went into the grammar school a year later than everyone else, too.

I was bullied at first because they were all in their cliques and I was the new boy, an outsider, and didn't know anybody or any of the places in Dover that they did. Plus, I was small. I became unhappy and didn't like the school.

I only made friends through football, which I was good at, until I started clowning about and doing things that other kids wouldn't. I'd throw the stone through the window, and do the mad stuff that they'd only talk about.

Not long after arriving in Dover, I broke my leg playing football and had a full-length cast put on my leg. I couldn't move my leg at all, so I had to sit still for the first time in my life, and couldn't go to school. This was for six months. I'd sit watching other kids playing football outside, and I started to get really depressed because I couldn't do anything.

Nicky 'Topper' Headon was only ever a member of one band, full-time: The Clash.

I developed alopecia and symptoms of depression, and so the doctor suggested I get a hobby or start doing something else to take up my time and attention. I was into music and was listening to The Who, and loved the sound of Keith Moon's drumming so I decided I wanted to be a drummer. A month later a drum kit was advertised for sale in the *Dover Express* and my father went and bought it for me.

MUSIC

My parents were musical. They're both Welsh, love to sing and my mum plays the piano. My mum loved The Beatles and I was brought up with music playing and being played around me. They encouraged me when I said I wanted to play drums, even though I had to play at home and made a hell of a noise. Yet they never complained.

I've never had a drum lesson in my life and when people ask me even now if I can teach them, I have no idea how to. I can't read a note of music, but I can play the piano and guitars; I just don't know what I'm doing on them. I inherited it from my parents, I think. According to my mum, when I was in my cot she'd sing a note to me and I'd sing it back at her.

Playing the drums became my first addiction – I'd play for eight hours a day. And my parents would let me; they were amazing.

Within six months of getting a drum kit I was gigging. There was a local family of musicians who lived nearby. The dad, Bill Barnacle, played the trumpet and he had three sons who were my age or slightly younger and they all wanted to be musicians. I went to see Bill one night at the Louis Armstrong pub when I was fourteen or so, and got up and played.

I was good enough to get regular gigs every Sunday night at the Louis Armstrong playing trad jazz, as well as at other pubs and clubs which I'd play with pick-up bands and was earning £5 a week at a time when other boys my age were getting five bob pocket money.

I used to love Gene Krupa and Buddy Rich records, but I also liked listening to rock stuff. I'd listen to as much music in as many different styles as I could and merge them into my playing. I really liked Steve Gadd, he was a brilliant drummer. I liked Herbie Hancock, too, and later Mick turned me on to Taj Mahal.

I don't know why, but I could play the drums. Behind the drumkit I was confident. It was my passport to confidence, I could talk to girls and felt like I could do anything. And my parents supported me in my drumming because they realized that it was the thing that I was good at.

Of course I didn't do any school work after learning to play drums. My parents tried to get me to work and I left school with two O levels, English Literature and English Language, both Grade As. But I didn't work and so failed all the others.

I moved to London on my own when I was seventeen. After a couple of nights in a B&B I met another guy from Dover who introduced me to some medical students who had a spare room in a house in Tooting, so I moved in there and worked at Initial Laundry. I stayed a few months but it was a bit

Nicky Headon, in school uniform, photographed before the family move to Dover.

hard at that age. I did some auditions at the time, one for Sparks where I came second, so didn't get the job. I ran out of money after a few months though and moved back to Dover. My parents took me back no problem. They've always been there for me.

I did some odd jobs in Dover for the next year or so. Like working on the Channel Tunnel construction; but I've never seen the point of working if you don't enjoy it. I kept auditioning for bands and when I was eighteen or so got a gig with a band called the IGs – they were all GIs – and all a lot older than me. I loved playing with them though. We'd stay in B&Bs and tour the US Army bases in England, and had to play all dressed in black.

We used to do Cloud 9 by The Temptations (I told people I'd played with the Temps, but hadn't) and Love Machine by The Miracles, the music was great. But I didn't like the actual touring with them because it was boring. The gigs were great, but the travel and hanging about wasn't.

BRAVE NEW WORLD

I moved back to London when I was nineteen and through *Melody Maker* magazine I got auditions with loads of different bands. One of them was London SS, which is when I met Mick and played with them for a week or so.

I met Bernie at the first audition for that band [London SS] and didn't like him from the word go. I never liked Bernie.

Before joining The Clash I played with a Canadian guitarist called Pat Travers for six months and he sacked me for not hitting the drums hard enough. After him I played with another band who were a couple of Canadian brothers playing heavy rock and the same thing happened. We rehearsed for months and they sacked me just as they were about to be signed because I didn't hit the drums hard enough.

Then I met Mick at the Rainbow and he asked me to audition for his new band and I thought, right I'll beat the shit out of the drums. So I did as we played London's Burning for the 200th time that day or something.

I remember the band asking all these other drummers who their influences were and them all going, Pistols, New York Dolls, that kind of stuff. Some of them were saying what they thought the band wanted to hear, but when they asked me I said, Billy Cobham, Buddy Rich and stuff I really liked.

After the audition I remember Baker the roadie showing me out of the audition and him saying, 'You've got it, if you want it'. I said, 'How do you know?' and he said, 'I know them. You've got it.'

Now, all this stuff about me not liking punk isn't true. When I met the band I loved the way they looked, they were intimidating the three of them, but it was exciting. And I loved their energy. I loved what they were doing. But it's not true that I never liked punk.

I wasn't a great drummer until I joined the Clash. I was a good drummer, had all the chops, but no power behind it. When I joined the Clash I had to relearn the whole thing. And we evolved together, our chemistry or whatever made us what we were musically.

1976

'The day I joined The Clash was very much back to square one, year zero. Part of punk was that you had to shed all of what you knew before.' JOE

The summer of 1976 was long and hot, the airwaves full of the sound of disco, prog rock and Abba. But in a few dark cellars and pubs in London a new sound and a new look was developing. The back room of a bondage clothing store in the Kings Road had spewed up the Sex Pistols who played a handful of chaotic gigs before landing a Tuesday night residency at the 100 Club. On 4 June, a Pistols show in Manchester organized by the Buzzcocks and attended by less than 100 people inspired journalists to hail the dawn of a new age of Punk. A month later, at a small pub in Sheffield, The Clash made their live debut as support act for the Pistols.

L-R: Joe, Mick, Paul. The Clash rehearsal rooms were part of the old railway buildings that backed onto the Roundhouse in Camden Town, which is seen in the background here. The area's decaying Victorian industrial buildings provided an enduring backdrop to the band's image. Joe's recently dyed hair and punk clothes make him almost unrecognizable from when he was lead singer with the 101'ers – only weeks earlier.

JOE: When I'd got back to London in 1974 I remember walking past an Irish pub and looking in the window and seeing this trio playing and thought, rather than being chased by the police around the Underground, that maybe I should try that. I was living in a squat in Maida Hill and thought that playing pubs could get me through the summer. That was the first time I'd thought about putting an electric rock 'n' roll band together, but my ambition was just to get through the summer without having to run around the Underground when the pubs kicked out, collecting pennies from drunks.

JOE: The squat was not only the one place I could afford to live in, but it was where we could rehearse, too. We started the 101'ers with one amplifier and one speaker. I built my equipment from a drawer, out of a skip. We got some

Paul (left) talking with Kris Needs, then editor of *Zigzag* magazine, a once hippie music magazine which reinvented itself under Needs' guidance to become a punk fanzine and big supporter of The Clash.

cheap speakers down the Edgware Road and put them in the drawers, put a facing board on them, stood them up and there were our cabinets. We booked our own club, too, 'cos no-one was gonna book us into a club or pub, so we found a room upstairs in a pub, rented it for a quid for the evening and that's how we learned to play. By doing it ourselves. That was the punk ethos.

JOE: We called the room the Charlie Pig Dog Club after this dog we had, and it got really jumping 'cos all the squatters from all over West London would come down and it soon became a big mash-up. One night there were these gypsies there ripping people off and throwing coats out of the window. The police raided the place and mayhem broke loose but we carried on playing. The police didn't know whom to search or arrest, the squatters or the gypsies. We played Gloria for about twenty minutes.

PAUL: The first time I saw the 101'ers was at this dump which had people running about with their dogs and giant hippies stomping around. There was one guy called Dave the Van or something who wore blue overalls, had a big beard and was jumping around completely sloshed while Joe was on stage. He'd be playing and there was a woman breastfeeding a baby and dogs running across the stage, but Joe was definitely the guy to watch.

JOE: In 1975 Kilburn And The High Roads were the top of the tree that we were on. Then Dr Feelgood came along and they were like a machine of intense proportions and we fell into that scene. One night Allan Jones [later editor of *Melody Maker* and *Uncut* magazines], whom we'd known in Newport, came to the Pig Dog Club to see us and wrote a couple of lines about us in the *Melody Maker*, saying the 101'ers could really rock. I cut it out and took it to some pubs in West London, and eventually in the Elgin the landlord went, 'Alright, a fiver. Monday'. And that was when we broke out of our little scene. The Elgin became a hotspot, the landlord switched us to a Thursday night because we were doing good business, and it really began to take off. Unknown to me the Sex Pistols would come there every Thursday and check us out. I didn't realize how good we were.

MICK: When Paul came into our basement rehearsal room he looked so stunning that we said, 'Can you sing?' He tried it and it didn't work out but he made an impression on me and we became quite friendly. He said 'Let's get a group together' one day while we were walking round Portobello Market.

JOE: The first time I heard the word 'Punk' was in *Time Out*, a London listings magazine, where they wrote that Eddie & The Hot Rods were a second-generation Punk band and I remember thinking, 'What is this word?' And then the Pistols came through and it was clear what they meant.

MICK: We borrowed a bass guitar from Tony (James) and Paul painted the notes on it and then we (Paul and I) sat down to try and learn. He turned out to be a fantastic bass player. He had his own style, plus the look, and was incredible. It was frustrating to begin with but he gradually built it up.

Paul onstage in 1976 in his self-decorated 'Jackson Pollacked' shirt with a patch showing Reggae band The Gladiators. His bass shows the notes he had painted onto the fretboard.

JOE: The 101'ers had been playing for two years or so when the Pistols burst onto the scene, and when I saw them I realized you couldn't compare the Pistols to any other group on the island, they were so far ahead. I mean it can't be stressed enough, it was a quantum leap. As soon as I saw the Sex Pistols in the Nashville Room – they were supporting the 101ers and we had plenty of attitude, we were squatters and we didn't care a damn about anything or anybody but when this lot came in I remember thinking, 'God damnit, look at these guys.' Sid Vicious was the last one in the queue as they came through the dressing room to do a soundcheck and I thought, 'I'm going to mess with one of these guys to see what they're made of', and he was wearing an Elvis Presley-like gold jacket so I said to him, 'Oi', he went, 'Wot?' and

Proto-punks watch and dance as the Sex Pistols perform in mid-1976. There were no brightly coloured Mohican haircuts among the first wave of punks.

I said, 'Where'd you get that jacket?' and I love Sid for this 'cos the groups were like that in those days, facing each other out, like dog eat dog, and he could have said, 'Piss off turd', or something and he didn't. He said, 'Oh it's really good innit? I'll tell you where I got it, you know that stall…' I thought that was great, Sid didn't have to put on an attitude. Anyway, they played and I went out front to watch and there was hardly any audience, it was a Tuesday or something. And I knew we were finished, five seconds into their first song I knew we were like yesterday's papers, I mean we were over.

PAUL: We saw the 101'ers at the Nashville with the Pistols. I knew Steve and Glen, though I'd never met John. He was fantastic on stage, really winding people up, blowing his nose, wearing a big, ripped red jumper and he just didn't give a toss. I thought they were great. I could really relate to them and didn't even notice the bad notes. When the 101'ers came on Joe was great and the rest of them were just sort of twiddling along.

MICK: We'd seen Joe with the 101'ers quite a few times and that he was out there playing was a big deal to us. We had this other singer called Billy, from Wycombe, but it didn't work out and I can't remember why, but we were looking for a new singer. I think it was Bernie who directed our thoughts to Joe. We'd seen him around, in the dole office and so on, and then we went to see the 101'ers with the Sex Pistols which ended up with the Pistols in a fight and that was the night we decided that Joe was the best guy out there.

PAUL: We had a singer named Billy Watts who was a nice bloke but his look was a bit old-fashioned and we needed fresh input. I think it was Bernie who suggested we try to nick Joe from the 101'ers.

JOE: The first time I saw Mick and Paul we were all in Lisson Grove Labour Exchange. I was queuing to get dole, which was about £10.64, and they were obviously waiting to see someone in there. I could see them staring at me and I didn't realize they'd seen the 101'ers the previous weekend and were probably going, 'Look there's that bloke from the 101'ers'. But I thought it was on, you know [a fight], so I ignored them, collected my dole and was expecting them to tangle with me on my way to the door or in the street, but they continued sitting there. They were eye-catching though, they already looked different to everyone else. But I thought there was going to be trouble so I was working out which one to punch first. I thought I'd punch Mick first because he looked thinner and Paul looked a bit tasty so I decided I'd smack Mick and leg it. That was my plan.

PAUL: I remember seeing Joe in the dole queue and I think he caught us looking at him and was a bit worried, like he might get done over. He looked, for a moment, quite timid and in terror. We were just going, 'It's that bloke out of the 101'ers'.

MICK: We decided to ask Joe if he wanted to join us and were all in the squat when Bernie and Keith went to see him play at the Golden Lion in Fulham. I think they gave him 48 hours to make his mind up but Bernie couldn't wait that long and phoned him after a day and Joe said yeah.

JOE: After seeing the Pistols I thought the 101'ers might as well give up there and then. The other members couldn't see it and we were beginning to splinter. The guitarist stormed off after a gig not much later at the Golden Lion in Fulham, but that night Bernie Rhodes came to the dressing room with Keith Levene and went, 'Hey, come with me, I want you to meet some people.' There was something about the way he and Keith looked I just said 'OK' and we went to Shepherd's Bush, to a squat in Davis Road where there were these two guys waiting who I'd seen in the dole office not long before. There were amps in the room and we started to practise either then or the next day.

Joey Ramone on stage at London's Roundhouse on 4 July 1976. Many British punks learned to play their instruments listening and playing along with The Ramones first album, including The Clash.

Afterwards Bernie said, 'Why don't you think about joining this band?' I thought about it for about 24 hours and then rang him and said, 'OK, I'm in.' It was the look of them more than anything else, you could see the new world.

MICK: He came to see us at Davis Road and we were all nervously waiting and then we went straight into it. We went into the little room where we'd put eggboxes on the walls to soundproof it and began. He didn't want to do his tunes so much but he was into changing, improving our songs. So we had a great lyric writer working with us and Bernie helping us to realize what we were about and what we should be writing about.

JOE: The day I joined The Clash was very much back to square one, year zero. Part of Punk was that you had to shed all of what you knew before. We were almost Stalinist in the way that we insisted you had to cast off all your friends, everything you'd ever known, and the way you'd played before in a frenzied attempt to create something new, which was not easy at any time. It was very rigorous; we were insane, basically. Completely and utterly insane.

JOE: When The Clash formed there was no real agenda, it was what everybody put in. There was only Mick and Paul, and Mick was teaching Paul how to play bass 'cos he'd only been playing for three weeks or something. Mick could already play really great guitar and I could hack it in there, but we didn't have a drummer. It was all new, all built from the ground up.

PAUL: When Joe came to see us at Davis Road we went into the little room to practise and me and Mick started throwing our guitars about, jumping around, and I think Joe enjoyed it 'cos he didn't get that from his other band, where everything had to be perfect. With us it was just bash it out and with me it was pot luck whether I hit E or G, which is why I painted the notes on the neck. Mick would say 'G' and I could just go to the G. Mick called it the Paul Simonon School of Music method.

JOE: Paul was practising bass to reggae songs and the first Ramones album, which was seminal. It can't be stressed how great the first Ramones album was to the scene because it gave anyone who couldn't play the idea that it was simple enough to be able to play. We all used to practise along with it. Paul and I spent hours, days, weeks playing along to the record. Anyone could see where the notes went and it gave everyone confidence. It was the first word of Punk, a fantastic record.

JOE: Our equipment was pretty rudimentary, we only needed three amps and cabs; we didn't have a drummer to begin with. Bernie bought us a PA and three microphones. One of our mics came from the English National Opera. I had a job there cleaning the toilets just before joining The Clash. I noticed a microphone high above the stage on the top gantry, for the man up there to talk to the wings or spot operators. One day when there was no-one around I climbed up this ladder to the very top with a pair of wire cutters in my overalls. I got hold of the mic, cut the wires, stuffed the mic down the front of my

trousers and climbed all the way down again. I was kind of sweating with the excitement of it all, and as I walked through the back corridor the manager of the Opera House walked towards me and I thought, 'He's sure to notice this microphone down my trousers', but he just walked straight past me. We used that mic in the early days.

EARLY CLASH SONGS

JOE: I brought in some stuff from the 101'ers, but Mick also had some songs they'd been working on. I think the most amusing story is about I'm So Bored With The USA, which was probably the first song that Mick, Paul and I started work on together. When Mick demoed it to me I thought he said it was called I'm So Bored With The USA and I jumped out of my chair going, 'Great, greeat' because then, like now, we live on a diet of American TV programmes and I said, 'Great, I'm so bored with the USA', and Mick says, 'No, I didn't say that, this is a song about my girlfriend, called "I'm So Bored With You"' and I said, 'Never mind that, let's write it now. "I'm So Bored With The USA".' It became a big favourite with American audiences; they used to scream if we didn't play it.

A very early Clash at Rehearsals Rehearsals, before the backdrop went up on the rear wall. L-R: Mick, Pablo LaBritain (later of punk band 999) on drums, Joe, Paul and Keith Levene.

An early Clash gig, 1976. Mick's speaker cabinet (centre) was to become the cover star of the single sleeve for Complete Control.

MICK: It was originally I'm So Bored With You, a kind of twisted love song, and Joe added the 'S-A' and it became about the Americanization of England. Although we'd all been brought up on American TV shows, we still thought there was too much American influence around us. We went into an ice cream shop on the Edgware Road one night, which was American-style, bought some ice creams and then went outside and wrote 'I'm So Bored With The USA' on the window, and it was filmed by Julien Temple (later to direct the Great Rock N Roll Swindle) who'd shot a lot of stuff with us, all without sound.

PAUL: The songs we started playing were a combination of Mick and Joe's, which helped build a unity between us. They'd both bring stuff in and we'd work on it. Bored With The USA, Protex Blue and Keys To Your Heart were all early ones. There were a couple of covers, too – Kinks songs.

JOE: At the time I was living in Orsett Terrace in a lovely squat, but it was cursed by flies. Paul came to live there for a while and Keith Levene. Sid Vicious was there, too, for a bit. One of the early Clash songs, I Can't Stand The Flies, was about that place, and was an interesting ditty about the cloud

L-R: Paul, Keith Levene, Mick, Joe. Photographed before one of the five gigs that the guitarist played as a member of The Clash. Levene went on to form Flowers of Romance with Sid Vicious, before Sid joined the Pistols (replacing Glen Matlock). After the Pistols split, Levene formed Public Image Ltd with John Lydon in 1978. Three years later he left PiL and recorded albums with various other musicians and producers, including Adrian Sherwood, Flea and Hillel of the Red Hot Chilli Peppers. His last musical project was titled Murder Global.

of a thousand flies which would gather in the kitchen. If you wanted to make a cup of tea you had to get on your hands and knees and crawl across the floor to get to the cupboard where the kettle was.

MICK: The second Clash song was probably 1-2-Crush On You, which didn't change much when Joe started playing it with us.

JOE: Mark Me Absent is a tune that I think Mick and Keith Levene were cooking up and went something like, 'Mark me absent baby, something something', but we soon got rid of it because it was a pile of old rubbish. It gave us something to practise on, though.

PAUL: Keith was great because his approach was always from another angle to Mick's and it made for an interesting sound. He was always experimenting, trying to push it a little further.

JOE: Paul Simonon was always humming this tune, Poison Flour On The Hour, which was about how bad flour had been made into bread which then poisoned people. Simonon brought it up as an example of how you could write about topical things. We got all that stuff from reggae music, the way they toast over music about what had just happened. It gave us a direction, to try and do that in our own way. That rasta/punk crossover was crucial to the whole scene.

MICK: I used to write a lot of the basic parts of songs on the bus from West London to Camden. So I'd be on my way to rehearsals and I'd hook into the rhythms of the bus. One day Janie Jones came into my head 'cos she'd been in the Sunday papers and so that song was a combination of the 31 bus and the Sunday newspapers.

PAUL: I think 1977 came out of Joe and I listening to the little record player we had in Rehearsals Rehearsals. We only had a few records, a couple of Kinks, The Who Sell Out, Sixties things.

JOE: Life at that time was so intense, we never stopped writing. It seemed to be that one huge body of work was created in one go. I can't remember in what order the tunes came.

MICK: There was a lot of struggling with our instruments at the beginning and, combined with our struggles with the stuff that Bernie was laying on us at the same time, it made us unlike anything else around.

YOU GOT THE LOOK

MICK: Keith, Paul and myself were walking down Portobello Road on a Saturday and we went to the second-hand end and found a stall which had all these car coats, like 1960s ladies' car coats in fetching lilac and pale green and we all bought one each. They were really cheap, and we put them on and walked around and it really felt like we were in a group.

PAUL: Mick's hair became a bit of a challenge for me, Joe and Bernie. He'd say to me, 'Your hair's getting shorter and shorter' while we were trying to stress the point to him that maybe he should get a haircut 'cos it looked as if he was from a different group.

JOE: In the world of squats where I was living there was no fashion sense at all. I had drainpipe trousers because I was never into flares but it wasn't a fashion statement, I'd buy them cheap in used clothing stores.

PAUL: I was aware of the look the Pistols had, Steve used to wear Malcolm

Joe decorates a punk's school shirt, backstage, after a gig. Before Punk fashions hit the shops, punks made all their own clothes, mostly by ripping, spraying, stencilling or otherwise defacing their 'normal' clothes.

One of Mick Jones' specially made shirts, created using screenprints of the photographs used in the artwork for the first *Clash* and *Blackmarket Clash* albums. They had been taken by Rocco Redondo at the 1976 Notting Hill Carnival during a riot.

and Vivienne's stuff, though John seemed not to be into that, he had his own look, which was interesting. We didn't have a shop to rely on though so we had to be self-sufficient, which helped us in the long run. We had to be more involved with what we were going to wear. Whereas the Pistols had it sewn up for them. Literally. Joe pretty much fell in straight away and while I was Jackson Pollacking shirts, Joe was painting his trousers.

MICK: I was always concerned about how a thing looked just as much as how it sounded and what it was about.

LEFT: Paul bursts through a door at Rehearsals Rehearsals.

RIGHT: Jamaican musicians of the 1970s showed a fascination with Westerns that was reflected in songs and even movies (see *The Harder They Come*). The Clash were similarly raised on Westerns and American movies portraying a gun culture that was all-pervasive. Paul poses with an air pistol alongside Joe and Mick at Rehearsals Rehearsals.

LEFT: Joe in his hand-stencilled '1977' shirt. The song became an early Clash live favourite and its chorus of 'No Elvis, Beatles or Rolling Stones' an instant punk catchphrase.

ABOVE: Paul (left) and Joe onstage at the Institute of Contemporary Arts, London, October 1976.

PAUL: We all realized that we needed a unified look. We came up with our own stuff and Bernie brought in this girl, Alex Michon, who was great. I'd do drawings of what I wanted and pass them to her and she'd sew them up for us. She made a Union Jack jacket which was the flag cut up and rearranged. We'd all discuss ideas with her, then I'd do the drawings and give her the specifications for each of us.

JOE: The only quote of mine that will go down in history is, 'Like trousers, like brain'. That flared look was a hangover from the Sixties and the new look was fast and trim. It was a big thing, you could see what people were into a mile off, which was quite handy, really.

PAUL: It shocked people if you walked down the road with Hate & War stencilled on your back. Joe asked me about being a skinhead once, and I said it's all about dressing to intimidate people and we brought that into the look, too. It connected Joe and me. We were both broke but he had dole money and used to share it with me. Once, after he'd been talking for a week about mirror shades and how intimidating they were, he got his dole and went and bought us both a pair. We walked around in them for ages. We were really hungry, but we had mirror shades. I repaid him later when I was given a $100 bill by somebody, and I bought him a boilersuit, 'cos I already had one.

First Dates

JULY TO NOVEMBER

LINE-UP: STRUMMER, JONES, SIMONON, CHIMES, LEVENE (UNTIL SEPT 20)

4 JUL: Black Swan, Sheffield
13 AUG: Rehearsals Rehearsals, Camden Town, London, private invite gig
29 AUG: Screen On The Green, Islington, London, Midnight Special
31 AUG: 100 Club, London, supporting the Sex Pistols
5 SEP: The Roundhouse, Camden Town, London, with Kursaal Flyers & Crazy Cavan. Keith Levene's last gig with The Clash
20 SEP: 100 Club, London Punk Festival (line-up Strummer, Jones, Simonon, Chimes). Also on the bill: the Sex Pistols, the Damned, the Buzzcocks, Subway Sect, Siouxsie & The Banshees, Stinky Toys
2 OCT: Institute of Contemporary Arts, London, with Fresh Air
9 OCT: Tiddenfoot Leisure Centre, Leighton Buzzard, with The Rockets
15 OCT: Acklam Hall, Ladbroke Grove, London
16 OCT: University of London, supporting Shakin' Stevens
23 OCT: Institute of Contemporary Arts, London, with Subway Sect
27 OCT: Barbarellas, Birmingham
29 OCT: Town Hall, Fulham, London, supporting Roogalator
3 NOV: Harlesden Coliseum, London
5 NOV: Royal College of Art, London, A Night Of Treason with The Jam and Subway Sect
11 NOV: Lacy Lady, Ilford
18 NOV: Nags Head, High Wycombe
29 NOV: Lanchester Polytechnic, Coventry

SONGS PLAYED:
Listen / Deny / 1-2 Crush On You / I Know What To Think Of You / I Never Did It / I Can't Stand the Flies / Janie Jones / Protex Blue / Mark Me Absent / Deadly Serious / What's My Name / Sitting At My Party / 48 Hours / I'm So Bored With You (+ USA) / London's Burning / 1977 / White Riot / Career Opportunities

Poster for the first ever punk festival, at London's 100 Club in Oxford Street. It was the first time that only Punk bands had played together and to a mainly Punk audience. For the first time that night Siouxsie and the Banshees performed, with Sid Vicious on drums.

'The first band to come along who'll really frighten the Sex Pistols'

The Clash
London

BEFORE WE begin, some clarification.

For a start, this isn't intended to be a 'review' as such; consider it rather as a somewhat peripheral cluster of observations regarding one The Clash.

Here's what you need to know: The Clash are a quintet, and feature among their number Mr. Joe Strummer, lately lead singer with the recently deceased 101'ers. The 101'ers were a sporadic but sometimes excellent rock 'n' roll band and all that remains of them is 'Key To Your Heart', a killer single (on Chiswick) and a few fond memories. The Clash are also a rock 'n' roll band. And there the resemblance begins and ends.

The Clash were unveiled last Friday evening in a small but rather splendidly decorated — by the lads themselves, no less — rehearsal room in darkest Chalk Farm, London.

The 'audience' was size-wise commensurate with the room — an informal gathering of press (including our own Mr. Ingham — he's that tastefully-attired gent languidly sipping his *vin blanc*, in the salvaged barber's chair) plus a handful of other hacks (that's me over there with the grubby jeans and acne scars) and potential bookers.

The invite was for nine. For an hour or so we amused ourselves with liqud refreshment from the amply-filled bar and music from the tastefully furnished juke-box.

Time. Five striking looking gentlemen strolled in. The four who carried guitars plugged them in to the waiting amplifiers, the fifth took his place at the drum-kit.

The gentleman on the extreme left (he looked not unlike a slightly more vicious Keith Richard in his striped shirt, leather trousers and centre-seamed Chelsea boots) gave a hoarse count-in and . . .

And for the next forty-odd minutes it was like being hit by a runaway fire engine — not once, but again and again . . . and again.

That first number was the one though, wasn't it boys and girls?

Wasn't it just like you're sitting peacefully at home and something taps you on the shoulder and you turn around and suddenly there's King Kong.

Or a runaway fire engine.

An Atom Bomb.

A hurricane.

An avalanche.

Or all these things, suddenly and very solidly right there above you. Screaming down.

I know, I know. It was only a rock 'n' roll band. So it was, but let me tell you, it was one

THE CLASH: unstoppable technicolour energy

picture by Eve Dadomo

monstrous entity in that first few minutes. Screaming down.

Clash could make it on looks alone practically. They all have that cropped hair, skintight trousers look that helps the Pistols' Mr. Rotten look so menacing. Only, like I said, there's five of them. Also their clothing, from collar to toe is spattered and daubed with paint, from the tiny flecks that look like maybe it just happened when they decorated the hall to the stripes on the afore-mentioned shirt. But it doesn't look at all silly — far from it — it looks the way a lot of kids will probably be dressing before very long, as much the anti-thesis of the bearded be-denimed latterday hippie as the mods were to the rockers.

Clash have plenty of that old mod flash too — posing f'sure, but impeccably done down to the last scowling spit.

But all this — striking as it is — is a secondary consideration, something my senses take in gradually. What hits first is the gut-curdling *power* of them. It's like the gleaming and totally unstoppable bastard son of the Pistols and the Ramones with the firepower of Status Quo. But get this — where all the aforementioned bands are basically simple, monochrome examples of electric violence The Clash generate an energy that's Technicolored Cinerama by comparison. By which I mean to dispel any notion that the music is one relentless semi-cacophony, because in all that nuclear glare there are incandescent gems of solos and references to everything from 'You Really Got Me' to **younameit**. Also, Strummer sems to have finally found his niche, his always manic deliveries finally finding their place in a compelling tapestry of sound and colour that only reveals its

full impact in the breathless silence that follows that first demonic show of hands.

Then we all breathe in and start to applaud — hesitantly at first, after all this is an 'informal' gathering — and then with increased delight.

Of course there were one or two little cock-ups, but considering the nature of the event The Clash still managed to come up with one of the most memorable debuts of the year so far.

I think they're the first band to come along who'll really frighten the Sex Pistols shitless.

I also think a hell of a lot of people are going to be knocked out by them.

And I know I can't wait to see them again, in front of a real audience this time, in a real hall.

Exciting isn't the word for it.

— GIOVANNI DADOMO

4 July 1976, Black Swan, Sheffield (with the Sex Pistols)

JOE: The line-up for the first gig was Terry Chimes on drums, Paul Simonon, Mick Jones, myself and Keith Levene, so we had a three guitar set-up.

MICK: I don't think we had been rehearsing that long before the first gig.

JOE: The first gig we ever played was at what we used to call the Mucky Duck (the Black Swan) in Sheffield. We had a song called Listen which had a bass line that went up in scale and then down a note to start, and Paul was so nervous that he just kept going up the scale and we all fell over laughing 'cos we didn't know when to come in.

PAUL: The day The Clash started really was when we played the Mucky Duck with the Pistols, which was great. It was the first time I'd ever played on stage. The night before it felt frightening but once we were on the way I began larking about. I tied one of Keith's shoes to a piece of string and hung it out the back of the van – the door had to be open so we could breathe. There we were sitting with all the amps and luggage with a plimsoll bouncing around behind us and all the cars behind us slowing down to avoid it. But the moment we walked on stage it was like I was in my living room. I felt really comfortable. Things went wrong and Mick had to come over and tune my guitar but it didn't bother me. I just wanted to jump around, but Mick wanted it to be in tune.

13 August 1976, Rehearsals Rehearsals, Camden (Showcase for journalists only)

JOE: Bernie organized a showcase gig at our rehearsal rooms for journalists: John Ingham, Caroline Coon, people who stuck their head above the parapet in order to publicize Punk, which was not an easy game. It would have been easier for them to have ignored us and carried on writing about Grand Funk Railroad or something – they took some flak by writing about us. Tony Parsons was another one who was there at the beginning.

MICK: We had to give the rehearsal room more than just a lick of paint. I remember spending days painting and listening to Rastafarian reggae, it was the soundtrack to that time.

JOE: Bernie had made us paint the rehearsal rooms before the gig, and we didn't really have any clothes except the ones we were wearing, or what we got from thrift stores. So there was paint everywhere, which is what I think gave Paul the idea of flicking it on our shoes and trousers, to jazz them up. It gave us an identity, too. So we came out resplendent, covered in paint. Just up the road from Rehearsals Rehearsals were the people who Bernie used to spray his cars, so we went to them and they sprayed the guitars and amps, jackets, ties, shirts and shoes using sprayguns. We must have looked fairly striking when we came on stage. If somewhat ridiculous.

MICK: By the second gig we had skinny ties and semi-smart jackets, but we'd gone through the painting thing. Paul made the connection between Jackson Pollock and our spritzing the paint on ourselves.

PAUL: I was walking down Denmark Street one day and I saw Glen Matlock. He was wearing what I first thought were Laura Ashley print trousers, but when I looked closer they were more Jackson Pollock. I realized that he'd splashed paint all over them. So thinking like Picasso, who'd pick up an idea and take it further, I went back to Rehearsals Rehearsals, got some gloss paint and splashed it on my shoes. It looked pretty good so I got a black shirt and did a bit on that with different paint and it was all about being aware of your textures (laughs). Because ideas were always discussed openly I only needed to do a few things for Mick and Joe to see what was going on and do their own stuff. It led to getting our guitars sprayed and then I got some stencils, probably from Bernie, which would clip together and so I sprayed words on jackets and shirts.

29 August 1976, Screen on the Green, Islington, with The Sex Pistols, Buzzcocks

JOE: Sometimes we'd take speed before a gig, but we didn't have a lot of money for that sort of thing. At this time Keith was still in the band and he always had some on him. But it wasn't very good for singing, 'cos your throat would dry out. It was fairly useless as a performance drug.

MICK: I don't think we played very well at the Screen on the Green because we'd spent the whole day looking after the equipment and watching *The Outlaw Josey Wales*. It was a Sunday and we had to wait until 1 a.m. to play, and we'd had to build the stage too. So we were a bit knackered by the time we got on the stage.

PAUL: I recall there was supposed to be some kind of deal where we would put up posters for the Screen on the Green gig and build the stage, but I don't remember doing any of that. Maybe someone gave me some posters and I

The Clash on stage at
The 100 Club, playing
to an audience of
punks, including Shane
MacGowan, later lead
singer with The Pogues:
seen here standing
facing Mick's guitar,
right.

chucked them in the bin. I wasn't going to stick up any posters that weren't my own. I couldn't understand why we sounded so awful on stage that night and then the Pistols came on and sounded fantastic, and it was that old trick of giving us a bit of the PA and not all of it. I suppose they were a bit scared of us, really. Or maybe it had something to do with Bernie and Malcolm's differences.

JOE: We didn't play very well that night, because we'd built the stage. At 8 a.m. we unloaded the scaffolding poles from a lorry and then built the stage. I was one of the posse hired to sit there all day watching the equipment that was stashed under the stage. I sat through *The Outlaw Josey Wales* three times and halfway through the third time, just as I was sinking into a coma, two young guys jumped out of the front row, dived under the stage and grabbed an amp before legging it out the side door. But because we were in position we went crashing right after them, and we nailed them to

the floor before they could get to the outside exit. We took the amp off them before kicking them out into the street. By the time the gig came up I was completely worn out. So we didn't play well. Though the Pistols were great.

31 August 1976, The 100 Club, London, with The Sex Pistols

JOE: Since the mid-1960s I tried to keep a transistor radio with me all the time so I could listen to the pirate stations in school break times. At The 100 Club, when we supported the Pistols, we'd decided that because we were punks we wouldn't talk to the audience, we'd just play, straight from one song to the next. That was great as long as you didn't have to stop, but Keith Levene broke a string and there was a horrible gap – there we were in a club with three or four hundred lunatics all lagered up and foaming at the mouth,

L-R: Mick, Paul, Bernie Rhodes, Joe. The band's first manager proves reluctant to have his photograph taken. Although he was never shy in front of journalists.

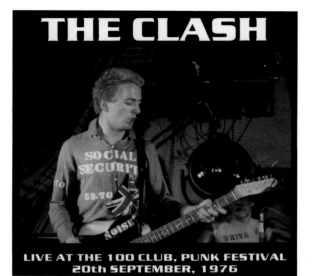

THE CLASH

LIVE AT THE 100 CLUB, PUNK FESTIVAL 20th SEPTEMBER, 1976

Like many of the first wave of punk bands, The Clash were bootlegged extensively. While original bootlegs of the 1970s were generally pressed onto vinyl and sold at high prices, in 2008 it was possible to buy many of those original bootleg recordings (as the above sleeve demonstrates) in CD format and at a cheap price.

and I couldn't just stand there and look at them, it would be ridiculous. So I grabbed my transistor radio from the top of the piano where I'd thrown it as we went on, turned it on and held it up to the microphone. It just happened that there was a really heavy news bulletin or panel discussion about the IRA and the bombing campaign that was going on in London being broadcast. Dave Goodman, who was the Pistols' soundman, had the nous to put a hip dub echo on the mic, so the announcer was saying, 'Bomb-bomb-bomb, Piccadilly-piccadilly-piccadilly', and it filled the gap so well that it's become a kind of punk folk tale. It was just a bit of luck. But after that gig we abandoned that stance and started speaking to the audience.

PAUL: Years later somebody told me that Malcolm had invited some Americans to The 100 Club that night to see the Pistols, but they saw us and went home thinking they'd seen the Pistols. They said to Malcolm: 'Yeah it's a really great show, but we didn't know you had two guitars.' It must have been a bit difficult for Malcolm to say they'd seen the wrong group.

5 September 1976, The Roundhouse, Camden, London, with Kursaal Flyers and Crazy Cavan

PAUL: The Roundhouse was an interesting gig 'cos it was just down the road from where we rehearsed. I used to walk there with Joe and we'd climb on the roof, and walk almost all the way to the top to find a way in. We went to see the Runaways and Patti Smith there but they wouldn't let us in. I don't think the promoter wanted any punks, so it was funny to get to play there. The problem was that you couldn't hear anything the audience was saying. Someone would shout 'wa wa wa', and the audience would laugh – but we had no idea what they were laughing about. That was Keith's last show with us.

MICK: Keith left the band after this gig because he couldn't be bothered to come to rehearsals. As I recall he actually said 'I can't be bothered to come to rehearsals,' so Joe said 'Well don't bloody bother to come again.'

PAUL: I'm not sure why Keith left, but he used to stand on my side of the stage, which was great for me, except Bernie always used to say 'stand further back, Paul.' I used to ignore him though and say, 'Not if I'm gonna be Pete Townshend', and stay at the front. When Keith left it was quite handy for me 'cos I had my own spot on stage and didn't have to share it anymore.

20 September 1976, The 100 Club, London, Punk Festival with Sex Pistols, Subway Sect, Stinky Toys and Siouxsie & The Banshees

JOE: There was a Punk Festival at The 100 Club which was quite important because it brought everyone together in one room for the first time. And it was historically important because of Siouxsie and the Banshees playing,

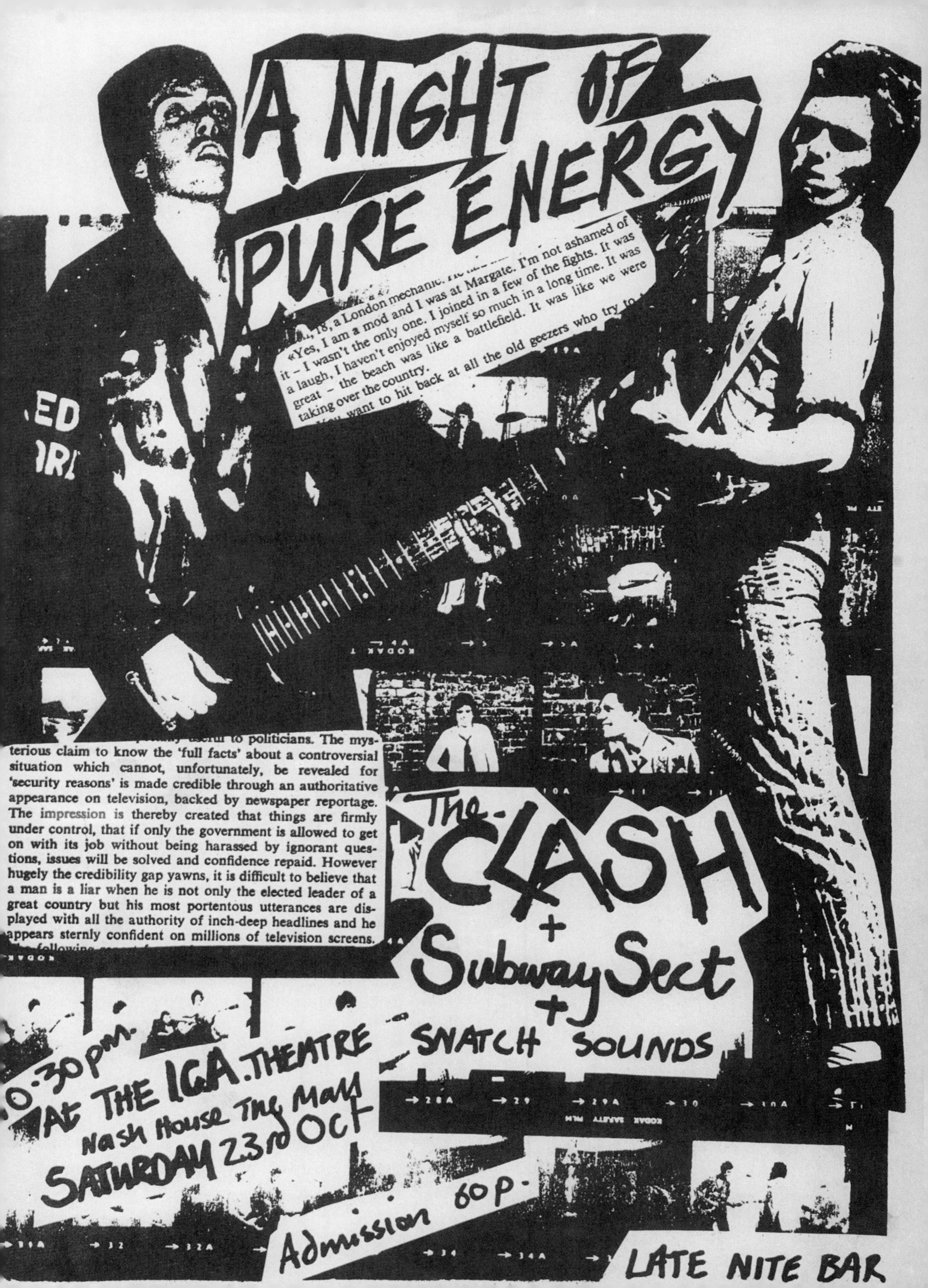

A NIGHT OF PURE ENERGY

«Yes, I am a mod and I was at Margate. I'm not ashamed of it – I wasn't the only one. I joined in a few of the fights. It was a laugh, I haven't enjoyed myself so much in a long time. It was great – the beach was like a battlefield. It was like we were taking over the country. [...] you want to hit back at all the old geezers who try to [...]

[...] useful to politicians. The mysterious claim to know the 'full facts' about a controversial situation which cannot, unfortunately, be revealed for 'security reasons' is made credible through an authoritative appearance on television, backed by newspaper reportage. The impression is thereby created that things are firmly under control, that if only the government is allowed to get on with its job without being harassed by ignorant questions, issues will be solved and confidence repaid. However hugely the credibility gap yawns, it is difficult to believe that a man is a liar when he is not only the elected leader of a great country but his most portentous utterances are displayed with all the authority of inch-deep headlines and he appears sternly confident on millions of television screens.

The CLASH
+
Subway Sect
+
SNATCH SOUNDS

0.30 p.m. at THE ICA THEATRE

Nash House The Mall

SATURDAY 23rd OCT

Admission 60p

LATE NITE BAR

SATURDAY NIGHT. The Clash are playing. It's a regular gig. In the foreground, two young lovers fondle one anothers earlobes . . .
Pic: RED SAUNDERS

CANNIBALISM AT CLASH GIG

(But why didn't anybody eat MILES?)

The Clash
ICA

A row of parked Vivas, Consuls and Zephyrs indicated that the ICA had an audience a little different to the usual. It was "A Night Of Pure Energy" with Subway Sect, who were terrible, Snatch Sounds, who I missed, and The Clash.

The Clash were real good. I enjoyed them a lot more than the Patti Smith Band the night before. They were not poseurs. They are everything that *Sniffin' Glue* magazine promised they would be.

It was as if they had crystalized the dormant energy of all the hours of crushing boredom of being an unemployed school-leaver, living with your parents in a council flat, into a series of three minute staccato blasts delivered like a whiplash at the audience, who were galvanised into frenzied dancing.

The audience stood out the disco, but now they demonstrated the choreography of the *West Side Story* knife-fight, the sparring partner bop, the villain seducing the virgin dance, the horse-ride, a little basic pogo dancing and even some old fashioned high-steppin' truckin'. Patti Smith was there, of course, and felt removed to climb onstage to dance.

The Clash have the musical intensity of the Ramones — a concerted high energy delivery — and their lyrics are much better. You can't hear too well, but if you do catch them it's an extra bonus to what's going down:

"In 1977, I hope I go to heaven
'Cos I been too long on the dole,
And I can't work at all.
Danger, stranger! You better paint your face,
No Elvis, Beatles or Rolling Stones,
In 1977!"
                    ("1977" by The Clash)

Lead singer-guitarist Joe Strummer was in the 101ers until they broke up. The other guys are Micky Jones on guitar, Paul Simenon on bass and Terry Chimes on drums.

The Clash weren't wearing pink plastic trous-ers, though a couple of dozen of their fans were. The Punk Rock scene — or New Wave Rock as it is better known — has already developed its merchant class of magazine importers, purveyors of 'punk paraphernalia' and, of course, journal-ists. The newly emerging independent record labels are doing fine work, but I personally find it hard to imagine a viable musical or social revolu-tion coming from a clothes boutique in the Kings Road, Chelsea.

Not that the clothes don't look good — many of the outfits were really neat and were certainly freaking the NW3 crowd who'd come to see one of the ICA's other shows that evening. There were imaginative combinations of tri-colour hair, fish-net stockings with plastic minis, the curious safety-pin fetish, the ubiquitous plastic trousers and, of course, a lot of Keith Richard look-alikes.

The Clash played some great numbers like "I'm So Bored With The USA" and "Career Oppor-tunities", all of which had a vicious treble ring to them. Then Joe peered down at the audience in front of the stage and muttered "I don't believe what's happening down here at the front . . ."

A young couple, somewhat out of it, had been nibbling and fondling each other amid the broken glass when she suddenly lunged forward and *bit his ear lobe off*. As the blood spurted she reached out to paw it with a hand tastefully clad in a rubber glove, and after smashing a Guinness bottle on the front of the stage she was about to add to the gore by slashing her wrists when the security men finally reached her, pushing through the trance-like crowd who watched with cold, calculated hiptitude.

Creepy, but not the much exaggerated violence that is rumoured to attend the new wave bands. I've seen rumbles at everything from Who concerts to pacifist folk singing sessions.

Meanwhile The Clash continued their 30 minute set, heads snapping forward like snakes on speed. They ended with their theme tune:
"White Riot. I wanna riot.
White Riot, a riot of me own!"
If anyone's got the energy for it, they have.
                                    Miles

TEN SECONDS LATER. My God, they're eating each other. These people are cannibals! The young man howls with pain as his blood-spattered young lady is dragged away, all the while trying to slash her own wrists. But for the dudes in the audience it's just a regular Saturday gig. Maybe they eat earlobes themselves? Edgar Froese (left) wonders if they'll be turning out for T. Dream. "Can't these Englishers afford sausages?"
Pic: RED SAUNDERS

LEFT: An original poster for the Night of Pure Energy gig held at London's Institute of Contemporary Arts.

ABOVE: At the gig, Shane MacGowan and 'Mad Jane Modette' enacted a fit of 'cannibalism' which thrilled the press.

with Sid Vicious on the drums. We could see for the first time that we [punks] had something, that we weren't on our own.

MICK: By the time of this gig things had started to pick up. There had been a few articles and reviews and people had started discovering Punk. It began to feel like something was happening.

PAUL: It was our event so we weren't pelted with bottles, and there were no people wanting to jump on stage and beat us up. It was great to have every-one there on our side; it was like a regular show. Groups just doing their stuff.

28 October 1976, ICA, London, with Subway Sect

PAUL: It was a good place to play. Bernie and I used to go there a lot. The night we played, Shane (MacGowan) and Mad Jane had a tumble and Shane's ear got bitten off or something and there was blood everywhere. Then someone jumped on stage with us and I thought, 'God, who's this? I'm gonna have to kick him off the stage,' and it turned out to be Patti Smith.

PAUL: After the show Patti invited me back to her hotel for a meal and I was starving so of course I went. I also got a boilersuit from her and the $100 bill with which I bought Joe a boilersuit, too. I went to Birmingham with her and the band and the support act was The Stranglers. They were really startled to see me, 'Cor, what you doin' 'ere?' they asked and I just said, 'I'm with the band' and kept walking past them.

5 November 1976, Royal College of Art (A Night of Treason)

PAUL: Just before the Night of Treason gig we went out putting up posters for it. I wasn't on the dole at the time and was bloody hungry. We got back to Rehearsals Rehearsals where I was living, and Joe might have been staying there too that night, anyway I was so hungry that I took a huge scoop of paste made of flour and water out of the bucket, made a cake of it, put it on the end of Bernie's saw, which was lying around, and held it over the fire. I cooked it and ate it. Nobody else wanted any, but I didn't care, I was hungry.

PAUL: The gig was difficult, 'cos the audience were against us. I remember the stage twinkling because of all the glass from the bottles that had been thrown at us. Terry Chimes adjusted his cymbals so that they were flat, facing the crowd so they couldn't see him.

PAUL: That gig was one of the reasons why we always moved about on stage — we got so used to dodging flying objects. While we were playing, Joe and I saw some guys fighting in the crowd so we dived in, threw our fists around and got back on stage. Sid was there that night — he was at the side of the stage and dived in with us. I did ask Mick after the show why he hadn't jumped in with us and he said, 'Well, someone's got to keep in tune.'

W.F.E. PROMOTIONS IN CONJUNCTION WITH ~~FOURTH EVER SIXTRIES REC~~

PRESENT

NEXT SATURDAY   *NEXT SATURDAY*

the
CLASH
+
the
ROCKETS

SAT. OCT. 9th · tickets:
65p AT THE DOOR

TIDDENFOOT · 8-12 P.M.
LEISURE CENTRE

Leighton Buzzard   LATE BAR

An original flyer for the band's seventh gig. It was the first performance by the band that editor of *Zigzag*, Kris Needs, attended. He wrote about the night in the April 1977 edition of his magazine: 'The Clash taking the stage was like an injection of electricity into the smoky air'.

STREET FIGHTING MEN

JOE: I know in America people think it ridiculous that one can fight to the death over articles of clothing, but in these islands it's a different story. Teddy Boys were rock 'n' rollers, so named after their Edwardian dress style, and punks came in and took the Teddy Boy jackets, which were lovely – long, fingertip-length with moleskin lapels – and ripped them and put safety pins in them. Johnny Rotten was particularly good at decorating a jacket. Teddy Boys didn't like punks because they thought it was disrespectful what they were doing to their clothes. Which I suppose it was. And for one summer in 1976 it was fairly dangerous to walk the streets of London dressed as a punk, especially on Saturday afternoons on the Kings Road, although you'd get involved with Teddy Boys on any day, really. It was their last stand, though, they were blown away by it all. They were the old thing and Punk was the new and there was never going to be a real contest.

John Lydon, then better known as Johnny Rotten, lead singer with the Sex Pistols, enraged Britain's Teddy Boys by daring to wear his hair as they did and to put on a drape jacket and frilly shirt (likewise, as they did) at a time when Teds and punks were fighting in the King's Road every Saturday. That a 'filthy punk' should wear their lovely clothes annoyed one gang of Teds so much that they attacked Rotten with chains and knives. He was hospitalized after the assault.

Paul leans against the back of Bernie Rhodes' Renault 16 car with its distinctive number plate. Many people thought Bernie was a Renault dealer at the time, although Joe thought he just sold the odd second-hand car.

PAUL: We did a show with Shakin' Stevens at the University of London and there were Teds everywhere and they didn't like us one bit. After our set we were in the dressing room and a bunch of them tried to get in and have a punch-up and Joe and I tore coke cans in half so we had a jagged half in each hand. We said, 'Alright come on then,' and opened the door for them but when they came in and saw the cans they figured that we were going to do them so they backed out of the room again.

MICK: I don't know if we were aware of Punk being an outlet for our anger. There were a lot of things that needed saying and they hadn't been said in that way before. We were just picking things out of the paper to write about. Even the name came out of a newspaper. Paul came up with the name The Clash because it was in the papers all the time. It was representative of how we felt and sounded.

PAUL: I met Sid (Vicious) at one of the Pistols' shows and we got on really well and started to hang out. One day Viv Albertine gave me and Sid a fiver to get some shopping for the Davis Road squat where we lived, so we went into the supermarket and filled two baskets each, getting carried away. We got everything Viv wanted and some extras, then legged it out of the shop. We were chased for a while and hid in a garden nibbling biscuits 'til it died down. Then we went back to the squat and on the way deliberated over whether to keep the money and split it, but we gave all the shopping plus the fiver back to Viv. It was kind of honour among thieves.

JOE: To begin with, things were really friendly between the Pistols and The Clash and it only got unfriendly when Malcolm realized that by preventing them playing they'd become more famous and they didn't like it, especially when we were out there doing it. They probably thought we were stealing their thunder and animosity built up. But at this time punk rock was the best time, when you had to be in league with each other because there were so many enemies out there. We'd play art schools and the audience would throw wine bottles at us, trying to fracture our skulls. I can't over-emphasize how people were against Punk. Not just Teddy Boys, it was incredibly vicious and dangerous. It was circle the wagons time.

BERNIE RHODES

JOE: When I first met Bernie I had no idea he'd had a life with Malcolm McLaren, or that they'd built a line of t-shirts and clothing. I had no idea about his past life so I just took him on spec and it was only later that I discovered he and Malcolm had fallen out. It was very much that Malcolm had the Sex Pistols so Bernie was going to find a band of his own and prove Malcolm wrong in a way.

MICK: Bernie had a bunch of these shirts with two cowboys on them [both with their dicks hanging out] and some other things, and there was a problem with the police who wanted to confiscate them all. So Bernie asked me to hide the silk screens and some shirts for him. He brought them up to my nan's flat and hid them under my bed. That was one of the first things I ever did with Bernie.

JOE: Bernie was the mentor. He constructed The Clash and focused our energies and we repaid him by being really good at what we did. It was Bernie who told us to write about what we knew i.e., the housing thing, lack of education, dead-end futures of just working your life away. If Bernie hadn't introduced us but we'd met anyway, I don't think we'd have been able to gel together in the same way. He was a wise head and we were like sticks of dynamite that could have gone off in any direction.

PAUL: I used to spend a lot of time with Bernie, discussing artwork and clothing. He got John into the Pistols and used to say that John would always go for the t-shirt that wasn't perfect. Bernie also found Rehearsals Rehearsals for us and I lived there on my own for a while. At weekends there was never anyone there and I wasn't on the dole so had to rely on Bernie to give me money for food. He gave me about £1 a week and I lived on coffee with lots of sugar for a while.

JOE: There was a rumour that Bernie had run a Renault dealership, but he hadn't; he just sold second-hand Renaults out of his backyard. He'd get a car, do it up, flog it, buy another one and live off selling the Renaults.

PAUL: Bernie was really quite sharp. He got John into the Pistols and me into The Clash and we were both non-musicians. He had that ability to pick up characters and put them in a situation that would challenge things, rather than just getting a bunch of musos together in a room. I have to thank him for that, really.

JOE: Bernie was the only one in our crew who understood how one should go about getting known. That's why his guidance was so crucial.

DRUMMER MAN

JOE: We must have auditioned every drummer in London that had a kit. I think we counted 205 drummers in all and every drummer who surfaced in a group for the next ten years would have tried out with us at some point. All those New Romantics like Rusty Egan (who formed Rich Kids with Glen Matlock and then Visage), John Moss (Culture Club) – every drummer in his infancy tried out with us in Camden.

MICK: We met Topper at one of our early auditions. He was really good and we wanted him to join but he wouldn't, I guess because we were too untogether for him. So he went off and did some more stuff.

JOE: Pablo La Britain drummed with us for about a week, 'cos at that time he was living down in Sussex on his old man's farm and things didn't work out.

An early photo shoot with new drummer Nicky 'Topper' Headon. Although he didn't join The Clash until 1977, Topper did play with London SS alongside Mick for a week, before quitting. He auditioned before Terry Chimes was hired, but declined the chance to join in 1976. When asked a few months later, he agreed.

ICA Theatre Benefit Party
Saturday October 2nd 10.30 pm
CLASH + FRESH AIR +
SHAFT INNERCITY SOUND SYSTEM
Min. Contribution 50p – All proceeds to ICA Theatre Bar

MICK: We couldn't work with just any drummer and Terry Chimes was with us from the first. He drummed on the first LP, but left just before it was released.

JOE: Terry Chimes was a bit freaked out by our lunatic, overboard, Stalinist behaviour because we were determined not to become like the groups who were ruling at the time, the monster stadium rock groups. Terry, as he later admitted, got into music so he would be able to afford a Lamborghini sports car. He wasn't ready to be thrown in with this bunch of lunatic, rabid dogs.

PAUL: Terry Chimes didn't ever really join the group. He was there and he played the drums but we used to have lots of political discussions about our lives and things that affected us. We'd say to Terry 'What do you want to do if you ever get any money?' and he said, 'Get a Lamborghini', and I said, 'I've never heard of a Lamborghini' – I thought it was some kind of pet budgie or something. He didn't spend much time hanging around with us.

JOE: Terry quit just before we were due to go out on the Anarchy In The UK Tour at the end of 1976. He said, 'I can't stand all this, I'm out.' That was like a death blow to me because Terry Chimes was a brilliant drummer. We were lost until we found Topper, absolutely lost.

ABOVE: The Clash played the Institute of Contemporary Arts twice in 1976, the 2 October gig for which the above flyer was printed was a more low-key affair than the Night of Pure Energy which took place at the same venue three weeks later.

RIGHT: Terry Chimes performs with The Clash for the last time. This photo was taken at Harlesden's Coliseum on 11 March 1977 when the band headlined with Subway Sect, Generation X and The Slits supporting. The drummer quit the band soon after.

MICK: The next time we saw Topper was at a Kinks gig at the Rainbow. We were really happening by then so I asked if he wanted to join and he said OK.

FIRST RECORDING SESSION MID-NOVEMBER 1976

JOE: Bernie Rhodes had hung out with Guy Stevens a lot in the Sixties when Guy was recording Free, Mott The Hoople and Procol Harum, groups like that. So Bernie brought Guy in. But Guy was drinking a lot at this time. We went into a demo studio off Oxford Street in Polydor and cut about six songs. It was the first time we'd recorded and the results were kind of disappointing. We had a very energetic unit but somehow it sounded flat and dull. I think Guy wasn't up to scratch. It didn't go too good.

MICK: I used to see Guy at Mott The Hoople gigs, which is when I first met him. Then Bernie got him to come and see a band I was lead singer with at the time, in a rehearsal place. He liked it and said he was gonna see if he could do something for us. The problem was that they wanted a keyboard player instead of my rhythm guitar and I was the least experienced member of the band so I was dropped. Then I met Tony James.

JOE: It was a debacle.

MICK: Polydor set us up to do some demo recordings and Bernie suggested we try working with Guy Stevens. We went in and banged out four or five numbers, the ones which were the first in our live set. I think Guy went to the pub or something, and didn't come back, so I don't know how they got finished.

PAUL: I don't remember Guy Stevens being there but the engineer was going on at Joe about having to 'Mind your p's and q's' which was ridiculous, as if Joe was going to pronounce every syllable. It was a complete disaster, really.

MICK: I was really excited about going into the studio and it was probably overwhelming. I didn't notice anything that was going on in too much detail because I was just getting carried away with it all.

SONGS RECORDED:
White Riot
London's Burning
Career Opportunities
Janie Jones
1977

All songs recorded at Polydor Studios, November 1976
Joe Strummer (rhythm guitar, vocals), Mick Jones (guitar, vocals), Paul Simonon (bass), Terry Chimes (drums). Produced by Guy Stevens.

Released in 1978, this professionally produced bootleg album contained all of the demo recordings made by the band in December 1976 at Polydor Studios, as well as the *Capitol Radio* EP given away free with *NME* in 1977 and three tracks recorded in late 1977 and early 1977. It was credited as 'A Fashion Mall Production' and 'made in Be-Jing Central Committee'. As well as the tracks listed left, it included 1–2–Crush On You, Pressure Drop, The Prisoner, Listen, *NME* Interview and Capitol Radio.

Anarchy In The UK Tour

DECEMBER

LINE-UP: STRUMMER, JONES, SIMONON, HARPER

The package tour headlined by the Sex Pistols also included the Damned and the Heartbreakers

1 DEC: Caird Hall, Dundee (cancelled and re-arranged)

3 DEC: Polytechnic, Norwich (cancelled)

4 DEC: Kings Hall, Derby (cancelled)

5 DEC: City Hall, Newcastle (cancelled)

6 DEC: Polytechnic, Leeds

7 DEC: Village Bowl, Bournemouth (cancelled)

9 DEC: Electric Circus, Manchester

10 DEC: Charlton Theatre, Preston (cancelled)

10 DEC: University, Lancaster (re-arranged date also cancelled)

11 DEC: Liverpool Stadium (cancelled)

13 DEC: Colston Hall, Bristol (cancelled)

14 DEC: Top Rank, Cardiff (cancelled and re-arranged)

14 DEC: Cinema, Caerphilly, Wales

15 DEC: Apollo, Glasgow (cancelled)

16 DEC: Caird Hall, Dundee (re-arranged date also cancelled)

17 DEC: City Hall, Sheffield (cancelled)

18 DEC: Southend Kursaal (cancelled)

19 DEC: Civic Hall, Guildford (cancelled and re-arranged)

19 DEC: Electric Circus, Manchester

20 DEC: Town Hall, Birmingham (cancelled)

20 DEC: Winter Gardens, Cleethorpes

21 DEC: Woods Centre, Plymouth

22 DEC: Torquay 400 Ballroom (cancelled)

22 DEC: Woods Centre, Plymouth

26 DEC: London Roxy Theatre, Harlesden (cancelled)

SONGS PLAYED:
White Riot / I'm So Bored with the USA / London's Burning / Hate & War / Protex Blue / Career Opportunities / Cheat / 48 Hours / Janie Jones / 1977

A poster ad for the Anarchy In The UK tour attempted to make sense of the cancellations and actual performances that would happen.

ANARCHY IN THE U.K.

TOUR

SEX PISTOLS

FIRST MAJOR U.K. TOUR
WITH SPECIAL GUESTS

THE DAMNED

JOHNNY THUNDERS HEARTBREAKERS

(Ex New York Dolls from USA)

THE CLASH

TOUR DATES

		Tickets From
FRI 3 DEC	NORWICH University	
SAT 4 DEC	DERBY Kings Hall	Students Union, U.E.A.
		Kings Hall, Derby
		R.E. Cords, Derby, Burton Slect a Disc
SUN 5 DEC	NEWCASTLE City Hall	Nottingham Record Centre, Long Eaton
MON 6 DEC	LEEDS Polytechnic	City Hall
TUE 7 DEC	BOURNEMOUTH	Village Bowl
	Village Bowl	Students Union, Leeds Poly
THU 9 DEC	MANCHESTER	Hime & Addamson, Manchester
	Electric Circus	Virgin Records, Manchester
FRI 10 DEC	LANCASTER University	
SAT 11 DEC	LIVERPOOL Stadium	Students Union, Lancaster University
MON 13 DEC	BRISTOL Colston Hall	Virgin Records
TUE 14 DEC	CARDIFF Top Rank	Top Rank, Cardiff
		Buffalo Records
WED 15 DEC	GLASGOW Apollo	Colston Hall
THU 16 DEC	DUNDEE Caird Hall	Apollo, Glasgow
		Caird Hall
FRI 17 DEC	SHEFFIELD City Hall	Students Union, Technical College
SAT 18 DEC	SOUTHEND Kursaal	City Hall — Wilson Peck Records
SUN 19 DEC	GUILDFORD Civic Hall	Usual Agents
MON 20 DEC	BIRMINGHAM Town Hall	Usual Agents
		Town Hall
TUE 21 DEC	PLYMOUTH Woods Centre	Virgin Records
WED 22 DEC	TORQUAY 400 Ballroom	Woods Centre
SUN 26 DEC	LONDON Roxy Theatre	400 Club
	Harlesden	Roxy Theatre

SINGLES AVAILABLE

THE DAMNED. NEW ROSE   HELP (BUY 6)
Available from even your dumbest dealer
SEX PISTOLS.   ANARCHY IN THE U.K. (EMI 2566)
Available from your cleverest

TOUR PRESENTED BY ENDALE ASSOCIATES
IN ARRANGEMENT WITH MALCOLM

ANARCHY IN THE UK TOUR, 1–26 DECEMBER INCLUSIVE, 1976

JOE: Terry Chimes quit just as we were about to start the Anarchy Tour and we found a replacement, a gentleman named Rob Harper. The tour was the Sex Pistols, Clash, The Heartbreakers and sometimes The Damned. It was the first national Punk tour, though most of it was cancelled due to them [the Pistols] swearing on TV on an early evening live show. Because the swearing was all over the front of the tabloids I think only nine out of an original thirty shows went ahead.

MICK: We learned loads of things from The Heartbreakers on the Anarchy Tour; like how to bottle people when they're looking the other way. . .

JOE: It put Punk on the map, even though the tour got severely cancelled, because now every truckdriver, builder, granny and uncle knew what Punk rock was, thanks to those swear words on an early evening TV show.

MICK: Punk exploded with the Grundy TV show. There was a lorry driver who smashed his telly in when the Pistols were on it and the whole thing started to affect us. Loads of dates on the Anarchy Tour were cancelled because of it, but Punk became massive then.

JOE: We were interviewed by Janet Street Porter for an early evening news programme (on LWT) and we displayed an attitude that we shouldn't really have had, since we were an unsigned act being interviewed on one of the few stations they had in Britain. It was quite hard to get on TV then but we didn't seem to give a monkey's whether we were on it or not, and that came over. But it was the attitude of punk.

PAUL: It always seemed to be night time on that tour. I think that was because we'd drive somewhere to play a gig and it would be cancelled, so we'd drive on to the next place. I remember being in a room constantly with the Pistols, waiting for sandwiches to turn up, or beers or whatever.

JOE: The Damned had released New Rose before the Pistols had put anything out, and there was a row between us over Punk solidarity. It was the Pistols who were banned from playing because they'd sworn on television and we weren't going to play anywhere the Pistols couldn't. The Damned decided to play anyway and that caused a rift. Soon everyone was at each other's throats.

PAUL: The first night we arrived at a hotel, we all had to pair up in double rooms, and someone said, 'Right, who's sharing with John?' and there was silence. I almost said 'I will,' 'cos I liked John, but Mick had teamed with Glen Matlock, so I thought I'd better share with Joe to keep a sense of unity.

MICK: I used to follow bands around, and Rod Stewart kind of let us down 'cos he never had any kind of relationship with the fans. I kind of felt betrayed by him, 'cos he sold out. I always thought that if you find yourself in that

Because of the Pistol's swearing on live tea-time television, the UK press had put Punk on every front page in the land. Before the Bill Grundy TV appearance, Punk had been an underground youth movement involving no more than a couple of hundred people at most. After the press decried the filth and the fury of Punk, the nation's disenchanted youth became punks almost overnight. The result was that all and any punk bands performing (or trying to) attracted lots of media attention. This photoshoot by Ray Stevenson captures the band on tour with the Pistols at the Ramada Inn, Plymouth.

LEFT: When The Clash began, Paul did not know how to play any instrument, and both Joe and Mick helped him to learn. Some of the learning happened live on stage.

BELOW, L-R: Sex Pistols' manager Malcolm McLaren and his band, guitarist Steve Jones, singer Johnny Rotten, bassist Glen Matlock and drummer Paul Cook wait around for a gig to happen. Paul recalled a lot of sitting around on the Anarchy Tour.

situation then it's not like 'I'm the greatest.' Always remember what it's like to be a fan.

PAUL: We arrived in Caerphilly and there were all these people outside the venue singing hymns and stopping us getting in. Steve Jones looks out of the window and says, 'There's a bloke out there with a banana wrapped round his face.' So we all looked and there was a guy with bright yellow sunglasses on, which made us laugh. It turned out it was Steve Strange.

JOE: None of us had ever been on tour before, and we were determined not to be like stadium-type acts where backstage was protected by goons and you had to have passes to get in and have a beer. We let the audience swarm backstage after a gig, and it was part of the ethos. It kept your feet on the ground.

MICK: We'd always let fans in through the back door or a window or something, and then they'd come backstage afterwards. We always wanted to meet people, 'cos we weren't apart from them; it was very important, that personal contact. Very often we'd also have them staying in our rooms and stuff, or we'd get them a room and there'd be fifteen or more fans in there.

White Riot

**NOTTING HILL CARNIVAL
31 AUGUST 1976**

'It's one thing to say, "Burn the cars and burn the ghetto", but you try setting a car alight.' JOE

PAUL:

Joe, Bernie and I went to Portobello Road, under the Westway, during the Carnival. I don't know where Mick was. We were hanging out listening to the sound systems when two squads of police turned up and picked on a couple of guys and tried to drag them off, and they're shouting that it's nothing to do with them. Somebody next to me said something about pickpockets. The next minute, paper cups were being lobbed at the police and then cans and then, because there were some building sites near us, it was bricks and suddenly there were police everywhere, charging the crowd.

So everyone's running away, people with babies in prams and us, and we get pushed up against a wire fence and Bernie's glasses go flying, Joe's tripped up and the police back off.

It just exploded after that. There were no-go areas for the police and we controlled those streets. The police station were at the top of the hill and their vans had to drive past us to get there, and as they came past people lobbed bricks at them, smashing all the windows. It was like shooting pigeons.

At one point a guy on a police motorbike came zooming down at us and I thought it was pretty brave of him, but I picked up a bollard and ran towards him and lobbed the bollard at him. It hit his wheel and he went flying. I was really worked up with the whole thing, along with everybody else.

That was how it was, though. Black people were picked on all the time. From the time I'd been a kid, going to Blues parties, there'd always be white guys having a go at me 'cos of it.

Don Letts walking towards the phalanx of police officers which formed in order to keep rioters confined to one area of the Portobello Road. The Roxy Club DJ and filmmaker was on his way home when the photo – which was later used as the cover of the *Blackmarket Clash* album – was taken by Rocco Macally.

**FOLLOWING PAGE:
Rioters in London's Notting Hill area in August 1976.**

Side 1   Side 2

The thing about the riot was that you felt relieved somehow, just to be holding that brick and lobbing it.

At one point Joe and I were trying to light a car to set it ablaze. Some kids had been trying and failed. We got an old shirt, stuffed it under the car and tried to light that, but it wouldn't go. Until suddenly it blazed, and smoke was pouring out.

I remember seeing a white guy dressed as a clown hiding in a basement while bricks were being thrown, looking dead scared.

Walking around the backstreets there were all these Rasta Generals who were in charge of what was going on, sending people to attack in different areas. They were always prepared for the police and sent them running back as soon as they tried to advance.

At one point Joe and I were cornered by a bunch of kids who tried to mug us, probably because we were white, and there in the middle of the riot. They went through our pockets and of course we were penniless but our pockets were stuffed with bricks. A Rasta General saw what was going on and came over and told the kids to clear off and then left us alone. It was then that I realized that this wasn't about us, this was not our story.

We got out, but went back that night with Sid (Vicious). We wanted to go to a black club, the Metro, but as we walked there people kept telling us not to go on. Not far from the club one guy said, 'Noooo, don't go there, you'll be dead' and we said, 'Fair enough' and that was it.

It was a great experience for Joe and I to have gone through; it was just us

Charging police officers photographed at the August 1976 Notting Hill Carnival riot by Rocco Macally/Redondo. This picture was used in this incarnation on the reverse of the band's debut album.

two running around there for a while. We met up with Mick the next day and Joe penned White Riot that evening.

There were various guys who took photos of the riot. One of them, Rocco, was a Spanish guy who took some photos that Bernie was really eager to use for our albums or posters or whatever. We ended up using one, of Don Letts walking towards a line of police, on the cover of *Black Market Clash*.

JOE:

There's a carnival every year in London. It was started by the Jamaican immigrants in 1957 or 1958, in Notting Hill, which had the highest population of Jamaican immigrants at the time. The housing was cheap and they were put into slums and ripped off, so to make themselves feel better they started the carnival. But that summer of 1976 there'd been heavy police pressure put on the black community. I believe we were there at the throwing of the first brick. Paul, Bernie and I were walking along and a conga line of policemen came through the crowd – they hadn't learned to keep their presence low back then. Anyway, they came through the crowd wearing the British police helmet, which kind of looks stupid. And when you see a line of them going through a carnival crowd it looks really stupid. Somebody threw a brick at them and all hell broke loose – and I mean hell!

The crowd parted and we were pushed into wire netting around a huge hole which was being excavated and we nearly fell in. Everybody started to throw rubbish at the police, which really had to be done, because the police were intolerable and there was no legal redress against their behaviour. It was your word against the policeman's and a judge would never believe you. It was a police state. Well, it still is.

But this was a case of people saying, 'I've had enough!', and that's what gave rise to White Riot. We participated in the riot but I was aware all the time that this was a black people's riot, i.e. they had more of an axe to grind and they had more guts to do something physical about it. After the riot I sat down and wrote the lyric. In its clumsy way it's trying to say to white people, if we're going to do anything, we're going to have to become anarchists or activists, we can't just sit around and be pummelled by society, or plastered over. That riot was like the biggest day of your life. I saw a police motorcyclist coming down Ladbroke Grove with people throwing stuff at him. One of our posse threw a traffic cone at him and he only just managed to keep going. People were turning over cars and burning them, so I decided to try to set light to one of these cars and it was ludicrous. We were standing around this car with a box of Swan Vesta [matches] and it's one thing to say, 'Burn the cars and burn the ghetto', but you try setting a car alight. This big, fat woman was screaming, 'Oh lord, they're going to set the car alight!' The wind was blowing out our matches and I couldn't get anything going on the car. It was a comedy, some of it. But it went on well into the night and was a hell of a day. They couldn't control it. The Grove burned.

1977

'I like the first album best, actually.'
MICK

The first edition of *Sounds* magazine that year, dated 1 January 1977, featured a full front-page photo of Mick, Paul and Joe along with the words: CLASH our pick for '77. They had only managed to play seven dates on the 1976 Anarchy In The UK Tour – eighteen other dates had been either cancelled or 'switched' to other dates and venues. Their final planned gig of 1976, at Harlesden's Roxy Theatre on Boxing Day, had also been cancelled. Yet those people who *had* seen The Clash play live, among them many rock journalists and wannabe rock writers who were inspired to start their own fanzines, were impressed by the band's energy, commitment and great songs.

Paul, Joe and Mick standing on a walkway leading to part of the stables block by the Roundhouse in London. The photograph by Kate Simon was used for the cover of the debut album and has become one of the iconic images of Punk.

That they looked cool also helped – as a review in *Sounds* magazine of a March 1977 gig at the Harlesden Coliseum by Vivien Goldman confirmed, 'The Clash's visuals (couture bezippered ensembles) are so hot that I can't make out which is the bigger plus, the music, the words or the image (dare I say)'. The same day that *Sounds* made the band their cover stars and pick for the year, The Clash headlined at the opening of a new, punk-only venue in London's Covent Garden, The Roxy.

JOE: The Roxy was started by Andrew C specifically for punk groups and its followers, and in a spirit of punk solidarity we agreed to kick it off on New Year's Day. It was the place where a really good Punk-Rasta interface began because the DJ was Don Letts. He'd play a lot of reggae tracks that we hadn't come across before. It was a great place to hang out.

MICK: The Roxy had opened unofficially before 1 January and Generation X had already played there. But we played at the big opening night, and did two sets.

JOE: The Roxy gave a start to loads of bands, hundreds played there that I don't remember the names of. Slaughter And The Dogs began playing there, I remember that.

JOE: People started hanging out at The Roxy to become part of the scene, now that it was headline news. Julien Temple was a film student at Beaconsfield Art School and he came down and filmed some footage. Then he sort of followed us around, filming us rehearsing.

THE DAY PUNK DIED

JOE: We signed to Columbia Records on 27 January 1977. Bernie Rhodes told us to sign the contract and we signed it. I suppose that he checked it out with his lawyer, but I've no idea.

PAUL: I thought we were signing to Polydor. We were outside the Polydor building in a taxi but at the last minute Bernie said, 'Right, over to Soho Square'. Within minutes we were signed to CBS. That afternoon we went to see *Battle of Midway* and that night I had dreams about bombing Dingwalls.

MICK: It didn't matter who you signed to. We trusted Bernie and left things like that to him. The morning we signed to CBS I thought we were going to Polydor.

JOE: I don't remember the day itself when we went into the CBS boardroom and signed. Maurice Oberstein (CBS managing director) must have been there and it was only due to him sticking his neck out to sign one of these damn punk bands, which he did in opposition to the whole of the rest of his company, that we signed with them.

MICK: I don't remember signing anything particularly at CBS – we didn't sign

FOLLOWING PAGES:
The band pose with new drummer Nicky Headon – nicknamed 'Topper' by Paul because he looked like the monkey which appeared on the comic's cover every week – under the Westway on Portobello Road, London W10.

GENESIS ◆ FEELGOODS ◆ GLUE

Sounds

CLASH
— our pick for '77
More predictions inside

CLASH: pic by Sheila Rock

COMPLETE CONTROL

THEY SAID RELEASE REMOTE CONTROL
BUT WE DIDNT WANT IT ON THE LABEL
THEY SAID FLY TO AMSTERDAM
THE PEOPLE LAUGHED BUT THE PRESS WENT MAD
OOH   OOHHH   OOH SOMEONES REALLY SMART
OOH   OOHHH   OOH COMPLETE CONTROL THATS A LAUGH

ON THE LAST TOUR MY MATES COULDNT GET IN
ID OPEN UP THE BACK DOOR BUT THEYD GET RUN OUT AGAIN
AT EVERY HOTEL WE WERE MET BY THE LAW
COME FOR THE PARTY COME TO MAKE SURE

OOH   OOHHH   OOH HAVE WE DONE SOMETHING WRONG
OOH   OOHHH   OOH COMPLETE CONTROL EVEN OVER THIS SONG

THEY SAID WED BE ARTISTICALLY FREE
WHEN WE SIGNED THAT BIT OF PAPER
THEY MEANT LETS MAKE A LOTTA MON-EEE
AN WORRY ABOUT IT LATER

OOH   OOHHH   OOH I'LL NEVER UNDERSTAND
OOH   OOHHH   OOH COMPLETE CONTROL
LEMME SEE YOUR OTHER HAND

I DONT TRUST YOU
WHY SHOULD YOU TRUST ME HUH
ALL OVER NEWS PAPERS
THEYRE FILTHY THEYRE DIRTY
THEY AINT GONNA LAST
THIS JOE PUBLIC SPEAKING
IM CONTROLED IN THE BODY
IM CONTROLED IN THE MIND
THIS THE PUNK ROCKERS
CONTROLED BY THE PRICE OF
THE FIRST DRUGS WE MUST FIND

TOTAL   C-O-N   CON-TROL

CBS FIVE-YEAR FINANCIAL SUMMARY

164.0
122.9
108.6
94.6
82.9

1972 1973 1974 1975 1976

Net Income
Millions of Dollars

any photos or anything, it seemed to be over so fast. I guess Bernie didn't have enough time to organize any stunts to celebrate it. So we went to the pictures.

PAUL: For days afterwards Joe and I deliberated over the content of the songs, saying we can't do Career Opportunities anymore, 'cos now we've got some cash.

JOE: We signed for £100,000 and at the time it seemed like a fortune, but later I found out that what I'd thought was a five-album deal was in fact a ten-record deal when you looked at the small print, like every corny story.

The boss of CBS records in the UK, Maurice Oberstein in his office, making up part of a spread from the first *Clash Songbook*, co-designed by Paul and Mick with Tess Van Eyck, Miles, Roger Day, Pearce Marchbank, Janey Coke, Susan Ready and Caroline Coon.

PAUL: But it didn't change very much because Bernie was in charge of the money and we all got £25 a week. Which was better than the £1 a week I had been getting.

JOE: I don't remember signing a publishing deal. We didn't even know what one was.

MICK: I don't remember having the contract, I can't remember it.

JOE: Because Punk was a roots movement, any comments were heard in the community. Mark P, being a leading light in the underground because of his fanzine *Sniffin' Glue*, wrote 'Punk Rock died the day The Clash signed to Columbia'. I remember thinking 'but we were never your toy to begin with'. *Sniffin' Glue* was the first great punk fanzine and it meant we had our own Punk commentators. We were miles ahead of most of the writers on the music papers, apart from say John Ingham, Caroline Coon, Tony Parsons and Julie Burchill, who were believers. Everyone else in the offices was probably sneering at them. So Mark P started *Sniffin' Glue*. It was followed by a million others, but it was a great scene because it gave punk criticism to punk groups and people could get information about what was going on, even if they lived in Wales or somewhere.

JOE: I guess the original followers have an attitude of, 'We were the first, it was ours', and got really bitchy towards new acts just breaking into Punk. Mark P wanted us to stay homemade, to make our own records, which people do. But we wanted to break out of it, to reach America and be global. Somebody had to take that bull by the horns and shake it.

MICK: We were very open to each other's input. We'd all come to it from different perspectives of what is now called popular culture, and it was the coming together of all that which made it spark.

JOE: The Pistols had signed to EMI by this time and our signing to CBS gave Punk a credibility in the big, bad old music business world.

JOE: We were moving too fast to take notice of the sniping from the fanzines though. I don't think we'd do anything different, even now.

A-side: White Riot (1.58)

[Strummer/Jones] Produced by Mickey Foote

B-SIDE: 1977 (1:40)

[Strummer/Jones/Headon/Simonon] Produced by
Mickey Foote

RELEASED 18 MARCH 1977

UK CHART PEAK: #38

PAUL: After we'd shot the photo for the cover of the White Riot single, someone told me about a Joe Gibbs record cover (for State of Emergency), which had three guys with their hands pressed against a wall as police are searching them, but I hadn't seen it. We were coming to the end of the photo shoot and there were only two frames left and I said, 'Why don't we go up against the wall, like this?' I don't remember having seen the Gibbs sleeve.

SINGLES

The answer is a Brick...

THE CLASH: *first meaningful event of the year?*

THE CLASH: White Riot/1977 (CBS). Last year's words belong to last year's language and next year's words wait for another voice. Look out, listen, can you hear it?

It's pointless to categorise this with the other records: "White Riot" isn't a poxy single of the week, it's the first meaningful event all year. Try and discount it. Go on, say they sold out to the enemy at CBS, say it's another idle London fad irrelevant to the lives of working people, say it's all a clever hype that's conned everyone, say it's just the 60s rehashed an' you can't make out the words.

Say what you like, you still can't discount it coz Clash aren't just a band, and this is more than just a single. There's a book written by a trad fan in 1963 saying how shoddy The Beatles were, how ripped off from R'n'B, how they could never last in the world of Tin Pan Alley. They didn't last in it, they took it to pieces.

Whatever your standpoint everyone basically agrees there are two sides. You know it's coming, we know it's coming and *they* know it's coming. Clash are the writing on *their* wall. The recorded version of "White Riot" is one minute 58 seconds of buzzsaw guitars, Simenon's pumping offbeat bass, an insolent-slurred vocal and sheer musical aggro. Won't pick up much airplay coz you can't make out the words — it'd pick up much less if you could: *"Black men gotta lotta problems but they don't mind throwin' a brick . . . white people go to school where they teach you how to be thick . . . White riot, wanna riot of my own . . ."*

Flip is "1977", already well known to those in the know: "*No Elvis Beatles or*

100 TON & A FEATHER: Just To Be Close To You (Pye). Jonathan King's okay. His records stink. A few honourable exceptions: this isn't one of them.

LYNSEY DE PAUL & MIKE MORAN: Rock Bottom (Polydor). Our song for Europe. The title sez it all.

HENRY MANCINI: Theme From Charlie's Angels (RCA). For sheer skill in Musak orchestration Hank is still streets ahead of upstarts like B. White and I. Hayes. This could've been a smash in the discos if he'd shot the drummer and producer in time.

JOHN CHRISTIE: Always Be Your Valentine (EMI). Within the MOR field, for what it's worth, Dave Clark's production pisses all over the MacCauley / Cook / Greenaways of this world. John Christie sounds a bit like Christopher Rainbow:

"*. . . They were people we knew, they blew out dinner for two, and I drank too much French wine.*" A miss.

THE BATCHELORS featuring CON CLUSKY produced by TONY HATCH: Torn Between Two Lovers (Galaxy). Violin count 10, *TOTP* quality 1, lyrical content 0, originality 0.

EDDIE RABBITT: Two Dollars In The Juki Box" (Elektra). Two minutes 22 seconds of classy rock'n'roll. Slinky piano/bass backbeat, apt guitar work and authentic vocals: "*Two dollars in the juke box, five dollars in the bottle . . . and ten more just in case that don't do the trick.*" Adding pedal steel was a bit suspect, and the production's too immaculate to really please the purists. Flip reminiscent of the American Housewives.

VICKI BRITTEN: Flight 309 To Tennessee (Arista). Julie Burchill's right about Arista — first The Kinks and now this ghastly MOR drivel. "Fl...

THE CLASH. WHITE RIOT. C/W 1977. CBS 5058

A-side: Listen (edit) (0:27)

[Strummer/Jones/Headon/Simonon] Produced by
Mickey Foote

**INTERVIEW WITH THE BAND BY
TONY PARSONS ON THE CIRCLE
LINE (PART ONE) (8:50)**

B-SIDE: CAPITAL RADIO ONE (2.09)

[Strummer/Jones] Produced by Mickey Foote

**INTERVIEW WITH THE BAND BY
TONY PARSONS ON THE CIRCLE
LINE (PART TWO) (3:20)**

RELEASED APRIL 1977 BY THE *NEW MUSICAL*
EXPRESS **MAGAZINE VIA MAIL ORDER ONLY
NO CHART POSITION**

**JOE: Tony Parsons was one of the journalists on the scene at the time
and we agreed to be interviewed by him, on the tube, going round and
round the Circle line, and for the recording of the interview to be given
away with the** *NME* **as a flexi-disc.**

**PAUL: It was OK doing the interview with Tony Parsons, but I got the
feeling that he just wanted to talk to Mick and Joe, which was fair
enough 'cos they wrote the songs. There was one bit when Mick said,
'Oh I hate him and he hates me' and I said, 'I hate everybody'.**

A RIOT OF YOUR OWN!

1977 is the Year Of The Clash — Hideous Bill Gangrene says so — and this is a chance to obtain some of The Sound Of The Westway X-CLUSIVE for those NME readers shrewd enough to buy, borrow or steal (**Cool it, Hideous old fellow! — Ed**) a copy of the band's first album which is going into the record shops now. What we're giving away (yeah, **giving away**) is a genuine collector's item — a 14-minute EP which contains two new Clash songs, "Listen" and the UTTERLY INCREDIBLE "Capital Radio", plus an extended burst of our very own gunslinger Tony Parsons interviewing the band about Clash Philosophy 1977. This is the stuff you read in last week's NME. Hear it from their own lips (if you don't believe us) on this FREE 45. To get this contemporary classic here's what you gotta do. On the inner bag of the first 10,000 copies of The Clash album you'll find a red sticker. Attach this to the announcement that you're now reading, legibly scrawl your name and address across the shaded area of the photo above and mail the lot to the following address: The Clash Offer, Pembroke House, Campsbourne Road, London N8 7PT. That's all. You don't need to enclose stamped addressed envelopes; we don't want any money. The whole deal (including postage and packing of the single) is FREE. A gift from NME and The Sound Of Westway to anyone who's interested enough in getting hold of a copy of the new Clash elpee. Got it? Right! Can you think of a better way to spend Easter?

N.B. This offer is open to readers in the U.K. only, and closes at the end of April '77.

The Clash

[UK LP CBS 32232]

RELEASED 8 APRIL 1977
UK CHART PEAK: #12
WAS NOT RELEASED IN THE USA IN THIS FORMAT
(An extended version of this album was released in the USA in July 1979, replacing Cheat, 48 Hours, Deny and Protex Blue with Complete Control, Jail Guitar Doors, Clash City Rockers, [White Man] in Hammersmith Palais and I Fought the Law)

Released almost exactly a year after the first Ramones album, and six months before the Sex Pistols only album, *The Clash* was the first long-playing record to be released by a British punk group of real note. Although two months earlier The Damned had released *Damned Damned Damned* on the independent Stiff label, *The Clash* was different, and not just because it was released via a major record label. Of the three UK punk acts who'd travelled on the Anarchy tourbus, The Clash were the newest. They had been press darlings almost from the moment that they'd appeared, and expectation for this release was high. 'If you don't like The Clash, you don't like rock 'n' roll,' said the full-page review in UK music weekly *Sounds*. Enough people liked them to put the album into the charts at number 12 the week of release.

SIDE ONE:
Janie Jones
Remote Control
I'm So Bored With
 The USA
White Riot
Hate & War
What's My Name
Deny
London's Burning

SIDE TWO:
Career
 Opportunities
Cheat
Protex Blue
Police & Thieves
48 Hours
Garageland

Joe Strummer (guitar, vocals), Mick Jones (guitar, vocals), Paul Simonon (bass), Tory Crimes [AKA Terry Chimes] (drums). Produced by Mickey Foote. Recorded in Whitfield Studios, London.

THE CLASH FIRST ALBUM

PAUL: When I think about the word 'Clash', it struck me that because we were in a confrontational situation all the time, even just walking the streets, our lives seemed to be a permanent clash. There was a clash of colours, clash of people – it's kind of self-explanatory.

MICK: It was so exciting for me, to actually be doing what I'd always wanted to do. It was great.

JOE: We didn't know it at the time, but Iggy Pop and the Stooges had recorded *Raw Power* in the No. 3 Studio at Whitfield Street, which was the smallest studio available to CBS artists. It was a very basic room and we went in there to make our first album.

MICK: We didn't write any new songs for the first album, it was really an extension of the live set that we were playing at the time. We went in over three or four weekends and played through the numbers, maybe used a rough vocal and then overdubbed the vocals later.

PAUL: The first album was recorded so quickly I can hardly remember doing it. We went in, bashed the songs out and left.

JOE: I got nicked by the police one night along with Mad Jane, Roadent [Clash roadie] and Mark Helfonment for being high-spirited in Whitfield Street. The cop shop was only half a block from the CBS studios and this copper says, 'I don't want to see you round here again'. After that as soon as I left the studio I'd go straight off somewhere else.

MICK: We were into helping each other out on the album. I wouldn't say I wrote any of the bass parts but I'd make suggestions to Paul. I didn't know much more than him anyway, I was winging it as we went along, too. Joe was the one who'd done it for a while.

JOE: There must have been something about that studio because we knocked our album out in about three weekends, in four day sessions. We were very strict about it. All the songs we could do live we just banged them out. There wasn't any studio trickery involved.

MICK: I don't know where our sound came from. I think your sound is a reflection of your personality, you'll always sound like you, no matter who you are. When I play you're hearing my whole life.

PAUL: The first time we went to the studio there was that guy who sang White Christmas... Bing Crosby? That's it. He was in the foyer when we walked in, which was a bit strange. I think he was there to record a duet with David Bowie.

MICK: Sometimes really good things come about by accident. With Police and Thieves we were trying to do our thing on a reggae song, it was a song that we heard all the time that year and we tried to do it our way.

Joe in the kitchen of his first legitimate London flat – a two-room place in West London, as he chatted with *Sounds* writer Peter Silverton. Elvis was still alive when the photo was taken and considered decidedly uncool by the music press of the day – although Peter was a big fan, as Joe knew.

JOE: CBS let us get on with it. They gave us a good engineer in Simon Humphries and Mickey Foote was supposed to keep our end of things up, 'cos we were very keen that it didn't become, like a lot of records, 'produced'.

MICK: The album was quite arranged, because I guess I had a talent for arranging. Probably because my dad, apart from being a cab driver, was also the manager of a betting office and is very quick with figures, which I inherited. Because music is mathematical, you solve a bit of the problem and then move on to the next bit.

PAUL: All the songs were pretty much formed, but the lyrics could change. At one point Mick pulled me aside and said, 'I want you to sing this bit about pensions', in Career Opportunities and I said, 'I'm not singing about bloody pensions', and Joe saw what the problem was and changed the lyric, using me like a filtering system.

MICK: I learned about music from asking people what they were doing, and when we went into the studio I was curious about how everything worked, about the actual process of making a record. I wanted to know about the

Joe takes the lead in yet another press interview.

boring stuff like how to make things sound bigger and compression, and was constantly learning.

PAUL: Bernie and I had a meeting with the head of the art department at CBS and he said, 'I've got a great idea for your album cover'. He showed us a picture of a cobbled street with a pair of dodgy old boots, and that was it. This was what we had to deal with. Luckily we had our own team so we did our own stuff.

JOE: We'd felt burned by the experience with Guy Stevens at the Polydor sessions, where it came out sounding boring. So we had Mickey Foote and Mick, too, overseeing the end result.

MICK: After the Guy Stevens demo Joe was very particular that he didn't want to sound like Matt Monro or something, didn't want to sound too polished, so we had our sound man Mickey Foote at the desk. And it was mixed like magic.

PAUL: Bernie and I spent a lot of time looking at album covers, especially Jamaican ones, which is where we got a lot of inspiration. We were checking out colours for the first Clash album cover at Bernie's place and there was a lot of green, and I liked it. Green seemed slightly militaristic, and with the black and white photo it was striking. We had one of Rocco's photos on the back from the Notting Hill Carnival riot, which Bernie had blown up to use as a backdrop when we played live.

Hate & War
JOE: I wrote the lyric in a disused ice cream factory behind the Harrow Road where I'd squatted. I wrote it by candlelight and the next day took it to Rehearsals Rehearsals and Mick gave it a tune straightaway. Paul was really into it.

What's My Name
MICK: A really early song that Keith and I had worked on before Joe joined. We had the music and chorus.

Deny
MICK: We had part of the song before Joe. Chrissie Hynde probably helped with the end bit, 'What a liar'. She'd write on her own and I'd write on my own but then we'd get together to sing.

PAUL: Mick and I were doing the backing vocals: 'What a liar, what a liar' and it goes on forever. We were gasping for breath and starting to go blue in the face, trying to finish this never-ending chorus.

London's Burning

JOE: I went to the back room at the very top of the squat at Orsett Terrace where me, Paul, Keith, Sid Vicious, Palmolive [of the Slits] and some others I don't remember used to crash. I wrote London's Burning there, very quietly, whispering it 'cos Palmolive was asleep in the same room. The next day I went round to Mick's and said 'Let's do it'. Sometimes we used to write apart, but not often.

Protex Blue

PAUL: When I first met Mick he had Protex Blue already.

MICK: It was the brand in all the pub condom machines. It was a valid subject for a song in those days.

48 Hours

MICK: For some reason we had to have another song and I remember us sitting in Rehearsals Rehearsals and knocking it off in half an hour, words and music.

Police & Thieves

JOE: We had a Bob Marley called Dancing Shoes on a b-side, and we decided to try and rock it up, Ramones-it. We used to play it a fair bit, but only to ourselves in Rehearsals Rehearsals. It was an attempt to fuse a style out of something but it wasn't getting anywhere so we dropped it. When we were recording I suggested doing Police And Thieves because we all loved it and Mick arranged it with that one big guitar hitting the front of the chord.

JOE: We weren't actually playing Police & Thieves at this point, though it was a big hit in the clubs. At least the clubs we went to, which weren't 'proper' ones. We had to crash Jamaican parties. We'd walk around until we found a place where they were selling beer and they'd tolerate us in there. The song was ringing out all over the town and eventually we tried to cut a version which, when I listen to Junior Murvin's original today, makes me think, 'What a bold brass neck we had to try and attempt that!' 'Cos he sings like a smooth river of silk. I'm glad we did it because we did it in a Punk Rock way which worked. I mean the song was strong enough to stand our kicking it and led to greater things in the future with Lee Scratch Perry and Bob Marley hearing it, and being hip enough not to diss it. By rights they should have said, 'Hey there man, you ruined it!' But they were sussed enough to know we'd brought our own music to the party.

JOE: I gotta say, and it hasn't been said enough: Mick Jones's talent is not only as a player, and he's a brilliant player, but as an arranger, like Gil Evans – he's an arranger of music and all through The Clash we hear his talent at arranging. Alright, it's a simple four-piece rock band, but to arrange those

Joe would often use boxing analogies to describe what it was that The Clash did, and here he tapes drummer Topper's hands before a performance in much the same way that cornermen prepare their fighters before a bout.

the clash

JOE STRUMMER (vocals/guitar)   MICK JONES (guitar/vocals)   PAUL SIMONON (bass)   TOPPER HEADON (drums)

Side One
1 I'M SO BORED WITH THE USA (Strummer/Jones)
2 HATE & WAR (Strummer/Jones)
3 48 HOURS (Strummer/Jones)
4 DENY (Strummer/Jones)
5 POLICE & THIEVES (Murvin/Perry)

Side Two
1 CHEAT (Strummer/Jones)
2 CAPITAL RADIO (Strummer/Jones)
3 WHAT'S MY NAME (Strummer/Jones/Levine)
4 PROTEX BLUE (Strummer/Jones)
5 REMOTE CONTROL (Strummer/Jones)
6 GARAGELAND (Strummer/Jones)
7 1977 (Strummer/Jones)

After the failure of the Anarchy In The UK tour in 1976, it was nothing short of a miracle that the second punk package tour, the White Riot tour, managed to play in as many cities as it did. The Clash, The Buzzcocks, The Slits, The Jam and Subway Sect took to the road at the beginning of May, 1977, the start of the summer of punk, and tore up almost thirty venues in as many days. As this was the first punk tour to travel the length and breadth of the country many classed this event as one of the most influential.

As the headline act, The Clash had to prove that they could stand shoulder to shoulder with the Sex Pistols, showcasing songs from their debut album they tore through their set at breakneck speed leaving the pogoing, sweating masses for dead.
This concert from the tour was captured on a wild Saturday night in Leicester, originally it had been scheduled for earlier in the month at the local Polytechnic, but the student union soon put a stop to that.

So as the month, and the tour, drew to a close the Clash finally hit the stage in Leicester at the De Montfort Hall, and you have the chance to relive that experience in full, glorious stereo.

Recording produced by The Clash
Front cover artwork: Westway td
Recording first published 1977

Goodtimes MUSIC   LONG PLAY 33⅓ R.P.M ● RELEASED AND UNDER LICENSE TO Goodtimes MUSIC

An early bootleg recording of the classic Clash line-up. The album cover's design is a pastiche of early Beatles' album covers, the image a reproduction of the poster for the gig.

pieces into something that works, so fantastically. Police & Thieves is a prime example. The way he told me to go, 'Rah!' And then kill it, as he went 'ra-ra' and then me hitting the on beat again. It was brilliant. Any other group would've all played the offbeat because we were trying to assimilate reggae. But it was very punk to have one guitar playing the on and the other the offbeat. He's a genius arranger.

Cheat
PAUL: We came up with Cheat when we were rehearsing for the album, just before going into the studio. We never played it live before we did the first album. I think we only played it a couple of times after that.

Garageland
JOE: At the time of the [Screen on the Green] midnight show, our media coverage was slim, so we were pretty done over when Charles Shaar Murray, who was one of the leading pundits of the day, wrote 'The Clash are one of those garage bands who should be swiftly returned to the garage and the doors locked with the motor left running.' At least it gave us the idea for Garageland.

MICK: That review really spurred us on, not only to write this song on behalf of all the garage bands, but to make us strong. Joe did the lyrics and it deserved a good tune.

PAUL: 'Complaints, complaints, what an old bag' comes from the woman downstairs at the Davis Road squat.

1977

JOE: I had the lyric to 1977 and Mick had the tune, we were piecing it together. I'd written 'No Elvis, Beatles or Rolling Stones in 1977' in my notebook, but thought it was too silly to start with. We were singing the song through and got to the bit where we didn't have any words, so I said I had something, but it was a bit silly. Mick said, 'What is it?' So I told him and he said, 'Great! That's great'.

JOE: It started off for Mick as a homage to the Kinks, because don't forget we had all that music, too. Mick was fooling with dragging that chord and then he put an E chord into it. We decided to write 1977 because it was easy to rhyme that with something like 'heaven'. We kinda did it as a joke but it got really good the more we wrote it.

London's Burning

JOE: I wrote it after walking around London, where there was nothing to do. Television stopped at 11 p.m. and that was it, there was only walking the streets at that hour to amuse yourself. I was walking around West London a lot at the time and it came to me, all at once. The bit I like best about the song is the intro, the guitar bit, because it's completely insane. Mick was living in his gran's flat overlooking the Westway at the time and the next morning I got up and I could still remember it from the night before, so I took it over to him and we licked it into shape. But we ruined that number by auditioning a load of different drummers to it, and after 200 drummers, we were sick of it.

JOE: One of the few things punks had for recreation was amphetamine sulphate. It was cheap and good value for money – and its effects lasted. But I grew tired of it because I didn't think the down you got was worth the up. The stuff you could get on the streets of London was of the base variety and heavily cut with whatever and you'd get so depressed after you'd had some. I decided pretty quickly that amphetamine sulphate was a terrible drug, it rotted people's teeth, minds and there was a high attrition rate with that drug.

Capital Radio

JOE: We recorded a track, Capital Radio, for the *NME* flexi-disc, which was slagging off the only London-based commercial radio station available at the time (and which was never gonna play Punk records). It seemed unfair to us that there was all this stuff going off in the capital and you couldn't hear it on the airwaves.

FOLLOWING PAGE: The lyrics of Police & Thieves as displayed in the first *Clash Songbook*. The image is of the Notting Hill riot of 1976.

POLICE & THIEVES

POLICE AN THIEVES IN THE STREETS
SCARING THE NATION WITH THEIR GUNS AN AMMUNITION
POLICE AN THIEVES IN THE STREET
FIGHTING THE NATION WITH THEIR GUNS AN AMMUNITION
FROM GENESIS   TO REVELATION
THE NEXT GENERATION   WILL BE NEAR ME
AN ALL THE CROWD COMES IN   DAY BY DAY
NO ONE TRIES TO STOP IT IN ANYWAY
AN ALL THE PEACEMAKERS TURN WAR OFFICERS
     HEAR WAT I SAY

PO LICE   PO LICE   PO LICE   AN TH IEVES

COMING IN
HERE COME   HERE COME   HERE COME   THE STATION IS BOMBED
LOOK OUT   LOOK OUT   LOOK OUT   YOU PEOPLE IF YOU DONT WANNA
                                      GET BLOWN UP

THE POLICE THE POLICE THE POLICE THE THIEF THE THIEF THE THIEF
HE GOT A NASTY CRIME   HE GOT AN AXE TO GRIND
AN CHOO WAN STUCK IN THE MIDDLE
    OF POLICE AND THIEVES

MICK: We all went into a photo booth first, then got a train and were just blabbering on for hours as the train went round and round. We were just joking about.

JOE: As a promotional exercise I decided to spray paint Capital Radio and the BBC with White Riot in six-foot letters in red paint. I was quite surprised when this didn't result in any airplay, but you live and learn.

Complete Control

MICK: Complete Control was one of Bernie's favourite phrases and he'd said to us once that he had to have complete control of the situation, and that stuck with us.

JOE: Bernie Rhodes was quite into the reggae end of our activities and he got hold of Lee 'Scratch' Perry and brought him in to produce a single that we'd written specially, called Complete Control. He did a great job and it was a real thrill for us to work with him.

PAUL: I was really excited to meet Lee Perry, it was like meeting my all-time hero. Unfortunately, though, I had a really bad cold so all I could do was play the song and then get out of the studio, so I missed the whole thing. But I have to say that listening to it I can't recognize any of Lee Perry's input. Maybe it got remixed once he'd left the building, I don't know.

MICK: We went back and fiddled with it a bit. What Lee did was good, but it sounded as if he'd recorded it underwater, that echo sound of his. We brought out the guitars, made it a bit tougher, but it's still his sound.

PAUL: Perry seemed as mad as Guy Stevens. He kept doing kung fu stuff all over the place and he had writing in biro up his arms, but he was a great character.

WHITE RIOT TOUR

TOPPER: When I joined The Clash, Mick, Joe and Paul hated funk and they hated jazz and anything that wasn't Punk. At the audition I went to there were five other drummers and they agreed with everything Mick, Joe or Paul said. When they asked me 'Who are your favourite drummers?' I said Buddy Rich and Billy Cobham, giving all the wrong answers.

PAUL: It was great to get Topper into the band at last, and resolve all our problems. Coming up with nicknames was my department and I decided to call him Topper because of his ears. He looked like a character from a comic book called *Topper*, a kind of Mickey The Monkey, especially when he had his hair cut off. But it was great to find him, he was our drummer mate.

JOE: We played London's Burning with all the drummers we auditioned, and were interested in volume. If we could hear them when we were playing, then

BY PUBLIC DEMAND

The CLASH

Tshirt, Now.
.3 COLOUR.
OBTAINABLE ONLY
FROM **UPSTARTS**
31 ALBANY St. N.W.I
LONDON 4LB.
£2·90 +25 P.P.P.
STATE SIZE · WIMP.
NORM, **TARZAN**
SUDDENLY —
· AVAILABLE SLITS
AND SUBWAYS ECT

White Riot Tour

LINE-UP: STRUMMER, JONES, SIMONON, HEADON

Support acts booked for the tour were The Jam, Buzzcocks, The Slits and Subway Sect. The Jam left after the gig at London's Rainbow, which ended in a riot. Seats were ripped out and thrown on the stage. (Cost: £28,000 damages.)

SONGS PLAYED:
White Riot / I'm So Bored with the USA / London's Burning / Hate & War / Protex Blue / Pressure Drop / Career Opportunities / Cheat / 48 Hours / Janie Jones / Garageland / Remote Control / Deny / Capital Radio / Police And Thieves / What's My Name / 1977

1 MAY: Civic Hall, Guildford
2 MAY: Rascals, Chester
3 MAY: Barbarellas, Birmingham
4 MAY: Affair Ballroom, Swindon
5 MAY: Erics, Liverpool
6 MAY: University, Aberdeen
7 MAY: Playhouse, Edinburgh
8 MAY: Electric Circus, Manchester
9 MAY: Rainbow, London. Support also included The Prefects. The Jam played and then quit the tour
10 MAY: Town Hall, Kidderminster (cancelled: Mick damaged his hand)
12 MAY: Palais, Nottingham
13 MAY: Polytechnic, Leicester
14 MAY: Brakke Grande, Amsterdam
15 MAY: Fiesta, Plymouth
16 MAY: University, Swansea
17 MAY: Polytechnic, Leeds
19 MAY: Rock Garden, Middlesbrough
20 MAY: University, Newcastle
21 MAY: City Hall, St Albans
22 MAY: Skindles, Maidenhead (cancelled)
22 MAY: Civic Hall, Wolverhampton, with Buzzcocks, Slits and Subway Sect
24 MAY: Top Rank, Cardiff, Wales
25 MAY: University of Sussex, Brighton, with Buzzcocks, Slits
26 MAY: Colston Hall, Bristol
27 MAY: Pavilion, West Runton
28 MAY: De Montfort Hall, Leicester
29 MAY: Chancellor Hall, Chelmsford
30 MAY: California Ballroom, Dunstable

From the very first day of performing, The Clash were rarely on the road without accompanying journalists or photographers. Having written one of the first big, positive pieces on the band, *Sounds*' Giovanni Dadomo was a welcome guest on the White Riot Tour.

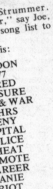

Continues next page

Strummer.
," say Joe,
song list to

is:
OON
77
RED
SURE
& WAR
HRS
ENY
ITAL
LICE
HEAT
MOTE
RREER
ANIE
RIOT

d tune up while I
s; first Mick and
an acoustic
Burning'. Then
forgotten how to
," says Paul. Joe
his bottom string
g the top of the
tween his teeth.

sh I was pissed,"

n't."
first two numbers are
the list, non-stop, no
between.
old geezers at the
they say this is a

ON THE ROAD WITH THE CLAS

By Giovanni Dado

The Clash

JOIN US ON THE WHITE RIOT — '77 TOUR

MAY		
Sun.	1st	Guildford, Civic
Mon.	2nd	Chester, Rascals
Tues.	3rd	Birmingham, Barbarellas
Wed.	4th	Swindon, The Affair Ballroom
Thurs.	5th	Liverpool, Erics.
Fri.	6th	Aberdeen, University
Sat.	7th	Edinburgh, Playhouse Theatre
Sun.	8th	Manchester, Electric Circus
Mon.	9th	London, Rainbow
Tues.	10th	Kidderminster, Town Hall
Thurs.	12th	Nottingham, Palais
Sun.	15th	Plymouth, Fiesta

MAY		
Mon.	16th	Swansea, University
Tues.	17th	Leeds, Polytechnic
Thurs.	19th	Middlesborough, Rock Gardens
Fri.	20th	Newcastle, University
Sat.	21st	St. Albans, City Hall
Mon.	23rd	Stafford, Top Of The World
Tues.	24th	Cardiff, Top Rank
Wed.	25th	Brighton, Polytechnic
Thurs.	26th	Bristol, Colston Hall
Fri.	27th	West Runton, Pavillion
Sat.	28th	Canterbury, Odeon
Sun.	29th	Chelmsford, Chancellor Hall
Mon.	30th	Dunstable, California Ballroom

... now out + THE LP + The CLASH

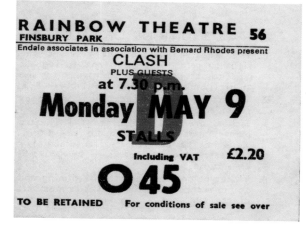

RAINBOW THEATRE 56
FINSBURY PARK
Endale associates in association with Bernard Rhodes present
CLASH
PLUS GUESTS
at 7.30 p.m.
Monday MAY 9
STALLS
Including VAT £2.20
O 45
TO BE RETAINED   For conditions of sale see over

LEFT: An original full-page ad for the White Riot tour from the *NME* of 30 April 1977. The dates show that the band had to travel in a non-linear route around the country, going from Cardiff to Brighton, from there to Bristol and then to the opposite side of the country (North Norfolk) on successive days.

ABOVE: A ticket stub for the Rainbow gig displays Bernie's role as co-promoter of the tour. The gig ended in a riot, with fans ripping seats out and piling them onto the stage. The band were billed for the damage, which Bernie was reported as saying was £28,000. Although the figure of £5,000 has also been quoted.

they were good. It took half the number for everyone to realize that Topper could whack 'em. He was dynamite.

TOPPER: I was in shock when I first got the job. But I listened to the album, which they'd just finished, I realized how incredibly powerful it was. I used to play everything on the hi-hat but Mick heard it being played on the tom-tom, and he hit it really hard, but it gave the drums more power. I had to re-learn the drums, basically. But it was worth it.

JOE: It was really great finding Topper Headon. There's a founding rule of rock 'n' roll that says you're only as good as your drummer. Topper had done the chicken-in-a-basket circuit since the age of 15 or 16, with American soul groups who'd come over and use a pick-up band. And nothing fazed him. He could play Funk, Soul, Reggae. He's why The Clash became an interesting musical unit.

PAUL: The tour was great fun. We had the Slits and Subway Sect with us so it was all friends together on the bus – Don and Leo [also from the Roxy] were there too.

MICK: We always tried to give the best performance we could but there were still gigs when one of us would have an off night. It could be that one of us had too much to drink and fell off the stage. You know if you fall off the stage and they catch you then you're happening, but if they make a space for you... Sometimes I'd be going so fast that I'd go off the end of the stage – but I'd be caught.

PAUL: I think I preferred the tension of the Anarchy Tour though, where it was us against them. On the White Riot Tour pretty much everyone was on our side.

TOPPER: My first gigs with The Clash were in France. Before we left I was lying on the floor at Rehearsals Rehearsals trying to get some sleep, thinking, 'What am I doing with this lot?' I only joined 'cos they were on the cover of the *NME*. I thought I'd do it for a year, make my name and then do something musical.

PAUL: One night in Scotland after we'd left the stage, one of the roadcrew said, 'You've got to see this' and I went back out and looked at the backdrop and there were about 20 darts sticking in it. They'd obviously been thrown at us. It was also going on at football games at the time.

TOPPER: It was great playing with Paul, because once he'd been taught a bass line, he'd always play it exactly right, every time we played the song. It gave me an incredible freedom to fill, knowing I wouldn't clash with Paul 'cos he'd be doing the right lines. I could always play around whatever Paul was playing, and it was especially good on stage.

JOE: Finding someone like Topper, who had the strength and stamina to play with us live the way he did, was our breakthrough. We'd never have gone anywhere without Topper on the drumstool.

Europe '77 Tour

LINE-UP: STRUMMER, JONES, SIMONON, HEADON

14 JUN: Grona Lund, Stockholm, Sweden

17 JUL: Rag Market, Birmingham (Punk Festival). The festival had been announced three weeks earlier but the local council had it cancelled at the last moment. The Clash turned up outside the venue in the afternoon to talk to local fans. Soon after the police arrived and moved everyone on, citing unlawful gathering and obstruction as their reason.

17 JUL: Barbarellas, Birmingham. The band had to borrow heavy metal band Warhead's gear and played a 45-minute set in front of 500 punks.

5 AUG: Mont de Marsan, France. Punk Festival including the Jam, the Boys, Eddie and the Hot Rods, Dr Feelgood.

11 AUG: 14th Bilzen Festival, Liège, Belgium, support acts included Elvis Costello and the Damned

26 SEP: The Paradisimo, Amsterdam, Holland

27 SEP: Brussels, Belgium

29 SEP: Bataclan, Paris, France

1 OCT: Kaufleuten Saal, Zurich, Switzerland, support act the Damned

2 OCT: Porrhaus , Vienna, Austria

4 OCT: Munich, Germany

5 OCT: Volksbildungsheim, Frankfurt, Germany

6 OCT: Winterhuder Fahrhaus, Hamburg, Germany

7 OCT: Dads, Malmo, Sweden

8 OCT: Ronneby, Sweden

10 OCT: Club 700, Stora Hotellet, Oreboro, Sweden

SONGS PLAYED:
White Riot / I'm So Bored with the USA / London's Burning / Hate & War / Protex Blue / Pressure Drop / Career Opportunities / Cheat / 48 Hours / Janie Jones / Garageland / Remote Control / Deny / Capital Radio / Police And Thieves / What's My Name / 1977 / Complete Control / The Prisoner / White Man In Hammersmith Palais / Clash City Rockers / City Of The Dead / Jail Guitar Doors / Time Is Tight

A setlist for a performance in Sweden, with Booker T And the MGs' Time Is Tight added on to the end. Despite both the Damned and Stranglers cancelling tours of the country that year because of anti-Punk feeling being high, The Clash played and won the admiration of lots of new fans. They suffered a bomb threat on the last night of the tour, but played anyway.

LONDONS BURNING.
1977
CAPITAL RADIO
BORED WITH U.S.A
THE PRISONER
POLICE + THIEVES
REMOTE CONTROL
HATE & WAR.
COMPLETE CONTROL
WHITE MAN IN HAMMERSMITH
CLASH CITY ROCKERS
CAREER OPPURTUNITIES
JANIE JONES
WHITE RIOT
GARAGE LAND
JAIL GUITAR DOORS

CITY OF THE DEAD
PRESSURE DROP.
CHEAT
WHATS MY NAME
DENY
PROTEX BLUE
48. HOURS.
TIME IS TIGHT

On stage at The Rainbow.

A-side: Remote Control (3.01)

[Strummer/Jones] Produced by Mickey Foote

B-SIDE: LONDON'S BURNING (LIVE) (2:10)

[Strummer/Jones] Produced by The Clash

RELEASED 13 MAY 1977
NO CHART POSITION

JOE: Columbia thought that Remote Control was the most radio-friendly track on the album so they released it. We thought it was one of the worst tracks, but they manufactured it while we were on [the White Riot] tour and so couldn't do anything about it.

PAUL: We were really pissed off about the record company releasing Remote Control, 'cos as far as we were concerned, we had artistic freedom. We had to make it clear to them that we knew what we were doing.

THE CLASH: 'Remote Control
(CBS) "Remote Control/ from the
city hall/ push a button/ activate
you got to work" . . . spiky lyrics
from the band you hate to love, in
Joe Strummer's half whine and the
typical Clash hard blur chords
taken at medium pace. The Clash
apparently wanted 'Janie Jones' as
the single but CBS, if rumour is to
be believed, insisted on this. I
reckon the band were right —
'Janie Jones' is both closer to the
Clash spirit and more immediately
listenable. As an album track
'Remote Control' is a great cut,
vicious and brooding, but I'd
imagine that airplay might be
limited. Maybe they'll ban it
anyway in fear of housewives
hysterically tearing up kitchen
chairs and throwing them in the
coalshed.

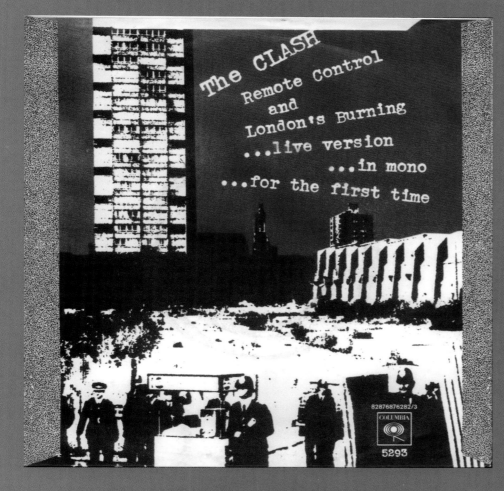

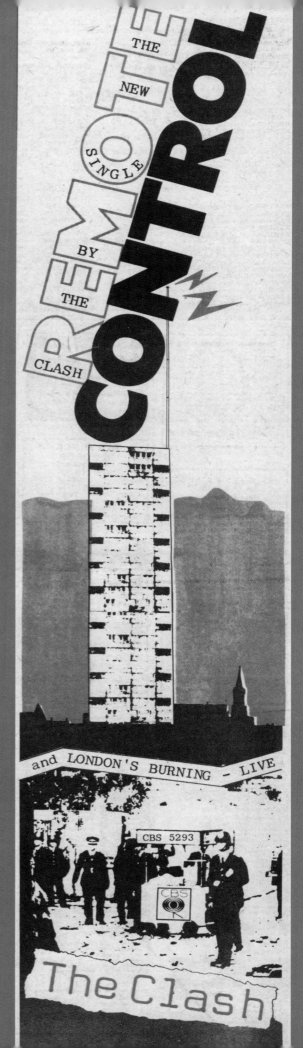

All profiles from the first *Clash Songbook* in which everybody tells their life story so far and then comments on each other. Joe on Mick: Egocentric bastard. Mick on Paul: Is selfish. Topper on Paul: Is a bad influence. Paul on Joe: Like having a dad in the band.

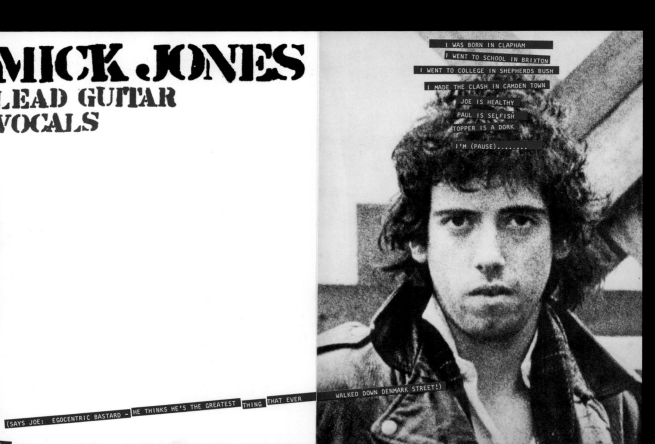

NICKY 'TOPPER' HEADON

BORN: BROMLEY 30.5.55.
(I'M USED TO DOING THIS FOR THE POLICE!)
PARENTS: TWO. DAD'S A HEADMASTER AT A PRIMARY SCHOOL
AND ME MUM'S A TEACHER.
I'VE GOT ONE YOUNGER BROTHER, DAVID.
DOG: BATTERSEA. (THAT'S WHERE WE GOT HIM FROM.)
MOTORBIKE: HONDA 125 TRIALS BIKE.
GIRLFRIEND: WENDY, WHO I LIVE WITH IN FINSBURY PARK - I CAN WALK
TO THE RAINBOW WHEN WE GIG THERE.
DRUMS: FIRST PLAYED WHEN I WAS THIRTEEN. I WAS WORKING AT THE BUTCHERS,
CLEANING UP AND STUFF, AND I SAVED THE MONEY TO BUY A KIT FOR £30.
SCHOOL: DOVER GRAMMAR SCHOOL. (I WAS PLAYING SEMI-PRO WITH LOCAL BANDS. SMASHED UP A CLASS ROOM.
LEFT SCHOOL: I WAS THROWN OUT WHEN I WAS SEVENTEEN. ME AND MY FRIENDS THE ODD PUB GIG.
WORK: ON THE DOVER FERRYS. THEN ON THE CHANNEL TUNNEL - WHICH NEVER GOT FINISHED. THEY WERE USELESS.
MOVED TO LONDON: DID A TOUR WITH A SOUL BAND FROM THE STATES AND SESSIONS AND
THE CLASH: I AUDITIONED WITH THE LONDON S.S. AND GOT THE GIG BUT LEFT 'CAUSE

(SAYS MICK: THAT'S WRONG! HE LEFT BECAUSE HE WAS INTO BILLY COBHAM..
......) THEN I BUMPED INTO MICK, JOE AND PAUL AT THE KINKS GIG AT
THE RAINBOW IN APRIL 1977. I REHEARSED WITH THEM THE NEXT DAY..... AND THAT'S IT.

10

PAUL SIMONON

I WAS BORN IN BRIXTON AND THEN I WENT TO
SCHOOL MORE OR LESS
EVERYWHERE.
SCHOOL WAS A LAUGH, ESPECIALLY ISAAC NEWTON IN LADBROKE GROVE. THAT WAS THE BEST ONE.
THE TEACHERS COULDN'T TEACH. AND ALSO IT WAS CLOSE TO PORTOBELLO MARKET WHERE YOU
COULD NICK LOTS OF THINGS. I HAD A PAPER ROUND AT SIX IN THE
MORNING. THEN I'D GO HOME AND MAKE ME DAD HIS BREAKFAST. THEN
I'D FUCK OFF TO SCHOOL. THEN I'D COME BACK AND COOK ME DAD
HIS DINNER AND DO ANOTHER PAPER ROUND AFTER SCHOOL AND THEN I'D
COOK ME DAD'S TEA. THEN I'D DO THE HOMEWORK ME DAD SET ME
'CAUSE HE WANTED ME TO GET ON. BUT I DIDN'T LEARN NOTHING -
OTHERWISE I'D BE A BANK CLERK, WOULDN'T I. WHEN I LEFT SCHOOL
I GOT A JOB IN JOHN LEWIS CARRYING CARPETS. THEN I TRIED TO
GET INTO ART COLLEGE BUT NONE OF THEM WOULD HAVE ME BECAUSE I
DIDN'T HAVE THE PROPER QUALIFICATIONS. THEN I FOUND ONE,
THE BYAM SHAW IN NOTTING HILL GATE WHERE YOU DIDN'T NEED
QUALIFICATIONS. I GOT A SCHOLARSHIP FROM THE LOCAL COUNCIL.
AND I SAID 'OY! DO YOU WANT TO JOIN MY BAND?' AND HE WAS REALLY DYING TO.
THEN I MET MICK (LAUGHS)
AND I TAUGHT HIM TO PLAY
GUITAR.......

(SAYS NICKY: PAUL IS A REALLY SOLID BASS-PLAYER AND A GOOD
LAUGH ON THE ROAD. HE IS A BAD INFLUENCE, HE LEADS US ON.
THE AIRGUNS ON THE ROOF INCIDENTS?
OH, THAT WAS MY IDEA.)

BASS VOCALS

9

Out Of Control Tour

LINE-UP: STRUMMER, JONES, SIMONON, HEADON
Support acts were Richard Hell and the Voidoids and the Lous on most dates, with extra local acts added in different places

20 OCT: Ulster Hall, Belfast, Northern Ireland
21 OCT: Trinity College, Dublin, Ireland, support act the Count Bishops
22 OCT: Eric's, Liverpool, support act the Toilets
24 OCT: Kinema, Dumfermline
25 OCT: Apollo, Glasgow, Scotland
26 OCT: Clouds, Edinburgh, Scotland
27 OCT: University, Leeds
28 OCT : Polytechnic, Newcastle
29 OCT: Apollo, Manchester
30 OCT: Victoria Hall, Hanley, Stoke-on-Trent
1 NOV: Top Rank, Sheffield
2 NOV: University, Bradford
3 NOV: Kings Hall, Derby
4 NOV: University, Cardiff, Wales
5 NOV: Exhibition Centre, Bristol
6 NOV: Market Hall, Carlisle
7 NOV: Top Rank, Birmingham
8 NOV: Tiffany's, Coventry
9 NOV: Winter Gardens, Bournemouth
10 NOV: Exhibition Centre, Bristol
11 NOV: Corn Exchange, Cambridge
12 NOV: Pavilion, Hastings
13 NOV: Top Rank, Southampton
15 NOV: Elizabethan Ballroom, Belle Vue, Manchester.
Arranged and filmed by Granada TV, with Siouxsie & The Banshees.
11 DEC: Apollo, Glasgow
13 DEC: Rainbow, London
14 DEC: Rainbow, London, support act Sham 69
15 DEC: Rainbow, London, support act Lovers of Outrage

SONGS PLAYED:

Complete Control / 1977 / Jail Guitar Doors / I'm So Bored With the USA / Clash City Rockers / White Man in Hammersmith Palais / Protex Blue / City of the Dead / Cheat / The Prisoner / Capital Radio / Police and Thieves / Career Opportunities / Janie Jones / Garageland / London's Burning / White Riot / What's My Name / Hate And War / Remote Control / Tommy Gun

An original full-page advert for the tour. Note that Birmingham is marked as being in Wales.

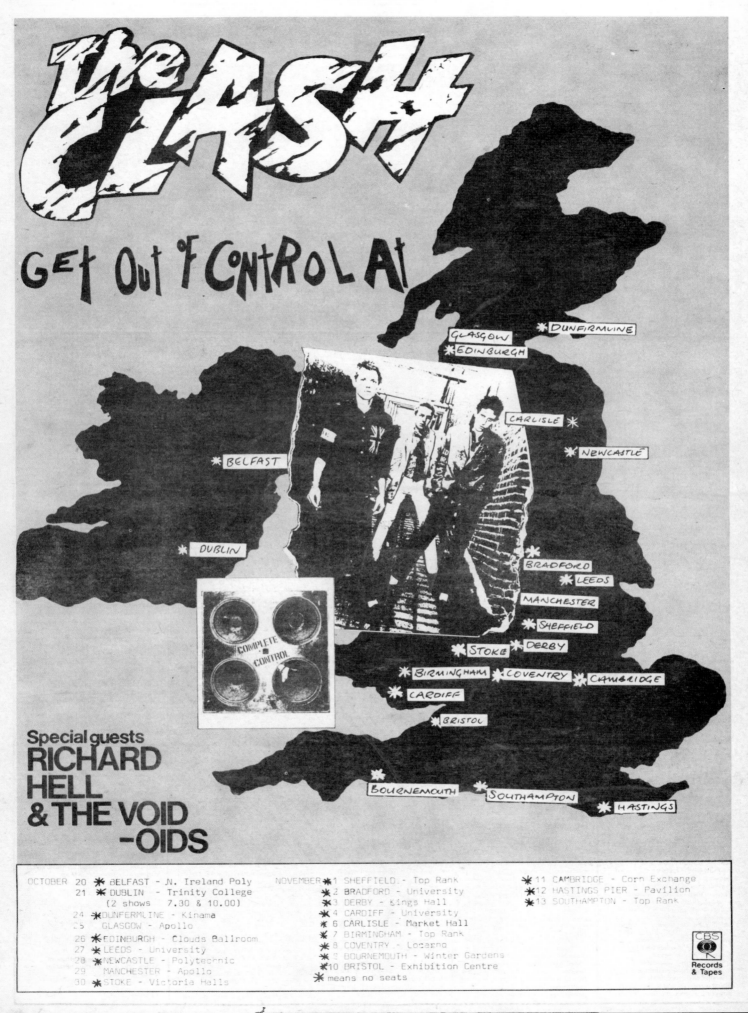

the CLASH

Get Out of Control At

Special guests
RICHARD
HELL
& THE VOID
-OIDS

OCTOBER 20 ✱ BELFAST – N. Ireland Poly	NOVEMBER ✱1 SHEFFIELD – Top Rank	✱11 CAMBRIDGE – Corn Exchange
21 ✱ DUBLIN – Trinity College	✱2 BRADFORD – University	✱12 HASTINGS PIER – Pavilion
(2 shows 7.30 & 10.00)	✱3 DERBY – Kings Hall	✱13 SOUTHAMPTON – Top Rank
24 ✱DUNFERMLINE – Kinema	✱4 CARDIFF – University	
25 GLASGOW – Apollo	✱ 6 CARLISLE – Market Hall	
26 ✱EDINBURGH – Clouds Ballroom	✱ 7 BIRMINGHAM – Top Rank	
27 ✱ LEEDS – University	✱ 8 COVENTRY – Locarno	
28 ✱NEWCASTLE – Polytechnic	✱ 9 BOURNEMOUTH – Winter Gardens	
29 MANCHESTER – Apollo	✱10 BRISTOL – Exhibition Centre	
30 ✱STOKE – Victoria Halls	✱ means no seats	

CBS
Records
& Tapes

White men in Glasgow melee

THE CLASH had yet another brush with the law last week during their British tour.

Joe Strummer and Paul Simenon were arrested by Glasgow police after the band's concert at the Apollo (the last rock show to be held there unless the latest moves to save the venue are successful).

The arrests happened as the band tried to make their way from the stage door to their cars after the concert. Reports of what happened vary, but Strummer was arrested by police first and Simenon was arrested soon afterwards.

The following morning both appeared at Glasgow District Court charged with a breach of the peace. Strummer was fined £25 for "smashing a bottle on the ground" and Simenon was £50 for "trying to rescue Strummer".

During the concert, which was virtually sold out, 50 seats were destroyed by fans. But press reports that fans in the circle were breaking off arm rests and hurling them into the stalls were denied by the theatre management.

STRUMMER: £25 fine.

LEFT: A music paper report on the band's troubles in Glasgow which ended with Joe and Paul both being fined by the court.

RIGHT: Mick performing in a customized shirt which has added buckles and patches. He wasn't arrested in Glasgow.

19 DEC: Belfast McMordie Hall, Queens University Students Union
20 DEC: Belfast McMordie Hall, Queens University Students Union

GET OUT OF CONTROL TOUR

PAUL: That tour with Richard Hell was pretty rough on the support acts. Skinheads kept jumping up and punching Richard Hell and then jumping off the stage. Same with Suicide, who were really good, 'cos they stuck with it. Richard Hell threw a wobbly though and wandered off. Suicide would carry on with their noses bleeding, things being chucked at them and skinheads jumping on stage to attack them. They stuck it out, like saying 'You ain't gonna get us off.' That was pretty admirable, I think.

JOE: Richard Hell and the Voidoids were on the tour and it was during the time of gobbing at bands, which was disgusting. Richard Hell took a lot of the early gob and by the time we'd come on they'd run out of spit, 'cos the Voidoids had taken the fresh load. It was beyond belief. People wouldn't credit it today.

MICK: We played our first gig in Amsterdam on that tour and we were really well received, but I thought it was one of our bad nights. I remember thinking, 'Bloody hell, they think this is good but we can do much better than this!' They lapped it up anyway.

TOPPER: The more we played together the better we got on. We became really good friends pretty quickly. Take the band away and we probably wouldn't have done, but because of The Clash we were all in it together.

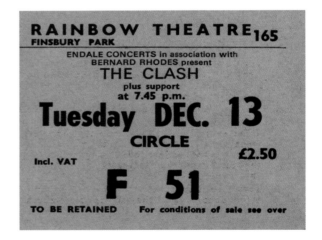

RAINBOW THEATRE 165
FINSBURY PARK
ENDALE CONCERTS in association with
BERNARD RHODES present
THE CLASH
plus support
at 7.45 p.m.
Tuesday DEC. 13
CIRCLE
Incl. VAT   £2.50
F 51
TO BE RETAINED   For conditions of sale see over

The May gig at the Rainbow ended with damage being done to the house seating, but the band were still booked to play three nights in a row in December at the crumbling venue.

A-side: Complete Control (3.13)

[Strummer/Jones] Produced by Lee 'Scratch' Perry

B-SIDE: CITY OF THE DEAD (2:22)

[Strummer/Jones/Headon/Simonon] Produced by
Mickey Foote

RELEASED 23 SEPTEMBER 1977
UK CHART PEAK: #28

JOE: Bernie and Malcolm had got together and decided that they wanted to control their groups. Bernie called a meeting in a pub after the Anarchy Tour and started with 'I want complete control', but Paul and I just ran out laughing. Paul was in hysterics about the phrase. Next thing I know Mick's come up with the tune and it was perfect.

MICK: I wrote it standing up in my bedroom. Bernie said write what affects us and this did.

HAVE YOU GOT...

THE NEW SINGLE FROM THE CLASH

COMPLETE CONTROL

OR IS IT

CITY OF THE DEAD

THE CLASH

---

have to buy the single to get a hold of that Barracuda Bass on the B side . . . 'cos it won't be on any album.

THE CLASH: 'Complete Control'/'City Of The Dead' (CBS 5664). The Westway Wonders meet up with rastaman Lee Perry who uses dem Trenchtown Echoplexes to give real depth to that ridiculously simple but supremely successful Clash formula. Chords like Council Demolition Squads. Anthemnilke refrains as strident as Ladbroke Grove graffitti. Pity the words on 'Complete Control' aren't too clear. But like E.C (Cochran, that is) said "WHO CARES? C'mon Everybody!" These two tracks EXPLODE!

RIGHT . . . AFTER THE SCENE

SAID RELEA

WE DIDNT WA

SAID FLY T

E THE PEOPL

OH OOOH OO

OH OOOH OO

COMPLETE CONTROL

CITY OF THE DEAD

CBS 5664

And The Dogs, Black Slate and Fruit Eating Bears.

...is talking about combining the two yet no-one has yet dared do anything about it.''

CLASH: new single

CLASH CONTROL

THE CLASH release their new single 'Complete Control'/'City Of The Dead' next Friday.

The band's manager has this to say about the record: "Complete Control' tells a story of a conflict between two opposing camps, both of which are using the tool of change to further their own beliefs . . . We all want change, so find out what side you're on and try to get complete control."

December 10, 1977   U.S. $1.10c/Canada 60c   18p

new MUSICAL EXPRESS

Pics: PENNIE SMITH

'CLASH'

'CLASH'

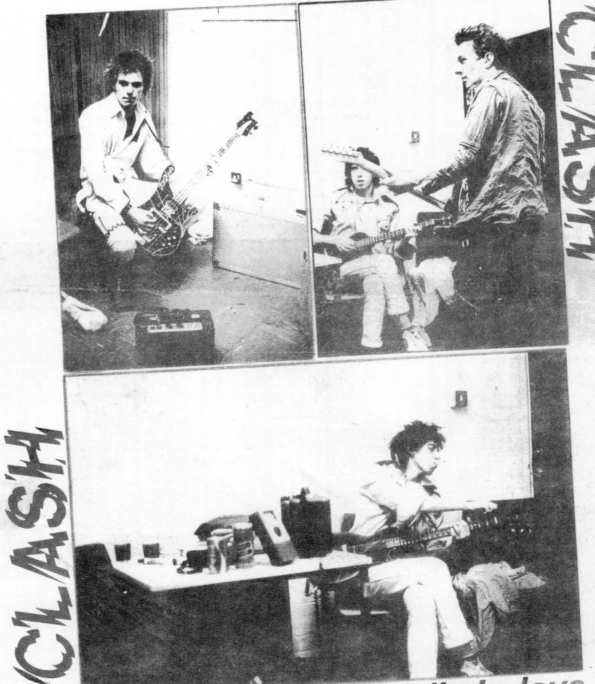

Lester Bangs falls in love (and sees the Promised Land)

Pages 31—34

SIX DAYS ON THE ROAD TO THE PROMISED LAND

When American music journalist Lester Bangs went on the road with The Clash and the *NME* ran his report over three successive weeks, it was considered a truly critical coup for the band (and the *NME*). That he was a stoner hippie wasn't seen to be a problem for either band nor writer, but it caused some merriment on the road.

PAUL: Lester Bangs was like a big cuddly bear and we were a bit funny to him at first 'cos he was American and a journalist. But he seemed so innocent and helpless and we couldn't but take a shine to him.

One night after a show, we were back at the hotel with loads of people sitting around in the foyer, drinking beer, and Lester was there, sitting quietly. I creeped under his chair, and stuffed newspapers up his flared trouser legs, then set light to them. He was rambling on about something and then suddenly, 'Aaaaah!' there's fire and smoke everywhere, coming from under his flares.

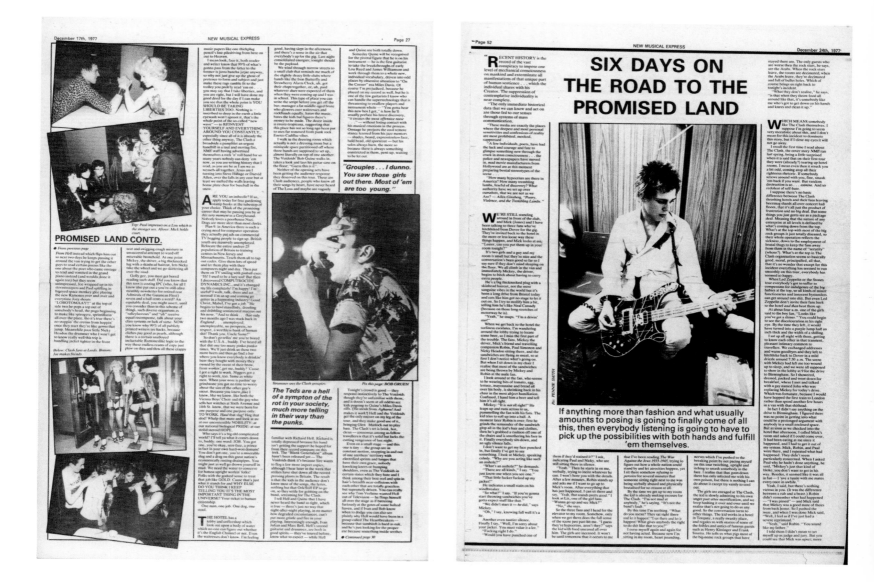

1978

'The situation with the record company was, there was no relationship. We were in full control of what we were doing, what our album covers looked like and what songs we put on them.'
PAUL

As 1977 came to an end, The Clash were playing to increasingly large crowds at increasingly large venues across the UK – and appearing as the headline act. On 13 December, during the last leg of their Get Out Of Control Tour, they played the Rainbow in London for three nights in succession, in front of 2,500 fans each night. For much of the tour they had played songs from the first album, along with the early singles and they had debuted [White Man] In Hammersmith Palais, The Prisoner, Clash City Rockers and Jail Guitar Doors.

As The Clash performed regularly they gained a well-earned reputation for being a fantastic live act. A big part of their act was not an act at all; they meant everything they played and sang.

While The Clash were playing some large venues, they still appeared at small (under 1,000 capacity) clubs, but it didn't matter what size the stage; the performance was always full-on.

At the Rainbow, though, they began to play two brand new songs: Tommy Gun and Last Gang In Town, neither of which would be released until November of 1978.

While Tommy Gun was a trademark Clash song, Last Gang was different. It showed that The Clash were about to begin a new phase musically and move away from the purely punk sound of the first album and singles. Its rockabilly rhythms and halting guitars pre-shadow the sound of London Calling and, unlike early Clash songs, it didn't just run straight through from 1-2-3-4 to the final ringing chord.

The message in the lyrics was how dumb it is to want to be the last gang in town, to have fought every other gang to the death. The song references the ongoing teds versus punks versus skinheads versus rastas versus what-have-you wars, which seemed to be going on across the UK at the time.

Last Gang was a radical musical and political move at the time since, from very small beginnings, the 'Punk' scene in the UK had grown to become dangerously close to being the mainstream musical movement for disaffected youth. Bands who'd caught on to the new wave later than the summer of 1976, such as Sham 69, were blasting out playground-level punk anthems (If The Kids Are United etc.) and playing to hormonally-driven teenagers who'd spend Saturday afternoons fighting at football grounds and Saturday nights fighting in clubs, stomping around to the new punk thrash on dancefloors which only weeks before had resounded solely to the sound of Tavares, The Bee Gees, Candi Staton and Motown.

As 1977 ended, the handful of original punks who'd bought *Sniffin' Glue* and had decided to be either Pistols or Clash fans were being joined by scores of new disciples to the Punk cause. And the new disciples wanted more of what had gone before – fast, furious, non-stop three-minute tunes to pogo and gob to. You couldn't pogo to Last Gang In Town. But the band knew they had to change in order to progress, to make it everywhere.

A-side: Clash City Rockers (3.48)

[Strummer/Jones] Produced by Mickey Foote

B-SIDE: JAIL GUITAR DOORS
(3:30)
[Strummer/Jones/Headon/Simonon] Produced by
Mickey Foote

RELEASED 17 FEBRUARY 1978
UK CHART PEAK: #35

PAUL: We were doing sporadic recording sessions. One day after Clash City Rockers had been written and we were on tour, Mick and I had an argument and it was getting too much. We were in a little van and Mick said something and I snapped and went to punch him. I got him on the ear so Topper and Joe grab my arms and I'm thrashing around trying to get Mick, who ended up with just a red ear. But Joe and Topper were covered in bruises from my elbows. We ended up in the studio with me on one side and Mick on the other, with Joe going back and forth to tell me when to change to E or C. The guy on the desk didn't know what had happened.

MICK JONES/GLEN/STEVE NEW: *"We do a better version of 'Pretty Vacant'."*

reputation into ready cash. Essentially it's a re-write of the old "Not Fade Away" riff, with the Bo Diddley beat allowed to slide languidly towards reggae. A very unusual mutant indeed. But there's also one of those choruses that strongarm their way into your memory and fight off all attempts to be bounced. In their way, too, the words are more effectively anarchistic than you get with more strident chaps. Oddly enough the B-side, "They Called It Rock", is even more formidable. But then the same thing happened with the "Bowi" EP and the "Halfway To Paradise" single. For all his sound commercial instincts, Lowe is evidently a touch perverse.

THE CLASH: Clash City Rockers (CBS). Having spent many months being gobbed upon in all parts of these islands, The Human Spittoons deserve some kind of reward for their sacrifice. As with Basher, their latest offering could be the one to do it. But at what expense? Sure, they've retained their punksh mannerisms, but there appear to be harmonies in among the braying that owe not a little to The Beatles. Pretty weird, right. Not only that, but you can actually hear — if not perhaps understand — a large proportion of the lyrics. All this is very surprising. New Wave music — as we used to call it — has pretty strict rules, and these guys could be reported to an international commission. But obviously something had to be done. The Clash couldn't continue to regard themselves as the most populist band in the universe if their records failed to get through. It's no good speaking up for the common man if the common man isn't putting his hand in his wallet. Watch for this act on *Top Of The Pops*. They're gonna be bigger than Darts.

BOB MARLEY AND THE WAILERS: Is This Love? (Island). Marley's least ethnic, least political, least mystical

Sandy Pearlman Dates

24 JAN: Barbarellas, Birmingham
25 JAN: Queensway Hall, Dunstable, Luton
26 JAN: Lanchester Polytechnic, Coventry
1 MAY: Barbarellas, Birmingham
21 MAY: Paris Hippodrome – Marxist Festival (Topper and Mick duetted White Riot at the end of the set; Paul had dropped his bass, Joe knocked over his mic and dropped his guitar in disgust at the terrible onstage sound)

In January of 1978 The Clash undertook a 'secret' tour of the Midlands in the UK and played three gigs. It seems that they were arranged mostly for the benefit of American record producer Sandy Pearlman, who was best known at the time for producing Blue Oyster Cult. He turned up at all three gigs and at the last (at Lanchester Polytechnic, Coventry, on 26 Jan 1978) tried to get into the band's backstage dressing room before the gig. The band's over-zealous roadie Robin Banks used undue force to keep him out, resulting in the long-haired American laying prostrate with a bleeding nose as the band stepped over him to get on the stage.

PAUL: The record company had this idea that they wanted a big name American producer for the second album. I think Mick probably had an interest in Pearlman, and anyway he kept turning up at our shows. Mick's old schoolmate Robin Crocker (AKA Banks) used to be our security and at this one gig we're trying to get changed before going on, and this guy's trying to get in, when suddenly there's a 'wallop' and Sandy Pearlman's lying on the floor with blood coming out of his nose. So he's dragged out as Mick shouts at Robin, 'He's our producer!' But he kept coming back even after the punch-up so he was obviously keen.

SONGS PLAYED:
Complete Control / London's Burning / Jail Guitar Doors / Clash City Rockers / Last Gang in Town / The Prisoner / White Man in Hammersmith Palais / Capital Radio / Tommy Gun / Police and Thieves / I'm So Bored with the USA / Janie Jones / Garageland / What's My Name / White Riot / Career Opportunities / English Civil War / Guns On The Roof

L-R: Mick and Joe with producer Sandy Pearlman. The fact that the band were using an American HM producer to make the eagerly anticipated, 'difficult' second album was viewed with suspicion by some parts of the music press (most of whom had been wholly supportive of The Clash up until this point).

An original full-page advert from the *NME* for the new Clash single. Big rock and pop acts had begun to put ads on the sides of London buses; the Clash just pretended to.

CLASH IN JAMAICA

After the Coventry gig and a brief recuperation for Joe, who claimed he'd caught hepatitis from someone having spit down his throat while he was playing, he and Mick flew to Jamaica to begin work on the second Clash album.

JOE: I suggested to Bernie that we go to Jamaica to write the next album as a joke. We wanted to get away for a couple of weeks and we couldn't go to Paris because we knew too many girls there and we'd be distracted, so I said what about Jamaica and he said no. But a couple of weeks later he came in with the plane tickets.

PAUL: I was really pissed off about them going to Jamaica because I really wanted to go and didn't. That really pissed me off.

JOE: I remember going to Jamaica with Mick for maybe a week or ten days and we came up with some tunes for the second album; Tommy Gun, Safe European Home and what have you, but mostly I remember searching for Lee Perry in Kingston. I don't know how we weren't filleted and served up on a bed of chips, 'cos me and Mick wandered around the harbour, and I think they mistook us for merchant sailors. But we were in our full punk regalia and we people just left us alone, probably because they presumed we were madmen or something – 'course me and Mick had no idea about anything, we were just wandering around Kingston like lunatics. We never found Perry, either.

PAUL I had a chat with John Lydon later and he said they [Mick and Joe] went over there and all they did was sit in their hotel room, which made me feel better because I was thinking at least they didn't go out on the town and have a great time.

MICK We only wrote a couple of songs in Jamaica. Safe European Home and Drug Stabbing Time, I think. The rest were written in Britain and even in the studio in New York.

Sham 69's Jimmy Pursey and Sex Pistol Steve Jones jamming on stage with Paul and Topper during a Clash gig encore (probably of White Riot).

Rock Against Racism

VICTORIA PARK, LONDON, SUNDAY 30 APRIL 1978

After a two-week stay in hospital, followed by three weeks in Jamaica for Joe and Mick, The Clash were back in rehearsals, putting together new songs for the second album. At the end of April they were booked to play at their first major outdoor gig, a benefit for the recently created Rock Against Racism organization (the headline act was the Tom Robinson Band). The idea for a rock 'n' roll anti-racism movement had formed in August 1976, as a reaction to dumb remarks made by Eric Clapton at a gig in Birmingham. From the stage he'd said that, 'England is overcrowded', and asked people to vote for Enoch Powell in the coming election, in order to stop Britain from becoming 'a black colony' (Powell preached repatriation). Clapton's remarks, combined with the growing popularity of the ultra right-wing National Front Party whose sole message was white supremacy, prompted a bunch of activists to create RAR. The Victoria Park gig was their first major event designed to highlight their cause. Numbers were estimated at around 100,000. In the wake of their appearance, during which Joe wore a Brigade Rossi t-shirt and Mick wore an all-black outfit, the band were accused by the British music press of jumping on the bandwagon of RAR and political naivety.

MICK: They were saying: 'How dare you play the Anti-Nazi League gig in a stormtrooper's outfit!' I was wearing a BBC commissionaire's hat which we nicked when we did the TV show, black shirt and black trousers. And all of a sudden I'm in a stormtrooper's outfit. And they're saying: 'You're disgusting.'

JOE: I wore [the Brigade Rossi t-shirt] because I didn't think they were getting the press coverage they deserved. After they shot Italy's answer to Winston Churchill, Aldo Moro, they shot down a new businessman every day. And it ended up on the back page of the *Evening Standard*, like who won the greyhounds and who got shot in Italy today. So I wanted to have my photo taken in it, and put it in the papers. Which of course it wasn't. I don't think anyone could actually see it at the gig.

SET LIST:

Complete Control / London's Burning / Clash City Rockers / Tommy Gun / Jail Guitar Doors / White Man in Hammersmith Palais / Last Gang in Town / Police and Thieves / English Civil War / Guns on the Roof / Capital Radio / White Riot

The Clash were passionate anti-racists and supporters of the Anti-Nazi League, so were a natural choice as the headline act for the Rock Against Racism outdoor gig in Victoria Park, Hackney.

AGAINST THE NAZIS

PAUL: I'm glad we did the anti-Nazi rally because it was important, but it was a bit off-putting with all these hippies wandering about with a giant bucket going, 'Put your money in here!' and shaking it around. We wanted to make the Left seem more glamorous 'cos at that time it was all hippies.

MICK: The National Front thing might have been slightly over-emphasized, but the whole thing is a much bigger ball game than just the Front. It's more than that. But we never needed to affiliate ourselves with little organizations.

JOE: We started playing reggae when everyone was saying white men can't play reggae, just like they used to say white men can't play the blues. On our tours we took lots of heavy dub stuff the kids had never heard.

MICK: We said we didn't want to top that bill. We just wanted to be part of it. No-one mentioned that other groups hired lots more bodyguards than us. I think it's important considering we couldn't get a glass of water backstage, but the others could.

The *NME* ran a four-page pull out special covering the gig.

An *NME* news report proving that The Clash didn't just write protest songs, they protested themselves, too. Here Mick and Paul help to man a protest outside the National Front ('is a Nazi Front!') headquarters.

Paul Simonon, Andy Bowen, Glen Matlock, Mick Jones and Michael Riley unite in silent protest outside the National Front headquarters.

PAUL: I remember we had a meeting with the guys from Rock Against Racism at Rehearsals Rehearsals and just before they turned up I was having a dig at Bernie over the Guns On The Roof episode, when I was banged up in Brixton prison and he hadn't done anything. I painted this mural on the wall of Bernie naked, and another on the ceiling of him with pigeons on his head. The naked one was over the fireplace and I hung a piece of silk material over it, and lit candles so it looked like an altar. Mick and Joe were laughing their heads off when Bernie came in with these guys from Rock Against Racism and we were singing, 'Praise Him, Praise Him' and they must have thought they'd come into some weird sect or something, us 'worshipping' this naked painting of Bernie on the plinth.

The Trouble with Bernie

(JUNE 1978)

'Whatever The Clash was it was something to do with Bernie Rhodes and The Clash, that's what I always maintained, for better or for worse.'
JOE

Two years after Bernie Rhodes had begun managing The Clash, his relationship with the band was showing signs of severe stress. In August he would announce a Clash gig in Harlesden, at the Roxy theatre, without having asked the band if they would or could play the date, which was subsequently cancelled. He was also insisting on sitting in on interviews with the press and answering questions, even though he hadn't been asked. In this extract from one such interview, with Tim Lott of *Record Mirror*, published in June 1978, it's clear from the comments of Joe and Mick towards Bernie that they both value and rubbish his input.

Conducted in the wake of the Rock Against Racism gig in Victoria Park, London, and on the eve of the 'Out On Parole Tour', the interviewer has been asking why the band haven't been touring for six months:

Bernie: You mentioned something...
Joe: Oh no, you shut up, you go on for 20 minutes.
[The tape is switched off until Bernie shuts up. When it comes back on the band are explaining the mechanics of the music business.]
Joe: We came out with this thing, we were helping groups. Normally in this business, people pay - if you want to support Black Sabbath, you've got to pay x thousand quid. We took groups on tour, and we were paying them, we were subsidizing everything, just like the Pistols had done for us on the Anarchy tour, although we had to pay them back later.

Bernie Rhodes, left, waits in the background while Joe and Mick talk with Mikey Dread.

Bernie: The Buzzcocks and all those bands, we paid everything for them.

Joe: Sitting behind Tom [Robinson] is Pink Floyd's management, and behind Jimmy [Pursey and Sham 69] is Mungo Jerry's management. And sitting behind us we've got (points to Bernie) him! You know what I mean? It's supposed to be right on and different and new, but if you look behind, it's just the same c— passing on the same money.

RM: But you've got CBS behind you. What's the difference?

Joe: We nearly had to cancel our tour because they wouldn't lend us the money to pay for the PA. That happened yesterday. Me and him were round there, and he was going: 'We'll have to cancel the tour then' and they said: 'Right, alright, we'll give you the two grand.'

RM: Why aren't they behind you then?

Bernie: Because Bob Dylan's in town.

Mick: Oi, hold it, that's enough of that. Show some respect.

Joe: What, about Bob Dylan? Oh yeah, he's the only one of the group going to see Dylan. Next question.

RM: *Let's pretend Bernie isn't present. How are relations with Bernie? We've been hearing rumours…*

Joe: Sometimes it's stormy, you know. The rumours are a load of bollocks. There's all kinds of bastards trying to take us over, because they see they can make a few bucks out of us. They started these rumours, they're trying to drive a wedge between us and Bernie.

Mick: We love Bernie really.

Joe: Yeah – even if he is short. We argue a lot, you know, because we're called The Clash and we have them. People say they ain't gonna last long like that, but we've been doing it for nearly a couple of years.

RM: *What do you argue about?*

Joe: Everything. We argue about dates, tours, songs, shoes, socks, shirts, television programmes, telephone bills, everything.

RM: *Another quote I saw somewhere was: 'We'll never get a Top 10 hit because they won't let us.'*

Joe: What I meant by that was the radio playlists. Unless it's played on the radio you might as well forget it. And I can't see anybody ever playing Clash records on the radio.

RM: *Why?*

Bernie: Because the music press hasn't backed us up, no-one else has backed us up, we're just five people working very hard. And you can't have five people working against maybe, twenty thousand.

RM: *Don't you think that's a bit paranoid?*

Joe: Better to be paranoid than pathetic.

Mick: The last time we phoned up Doreen Davies [head of CBS promotions dept] to say why aren't we on the playlist, she said: 'Well, it isn't exactly the sort of music you can work to.' And as an afterthought she added: 'Well, your lot don't work anyway, do they?' Well, why is that? Is our record too fast?

Bernie: It's not paranoid, it's realistic. The press at the moment are paranoid people, we ain't, we're dealing with it, right. We're getting on with it.

RM: *Why do you think it is they still dislike you? Is it just a hangover from the punk thing, or are you still doing something to get at them?*

Bernie: Of course we are. It's the naughty boy syndrome. If you're a good boy you get rewarded, if you're a naughty boy you get smacked. Art reflects society, and if Radio One reflects society, then you've got what you deserve.

RM: *Yes, but every group around hates Radio One, so what makes you any different?*

Bernie: We're not trying to be better than any groups, we're just trying to do a job that other groups maybe find hard to do.

RM: *What?*

Bernie: Like – get on with it.

Joe: Like make real records. Records that deal with real things. We're trying

Clash tune in, turn off

(I DON'T WANNA GO TO) HARLESDEN: The **Clash** gig at the Harlesden Roxy this Saturday has been postponed, the reason given being that the Clash feel unfairly treated by the radio and are going on strike in protest — all four of their singles have been critically acclaimed yet none of them have received more than a smattering of radio plays.

The gig will be rescheduled — possibly for September 22 or 23 and tickets for this Saturday's gig will be valid for whenever it is rescheduled. Beyond the obvious bizarreness of the reason given, rumours are running thick and fast (even thicker and faster than usual, that is) that the Clash are about to leave the warm and embracing clutches of manager **Bernie Rhodes** and that this and other forthcoming Clash gigs — mostly in Europe and the States — were set up while **Mick** and **Joe** were in the States and unaware of what was being done in their name.

Whatever the truth behind rumours of that split — and it's such a persistent rumour that the truth could be anybody's guess — Mick and Joe were still in the States on Monday and didn't look like returning to England immediately which certainly wouldn't have given them time to rehearse for the Roxy gig.

Meanwhile back in the States. . . getting to New York to finish off that long-long-long awaited second Clash album, Strummer took the unusual step of getting there from San

ONE DOWN, FOUR TO GO: Magazine is now — and has been for a while only they were keeping q about it — without a drummer, **Martin Jackso** left — musical difference of course, he wanted to something heavier. But, what, we ask ourselves, heavier than **Howie** in a temper tantrum?

HAVE INJURIES, WIL PLAY: If you've got nothing better to do toni (September 7), you might consider jaunting over to NYC where you could ca the Music Industry Casualties show at Max's Kansas City. Featured ar **Cheetah Crome, Jay Magnum** (who's he anyway?) and our own wonderful **Sid Vicious**.

APPLE LOOSE TALK: content with letting runn dog English music p hacks break up their ba **Television's Tom Verl**a and **Richard Lloyd** are b preparing solo albums the unwitting/expect world . . .

Chris Spedding is c there in Gotham City working with **Robert Gor**e — he certainly has as m leather clothes as one-t Gordon sidekick, **Link W** . . .

The **Helen Wheels** broken up (*oh really cynical Ed.*)…

Dillinger is gonna supp **Talking Heads** while **Syl** **vain** is now a real full-t member of the **Johann** band — the **Criminals** fully down the pan . . .

Noo Yawk roues rep

Music weekly *Sounds* publishes rumours of the split between band and manager, in September 1978.

to be the best group in the world. A punk rock group. A group that doesn't shirk out when it comes to it. Like telling the truth as we see it, and not being paid off. They offer you a bite of the big apple.

Mick: They've offered us every apple.

Joe: They say: 'If you change the words on this single, boys, you could have a hit.'

Mick: They say 'you could have the biggest hit in the universe if only you took the words piss and shit out of there'.

Bernie: How many copies of *Record Mirror* do you sell?

Joe: Oh my God. Bernie, go out and get some sandwiches.

(This leads into a long, rambling tangent from Bernie.)

RM: Bernie, why do you always insist on interrupting? Why can't you let the group talk for themselves?

Joe: Because he loves talking. He can't resist It. He'd rather be here, butting in, than sitting at home watching telly.

Bernie: Well, they're talking, aren't they.

Joe: Not when you're butting in.

Bernie: Sorry, you didn't send me the rules.

Within a matter of weeks of this interview appearing Bernie had been sacked. Looking back on the sacking the band simply state:

PAUL: Bernie set up a gig in Harlesden unknown to us, we were still in America when he announced it and it might have been Bernie trying to force some situation on us, in a kind of power play.

JOE: Bernie announced these gigs at the Harlesden Roxy and for some reason they were cancelled, I can't remember why but we had to go down there and apologize to the fans. I showed we weren't some tosspots swanning around somewhere not caring about them. About a month later Bernie was manoeuvred out of the managerial chair in a power struggle.

MICK: While we were away Bernie set up these gigs that we couldn't do of course. There were people around who were angling to change our whole set-up, there were always people trying to get in with us. Even Sandy, nice bloke that he was, tried to get us to sign a bit of paper and we were like, 'Uhh?' We didn't want anything to do with it all, had no interest.

PAUL: Bernie and Mick used to have serious falling-outs and I think the Harlesden gig was the last straw. We came back from the US and were unprepared for this gig, but we went down there and apologized to the fans. I can't remember exactly how it happened but that was when we parted ways with Bernie.

JOE: Losing Bernie created a vacuum that we never filled until he came back again two years later.

Rude Boy

DIRECTORS: Jack Hazan, David Mingay
WRITERS: David Mingay, Ray Ganges
STARRING: Ray Ganges, The Clash

At the RAR gig The Clash were being filmed by a small unit that had been following them around for a few weeks. Directors Jack Hazan and David Mingay had been filming the band with Bernie's agreement, and the band had simply gone along with it, they'd said, as long as the crew didn't get in the way. At the RAR gig, though, the filming became part of the show.

MICK: That was the most people we'd ever played to at that point, and I don't know if they were pushing Ray [Ganges] onto the stage to get some good footage, but they were trying to get some good footage of us and it was all a bit out of control.

JOE: At some point in 1977, this filmmaker came to us and said he wanted to make a film. He'd just made a film about David Hockney called *A Bigger Splash* and we said to him, 'OK, make your film just don't get in the way'. I like that we didn't say, 'what's the film about', or 'what's your agenda', or 'what are you trying to pull?' We just said 'OK, if you want to make a film about us go ahead, but we've got to go on tour, you can follow us around and film it but don't get in the way'.

MICK: It seemed like Bernie set up the film *Rude Boy*, then halfway through he stopped working with us, and we were just making it up as we went along. And they were filming it.

DAVID MINGAY: [director and writer, quoted in 1980 when the film was

CLASH PERFORMANCES FEATURED:
English Civil War (recorded 1/3/79, London Lyceum) / White Man In Hammersmith Palais (4/7/78, Glasgow Apollo) / I'm So Bored With the USA (4/7/78, Glasgow Apollo) / Janie Jones (4/7/78, Glasgow Apollo) / White Riot (4/7/78, Glasgow Apollo) / Complete Control (27/7/78, London Music Machine) / Tommy Gun (6/7/78, Dumfermline Kinema) / I Fought the Law (28/12/78, London Lyceum) / Safe European Home (27/7/78, London Music Machine) / What's My Name (27/7/78, London Music Machine) / Police & Thieves (12/7/78, Birmingham Top Rank) / London's Burning (30/4/78 Victoria Park, Hackney, London) / White Riot (30/4/78, Victoria Park, Hackney, London) / Piano Song (studio/film) Garageland (studio/film)

A Japanese flyer advertising a showing of *Rude Boy*.

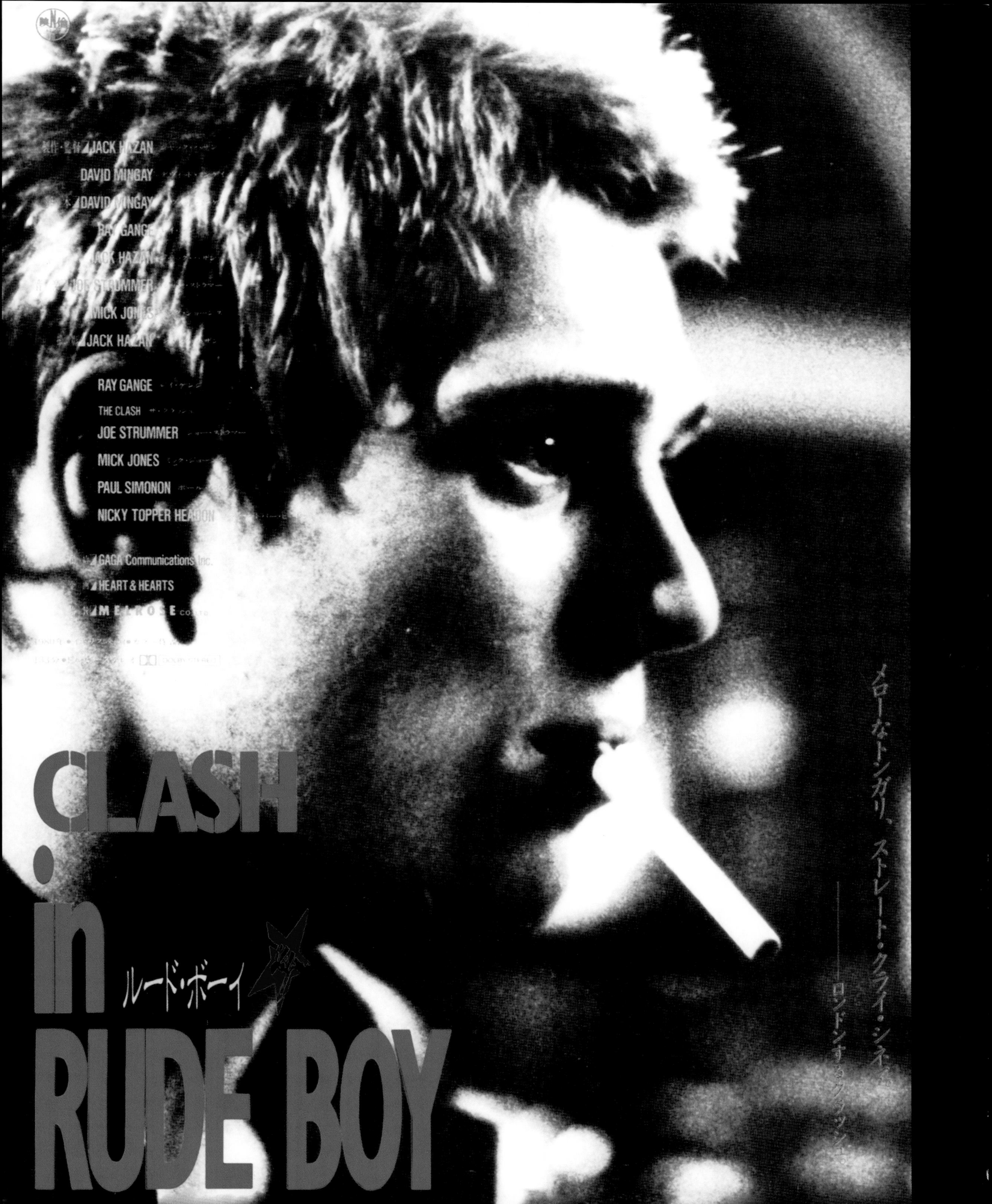

監 N 作 JACK HAZAN

DAVID MINGAY

DAVID MINGAY

RAY GANGE

JACK HAZAN

JOE STRUMMER

MICK JONES

JACK HAZAN

RAY GANGE

THE CLASH

JOE STRUMMER

MICK JONES

PAUL SIMONON

NICKY TOPPER HEADON

GAGA Communications Inc.

HEART & HEARTS

MELROSE co.,LTD

CLASH
in
ルード・ボーイ
RUDE BOY

メローなトンガリ、ストレート・クライ・シネマ
──ロンドンするクラッシュ

released]: What previously had seemed beautiful and correct had changed. When the Clash played the Rainbow and the seats were ripped up, it was just after the Irish bombs had gone off in London. There was an atmosphere about The Clash, and what they were doing was a long way from swearing on TV, which apparently launched the Pistols big.

MICK: With one thing and another, we were finishing our set at Victoria Park and roadies for the other bands started coming on stage, all being filmed of course, trying to get us off the stage. I don't know if we were running overtime, but if we were then we weren't doing it on purpose, we wouldn't at such a thing.

BERNIE RHODES [quoted in 1980 when the film was released]: It was hard work to get the group interested in the project because they were losing interest in me; it was difficult enough to get them to accept Ray. In the end they were going to get paid a certain amount, but basically it was supposed to be a labour of love.

JOE: I recreated some scenes with Ray Ganges, such as the one where he had actually come up to me in London and asked for a job as a roadie, and though some scenes were created for the film, most of it was true. Though he never was our roadie.

DAVID MINGAY [quoted in 1980]: The pressures on them are tremendous. You are what the music press sets you up as, because your every move is chronicled there, and so the demands from the fans are greater even than those from the business.

JOE: That film looks pretty good today, although at the time we fell out pretty badly with the filmmaker. After we saw it I don't think we really understood

Rude Boy **was meant to look like a documentary and for the most part, succeeded in that.**

Joe with Ray Ganges in a still from the film. By the time the film was released, relationships between the band and the filmmakers had become difficult.

what he was going on about – maybe we'd got fed up with him, maybe we were all fed up with each other, having to travel around together. It all became messy in the end. But I think the film stands up well.

[WHITE MAN] IN HAMMERSMITH PALAIS

PAUL: That was Joe's thing. He'd gone to Hammersmith to check out some sounds.

JOE: A lot of people have told me that when they first heard White Man they couldn't believe it because we weren't supposed to come out with something like that at the time. We were a big fat riff band, we were rock solid beats and so coming out with White Man in Hammersmith Palais was really unexpected. And those are the best moments of any career.

A-side: (White Man) In Hammersmith Palais (4.00)

[Strummer/Jones] Produced by The Clash

B-SIDE: THE PRISONER (2:59)

[Strummer/Jones/Headon/Simonon] Produced by The Clash

RELEASED 16 JUNE 1978
UK CHART PEAK: #32

MICK: White Man was Joe's experience of going to a reggae all-nighter. The music is a mixture of the reggae influence and punk, and was the next step after Police And Thieves. It was a bridge between the first and second album.

JOE: The audience at this reggae gig were really hardcore and I felt they were looking for something different from a showbiz spectacle. It was very Vegas. I was enjoying the show, but I felt like I saw it through their eyes for a minute or two.

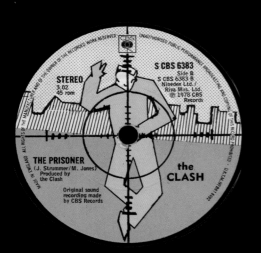

Give 'Em Enough Rope

[UK CBS 32444/US CBS 82431]

RELEASE DATE: UK 10 NOVEMBER 1978/US 10 NOVEMBER 1978
UK CHART PEAK: #2
US CHART PEAK: DIDN'T CHART

As 1978 wore on with no sign of its release, the UK music press complained that the second Clash album was taking too long to arrive; that the heavy metal American producer Sandy Pearlman would turn their once punk heroes into mid-Atlantic prog rockers; that they had 'sold out' and wanted only to be big rock stars in America. Which was laughable, since the American arm of the band's record label CBS didn't like what they'd heard of, or about, The Clash. Their debut album had only been sold there on import, via punk-minded independent record stores.

JOE: We didn't realize how weird the first album sounded to American record company people – they weren't keen to release it at all.

MICK: CBS wouldn't release the first album in America because they didn't think it was fit for human consumption at the time. In comparison to the rest of the music, it wasn't very polished or professional so they couldn't see it. It did all right on import though, and that was how a lot of the interest in The Clash in America seemed to grow – by word of mouth.

SIDE ONE:
Safe European
  Home
English Civil War
Tommy Gun
Julie's Been
  Working For the
  Drug Squad
Last Gang in Town

SIDE TWO:
Guns On The Roof
Drug-Stabbing
  Time
Stay Free
Cheapskates
All The Young
  Punks (New Boots
  And Contracts)

Joe Strummer (rhythm guitar, vocals), Mick Jones (guitar, vocals), Paul Simonon (bass), Topper Headon (drums). All songs arranged and performed by The Clash, produced by Sandy Pearlman, recorded and mixed by Corky Stasiak at Wessex Studios, London, and the Automat, San Francisco.

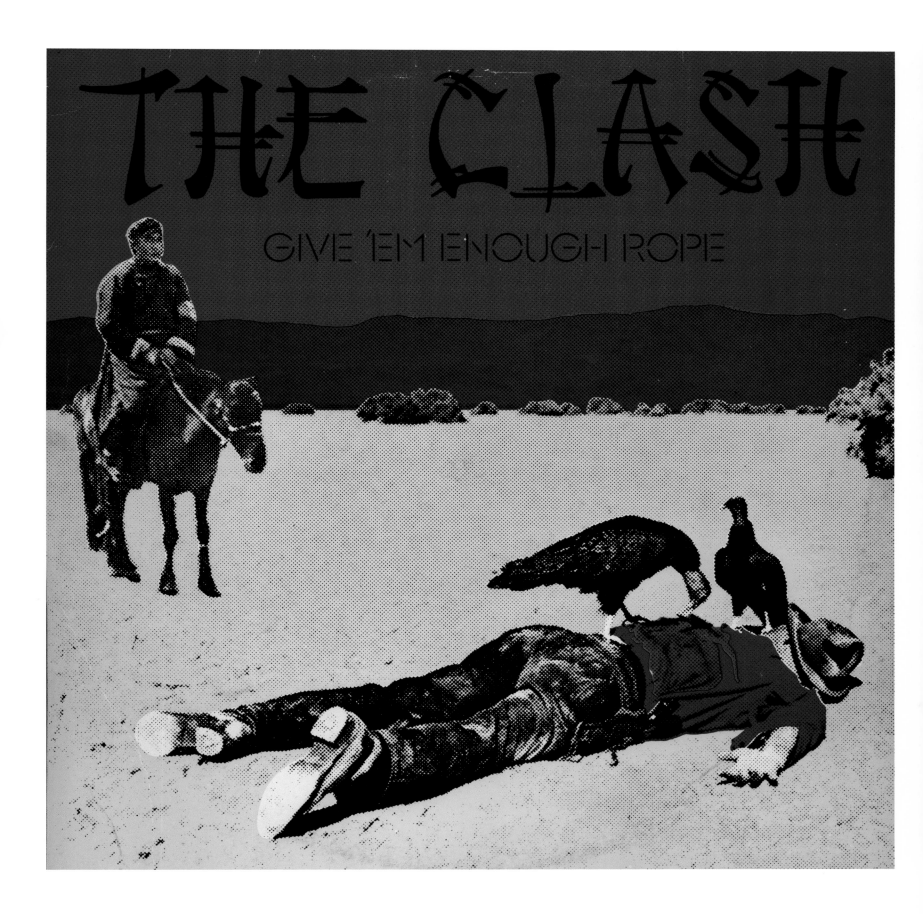

CLASH ON DELIVERY

INTERVIEW BY

GARRY BUSHELL,
PIX BY
JILL FURMANOVSKY

OR: how to beat the backstabbers and come up with a good second album. ('Good? It's bleedin' _great_ says the detached and objective Mr Bushell)

*'A spliff ana pound.
And half a pint of brown.
That's how we spell
Camden Town' ('All The
Young Punks').*

*'Just because we're in a
group you all think we're
stinking rich.
'N you think the cocaine's
flowing like rivers up our
noses.
'N every sea will part for
us like the red sea did for
Moses' ('Cheapskates').*

"I THINK the album's bloody great. Most groups after they've done their album they go 'aww, this could 'ave been better' or 'we mixed this badly cos we got stoned' an'all that. But we don't have that cos we spent like five days on each track getting it right."

Mick Jones laughed, it was like a Monty Python sketch, with him and me sitting on a 3d arrow, with 'admission free' stamped on it, plonked outside the Serpentine Art Gallery in Hyde Park with all these sculptured Morrismen behind us.

"I 'ate sculptures." Why meet here then? "Why not." Under the firm guidance of lensperson Furmanovsky, Jones and Topper wandered round the gallery posing, with me and Mick's long time mate Robin Banks (as we shall see, an appropriate name) bringing up the rear. It was a weird place, stuffed full of frightfully-frightfullys pretending not to see the star in their midst — me, dummy. Jonesy looked more like a lighterman with his red neckerchief and leather sports jacket with

CONTINUES OVER

The letter reads:

Dear Johnny,
For 9 months Im trying to get that white piano home I guess I'll be trying the Rest of the year too.
Ask Paul n Topper to keep our business STRICTLY to ourselves for the next 2 days, till we get back! No Newspapers. No Enemys
See you

LEFT: By the time that *Give 'Em Enough Rope* was released many music press journalists had decided that it would be a bad thing, mainly because it wasn't going to be a 'punk' record. There were writers who wanted the band to remain the leaders of agit-prop punk forever and play only fast, simple, three-chord protest songs.

ABOVE: The above note was discovered by Peter Silverton in 2008, having originally been given it by Joe Strummer in 1978. The note was intended for the Clash road manager Johnny Green, and had been given to Peter in America when he interviewed Joe and Mick for *Sounds*. Peter forgot to pass it on when he returned to England.

MAKING ENOUGH ROPE

By the middle of 1978 there was still no second Clash album in the shops and the music press were asking why not and accusing the band of being lazy. In an interview with *Record Mirror* in June, Mick said, 'We haven't had a day off since Christmas 1976!' But Joe put the 'delay' in releasing the album down to the fact that, 'We want to release an album that's 10 times better than the first one, and then one that's 10 times better than that. Not like the Jam and the Stranglers, they were rushed into theirs.'

JOE: The first I ever heard of [producer] Sandy Pearlman was in Bernie's Renault. He was checking out a Blue Oyster Cult tape and I thought he'd gone bonkers.

MICK: There was some suggestion [in the music press] at the time that our second album was being geared for the American market, which is why we got an American producer, but it was Bernie who introduced Sandy to the situation.

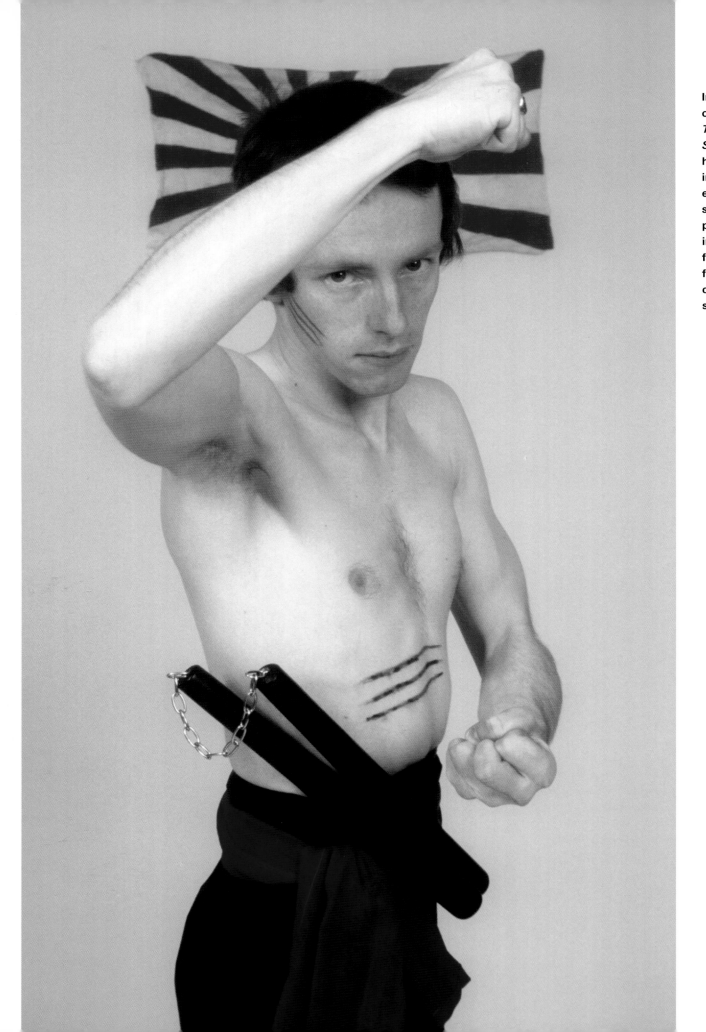

In a deliberate pastiche of Led Zeppelin's film *The Song Remains the Same*, in which the heavy metal Gods had individually filmed entire fantasy sequences, for a *Sounds* photo shoot The Clash indulged their own fantasies. Topper went for a Bruce Lee look, complete with scratches on his face.

TOPPER: That was my first album so it was a great buzz for me – and to get a producer who got such a great drum sound was really great. Sandy called me The Human Drum Machine because I didn't make one mistake on the album. Those were the days when I'd do my drum tracks and go, not entirely out of choice. Robin Crocker and all the nutters would be there and as soon as I'd finish my bit of work, they'd latch on to me and we'd cause mayhem. So once I'd done my bit we were told to go home, so there wasn't any trouble or damage bills.

JOE: After we recorded the first album, when the record company said, 'OK, let's talk about the second album', our attitude was, 'What do you mean second album?' We weren't really ready to make a second, I think it took so much out of us making the first. Behind the scenes I think they were pressuring Bernie to bring in something, they wanted an American angle to it. Bernie selected Sandy Pearlman off a list of producers that were presented to him as likely candidates by Columbia.

MICK: We recorded the basic tracks in Basing Street, West London, and then went to the Automat in San Francisco. Joe and I were virtually kidnapped and taken to America. All the time we were there we wanted to see Paul and Topper. Anyway, after the San Francisco sessions, I went to LA with Pearlman because he had this Blue Oyster Cult show. But on my first visit I was put in this bloody airport hotel and I felt so overcome, like, where's the rest?!? Joe had gone back to New York across the country in a pick-up truck with a friend of ours and I spent a week hanging out in LA. But by the end of the week I'd flown to New York where Paul and Topper joined us, 'cos we had missed 'em.

PAUL: That was the most boring situation ever, making that album. It was so nit-picking and a complete contrast to making the first album. There was no spontaneity and the only way I could get any kind of relief from the boredom of recording was to get some films from the Imperial War Museum and have them back-projected as we recorded, just to get some excitement going. So we had it running and I was enjoying it… but Pearlman then said he could hear the projector so we had to stop it.

MICK: That first trip to America had an effect [on me]. I'd been gearing up to go to there my whole life. I'd been fascinated by the stuff they had in the back of American magazines like BB guns and soldier sets and other things you couldn't get in England. But as far as songwriting was concerned, I don't think it had a great effect.

TOPPER: I'd never been to the States before, none of us had. We'd never been anywhere except Europe. Mick and Joe met us at the airport and I'll always remember driving over the bridge into New York from the airport and seeing it at night, the Manhattan skyline. It was breathtaking and gave me an amazing energy, too. I loved it, and even lived there for a while.

PAUL: I remember arriving in America with Topper to join Mick and Joe and the customs didn't want to let me in because my luggage was… well, it was a cardboard box that you put albums in, probably held about 12 LPs or something, but I just had some clothes in it. The customs couldn't understand why I didn't have a suitcase and they were on the verge of sending me back but somehow they didn't. It was really exciting driving into Manhattan, though, seeing the lights of New York for the first time.

Stay Free

MICK: It was about my old schoolfriends, and Robin especially. He was the guy who punched out Sandy Pearlman, who was producing the album of course. Which was kind of ironic.

Julie's Working for the Drug Squad

JOE: Operation Julie was carried out near Wales. There were these university graduates – chemists – and they were manufacturing LSD and distributing it. The only way for the cops to bust them was to put in some hippies of their own, who had to take the acid continually to maintain their cover. This stuff was the strongest outside Switzerland. The song's really about that, imagining tripping policemen.

GUNS ON THE ROOF

JOE: I think we were waiting for Mick to come to rehearsals [in Camden] and Topper and Paul got a bit bored. Topper had just bought a new airgun and so they went up on the roof and started firing away at these pigeons.

PAUL: Me, Topper, Robin and I think one of the Barnacle brothers was up from Dover, one of Topper's mates, and we had a couple of air rifles. This guy from Dover had a high-powered one and while we were waiting for Mick to turn up to rehearse we thought, we'll go and try out these rifles. So we went up on to the roof, saw these pigeons and started firing off a few shots. We missed and then they came back again. It was so weird, we'd take a shot and they'd keep coming back.

TOPPER: I love guns and had a couple of air pistols and an air rifle and I took them to rehearsals, on the bus. I walked all the way up Camden High Street with a rifle over my shoulder and two pistols down my belt. Didn't get pulled or nothing. Got to the studio, no Mick so I said, 'Right, let's go and shoot some pigeons on the roof.'

JOE: They started firing away at these pigeons which they didn't know were priceless racing birds, and belonged to one of the mechanics who worked round there.

PAUL: And then this big bloke comes over, like a builder or something,

TOP: The Press copy of *Give Em Enough Rope* came wrapped in a plain yellow card, printed on the other side of which was Joe's own account of how the band came to exist. The words 'THE CLASH' were printed onto the clear plastic sleeve. The release sleeve (see page 181) was also included.

A telegram was sent to members of the Press who'd been invited to an unveiling and play-through of the album, telling them that the venue had changed. Joe had been been born in Turkey, which was why the Embassy had been chosen for the launch. The reason for the switch is unknown.

shouting his head off and starts trying to get our guns off us and belt us around the head with them, and we're trying to belt him back.

TOPPER: Two big mechanics came over, whacked me on the arm with a monkey wrench, took the guns and that was it. Next thing I know there's a helicopter hovering overhead and the police come up with guns. Someone had reported an armed gang on the roof firing at trains, and this was around the time the IRA were active in London, so they pressed the red alert button.

PAUL: Next thing we know we're looking up at a helicopter, going, 'Cor, look at that, it's really close!' and it keeps getting closer and then there's police coming over the roofs with guns, yelling 'FREEZE!' So we froze, got nabbed by the cops and were taken down into the courtyard where there were about six police vans. They took us off to the police station and interrogated us, trying to get us to admit shooting at the trains. I remember having a pistol held to my head by one of them at one point, with him shouting, 'Tell us the truth!'

TOPPER: It was pretty scary when the police popped up yelling 'FREEZE!', pointing guns at us. But when they eventually realized that they couldn't really do us as IRA or keep pretending that we were a danger, then it became quite amusing. I think I got fined more for giggling in court than for the actual offence.

PAUL: Eventually we were dragged off to Brixton Prison and as we were waiting to be put in one of the cells, a prisoner starts laughing at me because I've got these big rips in the knees of my jeans. 'Oh look,' he says, 'he's been trying to get bail by begging on his knees.' Fortunately I didn't have to spend the night in there because Joe came down with Caroline Coon and bailed me out. Which I was grateful for. But Bernie was nowhere to be found throughout that whole scene.

JOE: They were eventually fined for killing five or six of these hard-to-train, expensive birds. But it was a bit of a farce.

MICK: Where was I? Inside the rehearsal room when I heard the helicopter. What was I doing? I was probably going, 'Help!'

FOLLOWING PAGE: Both pages are taken from the second *Clash Songbook*, art direction for which came from 'Paul, Mick, Nicky and Joe (The Clash)', design © Riva Music Ltd/ Derek Boshier 1979.

JULIE'S IN THE   STRUMMER/JONES
DRUG SQUAD:

IT'S LUCY IN THE SKY AND ALL KINDS OF APPLE PIE
SHE GIGGLE AT THE SCREEN COS IT LOOKS SO GREEN
AND THERE'S CARPETS ON THE PAVEMENTS
AND FEATHERS IN HER EYE
BUT SOONER OR LATER HER NEW FRIENDS WILL REALIZE
THAT JULIE'S BEEN WORKING FOR THE DRUG SQUAD.

WELL IT SEEMED LIKE A DREAM TOO GOOD TO BE TRUE
STASH IT IN THE BANK WHILE THE TABLETS GROW HIGH
IN THEIR MILLIONS
AND EVERYBODY'S HIGH   HI MAN....
BUT THERES SOMEONE LOOKING DOWN FROM THAT MOUNTAINSIDE
COS JULIE'S BEEN WORKING FOR THE DRUG SQUAD.

AND ITS TEN YEARS FOR YOU
NINETEEN FOR YOU
AND YOU CAN GET OUT IN 25
THAT IS IF YOU'RE STILL ALIVE.

AND THEN THERE CAME THE NIGHT OF THE GREATEST EVER RAID
THEY ARRESTED EVERY DRUG THAT HAD EVER BEEN MADE
THEY TOOK 82 LAWS
THROUGH 82 DOORS
AND THEY DIDN'T HALT THE PULL TILL THE CELL WERE ALL FULL
COS JULIE'S BEEN WORKING FOR THE DRUG SQUAD.

THEY PUT HIM IN A CELL AND THEY SAID YOU WAIT HERE
YOU'RE GOT THE TIME TO COUNT ALL OF YOUR HAIR
YOU'VE GOT FIFTEEN YEARS
A MIGHTY LONG TIME
YOU COULD HAVE BEEN A PHYSICIST BUT NOW YOUR NAME IS ON THE MAILBAG LIST
COS JULIE'S BEEN WORKING FOR THE DRUG SQUAD.

ENGLISH CIVIL WAR

WHEN JOHNNY COMES MARCHING HOME AGAIN
HE'S COMING BY BUS OR UNDERGROUND
A WOMEN'S EYE WILL SHED A TEAR
TO SEE HIS FACE BEATEN IN FEAR
AN IT WAS JUST AROUND THE CORNER IN
THE ENGLISH CIVIL WAR.

IT WAS STILL AT THE STAGE OF CLUB+FISTS
WHEN THAT WELL KNOWN FACE GOT BEATEN
TO BITS
YOUR FACE WAS BLUE IN THE
LIGHT OF THE SCREEN
AS WE WATCHED THE
SPEECH OF AN ANIMAL SCREAM
THE NEW PARTY ARMY
CAME MARCHING OVER
OUR HEADS.

40

ALRIGHT

THERE YOU ARE HA HA WE TOLD YOU SO
SAYS EVERYBODY THAT WE KNOW
BUT WHO HID A RADIO UNDER THE STAIRS
AN WHO GOT CAUGHT OUT ON THEIR UNAWARES?
WHEN THAT NEW PARTY ARMY CAME MARCHING
RIGHT UP THE STAIRS.

WHEN JOHNNY COMES MARCHING HOME AGAIN
NOBODY UNDERSTANDS HOW IT HAPPENED AGAIN
THE SUN IS SHINING AN THE KIDS ARE SHOUTING LOUD
BUT YOU GOTTA KNOW ITS SHINING THROUGH A
CRACK IN THE CLOUD
AS THE SHADOWS KEEP FALLING WHEN JOHNNY
COMES MARCHING HOME.

OK JOHNNY
ALL THE GIRLS GO WHOAH
GET HIS COFFIN READY
COS JOHNNYS COMING HOME.

ENGLISH CIVIL WAR' (TRADIONAL. ARRANGED BY
STRUMMER/JONES)
(LYRICS (C) 1978 NINEDEN LTD. CONTROLLED BY
RIVA MUSIC LTD FOR THE UK +
EIRE, CONTINENTAL EUROPE +
AUSTRALASIA

Out On Parole Tour

LINE-UP: STRUMMER, JONES, SIMONON, HEADON

Support acts were the Specials and Suicide

28 JUN: Friars, Aylesbury

29 JUN: Queens Hall, Leeds

30 JUN: Top Rank, Sheffield

1 JUL: Granby Hall, Leicester

2 JUL: Apollo, Manchester

3 JUL: Rafters Club, Manchester

4 JUL: Apollo, Glasgow

5 JUL: Music Hall, Aberdeen

6 JUL: Kinema, Dunfermline

7 JUL: Deeside Leisure Centre, Chester

8 JUL: Sports Centre, Crawley

9 JUL: Locarno, Bristol

10 JUL: Town Hall, Torquay

11 JUL: Top Rank, Cardiff

12 JUL: Top Rank, Birmingham. Spizz 77 also played, Steve Jones joined the Clash for an encore of Pretty Vacant

13 JUL: Empire, Liverpool (cancelled)

13 JUL: King George's Hall, Blackburn. Steve Jones joined the Clash again for encores.

14 JUL: Corn Exchange, Bury St Edmunds

15 JUL: Picketts Lock Sports Centre, Edmonton. Cancelled due to local residents' complaints.

21 JUL: Eric's, Liverpool

22 JUL: Eric's, Liverpool – matinee for under-16's

22 JUL: Eric's, Liverpool – evening

24 JUL: Music Machine, London

25 JUL: Music Machine, London

26 JUL: Music Machine, London

27 JUL: Music Machine, London

SONGS PLAYED:

Complete Control / Tommy Gun / Cheapskates / Jail Guitar Doors / Drug Stabbing Time / All the Young Punks / Clash City Rockers / White Man In Hammersmith Palais / Capital Radio / Stay Free / Police and Thieves / Blitzkrieg Bop / English Civil War / Safe European Home / London's Burning / Garageland / I'm So Bored With the USA / Janie Jones / White Riot / What's My Name / Garageland / Guns On The Roof / The Prisoner / Capital Radio

Paul Simonon might not have been able to play when The Clash formed, but he soon became an accomplished and rock-steady bass player. Topper loved playing with him because he could keep perfect time. As Topper said in the first *Clash Songbook*, 'Paul is a really solid bass player'.

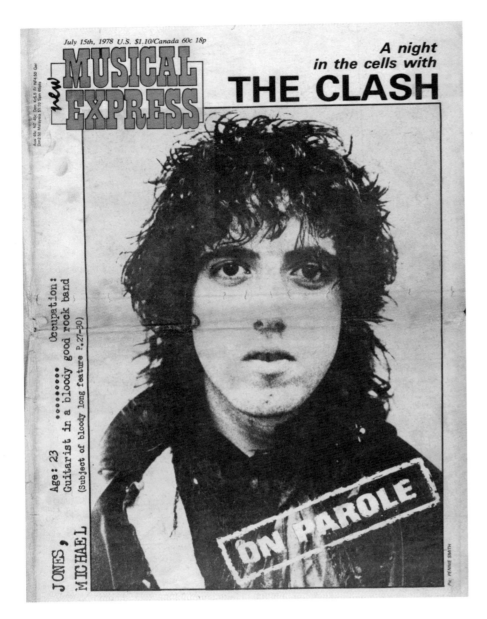

July 15th, 1978 U.S. $1.10/Canada 60c 18p

new MUSICAL EXPRESS

A night
in the cells with
THE CLASH

Occupation:
•••••••• Guitarist in a bloody good rock band
(Subject of bloody long feature P.27-30)

Age: 23

JONES, MICHAEL

ON PAROLE

Pic: PENNIE SMITH

The Clash's capacity for attracting police attention didn't wane in 1978, which is why the *NME* dummied up a fake Police arrest card for Mick's photo on their cover in July.

OUT ON PAROLE TOUR

After the debacle of the Guns On The Roof incident, the next tour of the UK was given the title of Out On Parole. Which was to prove doubly prophetic. The band were arrested in Glasgow on 4 July, and in Blackburn on 13 July. Mick was charged with possession of marijuana, Joe with stealing a hotel towel.

JOE: We were travelling on the bus with the Slits and Subway Sect and it wasn't very comfortable, given we were doing a lot of overnight runs. So people started to remove pillows from hotels where we did stay to try and make the bus a bit more comfortable. The police were out in force trying to suppress Punk Rock and they decided to raid our bus somewhere up north, so they came on board and searched everyone. They found about 34 pillows

ON THE WAY IN, OR STILL IN

ON THE WAY OUT MAYBE

JULIE'S IN THE DRUG SQUAD
I'M SO BORED
WHITE RIOT
LONDON'S BURNING
PROTEX BLUE
POLICE & THIEVES

DRUG STABBIN' TIME
I FOUGHT THE LAW.
STAY FREE
LAST GANG IN TOWN
JANIE JONES
CAPITAL RADIO
SAFE EUROPEAN HOME
THE MAN IN ME
TOMMY GUN
1, 2, CRUSH ON YOU
GUNS ON THE ROOF
CHEAPSKATES
ENGLISH CIVIL WAR
GROOVY TIMES

JULIE'S IN THE DRUG SQ
JAIL GUITAR DOORS
CITY OF THE DEAD
ALL THE YOUNG PUNKS
GATES OF THE WEST
WHITE MAN
CLASH CITY ROCKERS
COMPLETE CONTROL
SHOOTIN' IN SOWETO
GARAGELAND

One of Joe's set lists from the Out On Parole Tour. The number of songs that they could, and would, get through was astonishing.

and 20 room keys that people had forgotten [to leave at the hotels] and wouldn't let us go until they'd charged someone. So that we could continue to the next gig, Topper and I were elected to be charged for this offence. Later, when I was arrested in London [for spraying 'The Clash' on a wall] the police found the charge and Topper and I were driven hand-cuffed together all the way to Newcastle. We spent the weekend in jail there before being fined on the Monday morning for stealing bed linen and keys.

PAUL: We played the Apollo in Glasgow and weren't aware that there was a running battle every week between the bouncers and the audience, so we kept stopping the gig to tell the bouncers to leave the fans alone. After the gig, the bouncers turned on us and we had to barricade the door and escaped out the back way. In the street some characters came up and started having a go at Joe, saying he'd let them down because of the violence in the Apollo. Joe got frustrated and threw a bottle to the floor, and it smashed. As if from nowhere the police arrived, grabbed Joe and tried to drag him off. That annoyed me because there were loads of them and just him, so I leapt on top of Joe to protect him and a scuffle started. We were dragged off to separate cars. A cop asks, 'Where you from?' and I say 'London', so he slaps the handcuffs on me and says, 'Well this is Glasgow'.

At the station, I was dragged in by the handcuffs and stood next to Joe, and we leaned on each other. The cops go, 'Ah, they must be gay'. All these kids from the show are being dragged in, too, and they all see us. That night, Joe and I are in a cell and the fans are singing Clash songs throughout the night. Because we had trousers and jackets with so many zips in them the police got bored of searching us, and Joe had some speed in one pocket so we licked that and stayed up all night. The next morning, waiting to go in to the court, the rest of the prisoners were giving us fags and chatting and the warder was surprised when he came back that we hadn't been beaten up. Joe was done for drunk and disorderly, I was done for the same thing, plus attempting to rescue a prisoner, which I'm quite proud of.

JOE: I remember the tour chiefly because we were arrested for carousing at a hotel, and the support act we had with us, Suicide from New York, were the ones dragged out of their beds and taken down to the police station, not any-one else. Which was a bit of bad luck, 'cos they were nice guys and didn't deserve that. In fact Alan Vega was one of the bravest men I've ever seen on stage. No-one in England had seen anything like Suicide and the skinheads weren't standing for it. I saw one guy jump up on stage and smash him in the face while he was singing, I saw a bottle just miss his head and he bent down and threw it at his own head as if to say, 'You idiot!'. He faced them down.

PAUL: There were a few incidents with the police on that tour, but that sort of seemed a regular occurrence, us and the law.

A-side: Tommy Gun (3.16)

[Strummer/Jones] Produced by Sandy Pearlman

B-SIDE: 1-2 CRUSH ON YOU (2:59)

[Strummer/Jones/Headon/Simonon] Produced by
The Clash

RELEASED 24 NOVEMBER 1978
UK CHART PEAK: #19

JOE: It's about the ego of terrorists. It suddenly struck me that they must read their press clippings, like rock stars or actors and actresses do.

TOPPER: It used to start '1-2-3-4 Tommy Gun' and I said, 'Hang on a minute, how about a bit of machine gun drumming at the beginning?' and the others said, 'What do you mean?' It was my first contribution to a Clash song.

Ray Conniff singing Earth Wind and Fire.

THE CLASH: Tommy Gun
(CBS)

After the brouhaha with "Remote Control" has the position been laxed for this album cut to attack the singles market? For long-time followers of Clash this track has been around since early this year, and isn't made any more attractive by a shabby rendering of the ancient "1, 2 Got a Crush On You" on the B side (complete with Pleasers style rising "AH's" intro). With "White Man In Hammersmith" I thought Clash were untouchable, but this is a sad report on the state of things. Collectors item?

STEVE HAYNES BAND: Save Me *(Black Bear)*

An accusation often levelled at reviewers is the amount of

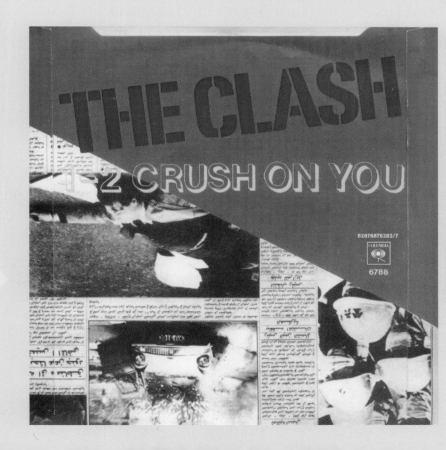

Sort It Out Tour

LINE-UP: STRUMMER, JONES, SIMONON, HEADON

Support act was The Slits

13 OCT: University Students Union, Queens Hall, Belfast
14 OCT: Top Hat, Dun Laoghaire, Dublin, with Berlin
18 OCT: Le Stadium, Paris
20 OCT: The Stokvishal, Arnhem, Holland
21 OCT: Leuven, Belgium
22 OCT: Ancienne Belgique, Brussels
23 OCT: The Paradiso, Amsterdam, Holland
25 OCT: Roxy Theatre, Harlesden, London. Postponed on 9 September, rescheduled date of 25 September postponed and also further rescheduled date of 14 October postponed. New GLC restrictions limited tickets to 900, so a second night was scheduled for the other 700 ticket-holders.
26 OCT: Roxy Theatre, Harlesden, London
9 NOV: Village Bowl, Bournemouth
10 NOV: Winter Gardens, Malvern
12 NOV: Odeon, Canterbury
14 NOV: Locarno Ballroom, Coventry
15 NOV: Belle Vue, Manchester
16 NOV: Odeon, Edinburgh,
17 NOV: Town Hall, Middlesbrough
18 NOV: University, Leeds
19 NOV: Top Rank, Sheffield
20 NOV: De Montfort Hall, Leicester
21 NOV: Locarno Ballroom, Bristol
22 NOV: Odeon, Birmingham
22 NOV: Village Bowl, Bournemouth
23 NOV: Gaumont, Ipswich
23 NOV: Apollo, Manchester
24 NOV: Kings Hall, Derby

SONGS PLAYED:
Complete Control / Tommy Gun / I Fought The Law / Jail Guitar Doors / Clash City Rockers / White Man in Hammersmith Palais / Drug Stabbing Time / Protex Blue / Guns On The Roof / Stay Free / Police and Thieves / Blitzkreig Bop / Capital Radio / Janie Jones / Garageland / What's My Name / English Civil War / London's Burning / White Riot / Safe European Home / City Of The Dead / Julie's In The Drug Squad / Cheapskates / 1-2 Crush On You / Complete Control

Joe and Mick in action.

26 NOV: Top Rank, Cardiff,

27 NOV: University, Exeter

28 NOV: Locarno Ballroom, Coventry

29 NOV: Victoria Hall, Hanley, Stoke-on-Trent

30 NOV: Wirrina Stadium, Peterborough

2 DEC: Polytechnic, Newcastle

4 DEC: University of Strathclyde, Glasgow, Scotland. Cancelled due to student-only policy which Joe found out about and objected to.

6 DEC: University, Liverpool

10 DEC: Top Rank, Brighton

12 DEC: Pavillion, Bath

17 DEC: Locarno, Portsmouth

18 DEC: Tiffany's, Purley

19 DEC: Music Machine, London. Sid Vicious Defence Fund benefit

20 DEC: Civic Hall, Wolverhampton

21 DEC: Pier Pavillion, Hastings

22 DEC: Friars, Aylesbury

28 DEC: Lyceum, London

29 DEC: Lyceum, London

3 JAN 1979: Lyceum, London

```
                    THE MUSIC MACHINE

              I M P O R T A N T   N O T I C E


Due to a mis-understanding by Music Machine management, the Music
Machine has over-sold the Clash 'Sid Vicious' Benefit on December 19th.

The Music Machine sold tickets in excess of the capacity of the venue
according to G. L. C. restrictions.

THE CLASH HAVE JUST ADDED AN EXTRA LONDON DATE AT THE LYCEUM ON WEDNESDAY,
3rd JANUARY, 1979, TO THEIR CURRENT U. K. TOUR.

It is essential that those people who are unable to gain admittance to
the Music Machine tonight retain their un-torn tickets and this notice,
as these will be exchanged on 27th December at the Lyceum Box Office for
the Clash show on 3rd January.

On 27th December, tickets will also be on sale at the Lyceum Box Office
for the 3rd January show, at £2.50 in advance.

The Music Machine apologises to both the Clash and their fans for any
inconvenience caused.

N.B.  NO EXCHANGE LYCEUM TICKETS WILL BE GIVEN OUT WITHOUT AN UN-TORN
MUSIC MACHINE TICKET.
```

A statement issued to ticket-holders for the band's performance at the Music Machine in Camden in December 1978 which had been over-sold. The gig was a benefit for former Sex Pistol Sid Vicious, who was on bail in New York on a charge of having murdered his girlfriend Nancy Spungeon. The proceeds would have gone to aid his defence. He didn't live long enough to stand trial though, dying from a drug overdose on 2 February 1979, before proceedings could begin.

he band's stage
w grew, they added
kdrops to the
formance. Paul had
de one from film in
Imperial War
seum of WWII
man bombers in
on. The far left photo
image of people
ying a body after a
tary shooting on the
ets of Northern
and in the early
0s. The central flag
ommunist Chinese.

Sort It Out

PAUL: Steve Jones turned up on stage a few times on the Sort It Out Tour and would do a couple of numbers. He travelled around with us occasionally. Pete Townshend turned up when we were playing Brighton and he was great. He came back to the hotel with us, too.

JOE: During that tour we went up North and Steve Jones joined us on stage for a few nights, I think 'cos The Sex Pistols were off the road or something. This was when Sid and Nancy were in New York and he was arrested for murdering her. We ended up doing a Sid Vicious benefit at the Music Machine, at the end of the tour.

JOE: We'd learned from Bernie Rhodes that the bill on the night has to have cultural importance. He brought in Suicide and Richard Hell and it was really good for British fans to see that. Likewise, when we went to the States, we tried to think about what we'd bring with us, 'cos it had to be a memorable evening. That's taking care of people, not pissing on them.

JOE: When we played we weren't playing along to backing tapes, so we could stop, and this might seem like a small thing, but when you see some-

1979

'When you've been into American music as long as I have, to go there and ride across the country on a bus is a real trip. To go to places you've only heard of in songs is fantastic.' JOE

Give 'Em Enough Rope was released in the UK in November 1978, but it was not due for release in the USA until April 1979. In January the band embarked on a pre-promotional tour of America, their first in the US. Displaying their usual tact and diplomacy, they chose to name the nine-date romp across North America the Pearl Harbour Tour. It began in Canada where a reception committee of customs men waited to greet them at Vancouver airport.

Joe on stage in the US for the first time. Unintentionally perhaps, the pose echoes a classic shot of Elvis Presley from the 1950s. The newspapers pinned up along the drum riser are all American and reinforce the visual idea that The Clash were a band of their time, concerned with what was in the news, making headlines.

Pearl Harbour Tour (USA)

LINE-UP: STRUMMER, JONES, SIMONON, HEADON

Support act Bo Diddley

31 JAN: Commodore Ballroom, Vancouver, Canada, extra support the Dishrags
7 FEB: Berkeley Community Center, Berkeley CA
8 FEB: Geary Temple (Fillmore), San Francisco CA, extra support the Zeros and Negative Trend
9 FEB: Civic Auditorium, Santa Monica CA
13 FEB: Agora, Cleveland OH, extra support Alex Bevan. A Larry McIntyre Fund Benefit gig
15 FEB: Ontario Theater, Washington D.C., extra support the D-Ceats
16 FEB: Harvard Square Theater, Cambridge, MA, extra support the Rentals
17 FEB: Palladium, New York NY, extra support the Cramps
20 FEB: The Rex Danforth Theater, Toronto, Canada

SONGS PLAYED:
I'm So Bored with the USA / Drug Stabbing Time / Jail Guitar Doors / Tommy Gun / City Of The Dead / Hate and War / Clash City Rockers / White Man in Hammersmith Palais / Complete Control / Julie's In The Drug Squad / Safe European Home / Stay Free / Police and Thieves / Capital Radio / English Civil War / Guns On The Roof / Capital Radio / Janie Jones / Garageland / What's My Name / London's Burning / White Riot / Career Opportunities

MICK: 'Cos Epic didn't release the first album in America, and people had only heard it on import, our reputation kind of grew over there. People didn't see us in the same way as they did in Britain. I always thought that people would be really proud of us in England, because we'd almost made it in America when Give 'Em Enough Rope came out and we went on our first tour. Hopefully it was inspiring to people.

JOE: People would ask me if American audiences were any different to European ones, but when you're up there you can't see the difference. Some nights the crowd is good, some nights the crowd is bad, but I could never see a national demarcation line or anything like that.

MICK: Coming into the States through Canada they'd always give you a spin. At some places we'd be lined up against a wall and they'd get the dogs out and walk them over the suitcases, which were a way off.

A live action photo from above and behind the band on the first night of the Pearl Harbour Tour to hit the USA, in Berkeley.

MICK: I remember it was snowing when we arrived in Vancouver where, for some reason, every time you touched anything you got an electric shock because there was so much static. We got on a bus and did the tour the traditional way with overnight bus rides.

PAUL: That first tour of America was great, with Bo Diddley on the bus with us. He used to drink this stuff called Rock 'n' Rye, which was a whiskey with fruit at the bottom of it and we thought it was pretty delicious. Joe adopted it as his 'before-stage' drink. Bo was great, he'd sit up all night telling us jokes, his guitar in his bunk.

MICK: I can't remember many of the gigs on that first tour, which was really short. I just remember the bus and watching America go by outside, like some big movie.

JOE: It never occurred to us that taking songs from London to America was odd. We'd go on to *Saturday Night Live* or *Fridays* on ABC and do our normal thing.

ABOVE: **Touring the USA meant that the band could buy American clothes and equipment direct from the source – and Mexican food too.**

RIGHT: **The Clash might no longer have been considered just a punk act by the time of their first US tour, but they still made clear their political stance. This original tour advertising poster works hard to sell the band – note the 'Album of the Year' award from** *Rolling Stone* **magazine.**

WE MEET AT THE AIRPORT AND GET ON A PLANE TO VANCOUVER. THERE SEEMS TO BE QUITE A LOT OF US. WE GOT BAKER AND JOHNNY GREEN OUR BACKLINE CREW, AND ROB AND ADRIAN WHO ARE WELSH SOUND MEN, WARREN "GANDALF" SPARKS LIGHTING ENGINEER, AND BARRY 'SCRATCHY' MYERS, THE FAMOUS D.J. THEN THERE'S THE FOUR OF US AND CAROLINE CROON TO HANDLE THE BUSINESS.

"EVEN AEROSMITH DONT TRAVEL WITH SO MANY PEOPLE," SAYS EPIC RECORDS. "AH YES WE REPLY," BUT WE VE GOTTA DO IT PROPERLY!".

SO, 17 HOURS LATER HERE WE ARE VANCOUVER, CANADA. NO BLIZZARDS NO SNOW NO MOUNTIES — JUST THE CUSTOMS. THEY GO THROUGH EVERYTHING, CONFISCATING STUDDED BELTS, ARMBANDS, KNIVES, COS THEY CANT FIND ANY DRUGS. "IF WE'D KNOWN IT WAS GONNA BE LIKE THIS, WE'D HAVE BROUGHT SOME DRUGS FOR YOU" WE TELL 'EM. BUT THEY DONT SMILE THEY JUST KICK US OUT, KNIFELESS AND BELTLESS.

ANYWAY, ON WITH THE SHOW. WE PLAY THE AGORA BALLROOM, WHICH SHOLD BE CALLED THE AGORA COWBOY SALOON. Q. ARE WE NOT MEN? ANS. NO, WE ARE NERVOUS.

BUT THE SHOW GOES OFF REAL GOOD AN WE MEET BO DIDDLEY AT LAST. BO IS COMING ON THE TOUR AND THE NEXT MORNING A BIG SHINY GREYHOUND BUS DRAWS UP OUTSIDE THE HOTEL WITH TWO NASHVILLE DRIVERS. ITS ALL ABOARD FIRST STOP, CALIFORNIA.

THE BUS IS REAL NEAT WITH BUNKS A PISSHOLE AN A TV VIDEO. ITS JUST COME OFF A WAYLON JENNINGS TOUR. WE CROSS THE US BORDER REAL EASY, NO SEARCH, NOTHING, THEN ITS NON STOP ACROSS OREGON.

ABOUT MIDNIGHT WE DOSS IN A FACELESS MOTEL. I WAKE UP AND AS I'M SEARCHING FOR SOME BREAKFAST, ACE PENNA OUR US TOUR MANAGER TELLS ME" HEY, DIDJA KNOW SID IS DEAD?" I GRAB HIM BY THE THROAT "WHAT DO YOU MEAN" I SNARL. THEN AS IT SINKS IN I DONT WANT NO BREAKFAST. OUR FIRST MORNING IN AMERICA.

IN CALIFORNIA THE SUN IS SHINING WEAKLY. THE OTHER PEOPLE WALK ABOUT THE STREETS, WEAKLY. IN FACT EVERYTHING HERE IS DONE WEAKLY, EXCEPT FOR WHEN THE COPS GET HOLD OF YOU. WE PLAY THE BERKELEY COMMUNITY THEATRE ON THE COLLEGE CAMPUS. OUR FIRST MISTAKE, MEANING, IT AINT OUR SCENE. BUT WE PLAY AND THEY DIG IT, TAPPING THEIR BIOLOGY BOOKS IN TIME TO THE TUNES.

BILL GRAHAM, FAMOUS HIPPIE PROMOTER, IS PROMOTING THE SHOW, IE MAKING ALL THE MONEY, BUT HE LEAVES TOWN JUST BEFORE WE ARRIVE. NEXT NIGHT HOWEVER WE AGREE TO PLAY A BENEFIT FOR THIS YOUTH ORGANIZATION WHO ARE TRYING TO OPEN UP THE S.F. SCENE BY PROMOTING COST PRICE ROCK SHOWS. THE SHOW IS REALLY GRLAT, THE HALL IS REALLY GREAT, THE AUDIENCE IS REALLY GREAT BUT WE GOTTA LEAVE STRAIGHT AFTER THE SET TO DRIVE THE 400 MILES TO LOS ANGELES.

THE DRIVE TAKES ALL NIGHT AN WE TEST OUT THE BUNKS WHICH ARE LIKE COMFY SHELVES. WE HIT L.A. IN THE MORNING AN WE GOTTA PLAY THE SANTA MONICA CENTRE THE SAME NIGHT. ME AN MICK TRY TO GET A LOOK AT HOLLYWOOD BUT WE COLLAPSE INSTEAD. LATER MICK TELLS ME HIS HOTEL BED JUST KEPT MOVING ALL THE TIME, JUST LIKE MINE, AND WE WORK OUT IT IS BECAUSE WE WERE ON THE BUS ALL NIGHT.

THE SANTA MONICA CIVIC CENTRE TURNS OUT TO BE A CONCRETE BARN. I ONLY REMEMBER THE REALLY GOOD SHOWS OR THE REALLY BAD SHOWS, SO THIS ONE MUST HAVE BEEN JUST O.K. COS MY MEMORY IS BLANK.

RIGHT AFTER THE SET THEY DRAG IN SOME EPIC PEOPLE, QUITE A LOT OF 'EM, LINE 'EM UP AND TRY TO GET US TO

POSE WITH THEM. I'M FED UP WITH THIS, SO I LOOK AT TOPPER AND HE READS MY THOUGHTS, "LETS FUCK OFF OUT OF IT" HE SAYS ALMOST SIMULTANEOUSLY AS MICK AND PAUL SAY IT. SO WE DO. WHEN THE EPIC PEOPLE LEAVE THEY DO NOT SPEAK AND THEY DO NOT LOOK. THE AIR IS THICK AS THEY FILE PAST.

AGAIN STRAIGHT AFTER THE SHOW WE GOTTA HIT THE ROAD. A LOAD OF FANS GIVE US A GREAT SEND OFF SO WE ARE ALL IN A GOOD MOOD AS WE HEAD FOR OKLAHOMA CITY.

ON THE BUS BO SITS UP FRONT SLUGGING "ROCK N RYE" AND POURING OUT ANECDOTES FROM HIS 23 YEARS ON

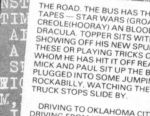

THE ROAD. THE BUS HAS THREE VIDEO TAPES — STAR WARS (GROAN) KING CREOLE (HOORAY) AN BLOOD FOR DRACULA. TOPPER SITS WITH HIS FEET UP SHOWING OFF HIS NEW SPURS WATCHING THESE OR PLAYING TRICKS ON BO WITH WHOM HE HAS HIT IT OFF REAL GREAT. MICK AND PAUL SIT UP THE BACK PLUGGED INTO SOME JUMPING ROCKABILLY, WATCHING THE ENDLESS TRUCK STOPS SLIDE BY.

DRIVING TO OKLAHOMA CITY IS LIKE DRIVING FROM LONDON TO GLASGOW 10 TIMES. SO I GET MY HEAD DOWN AND WHEN I WAKE UP WE ARE IN TEXAS. I KNOW THIS BECAUSE JOHNNY GREEN AND BAKER ARE WEARING THE BIGGEST COWBOY HATS I EVER SEEN.

TEXAS IS ONE OF THE BEST PLACES ALTHOUGH I CANT SAY WHY. WE ARE TRYING TO REACH CLEVELAND OHIO HOPING TO CATCH A PLANE IN OKLAHOMA CITY. THERES PLENTY OF SNOW FOG AND ICE AT THE AIRPORT BUT NO PLANES. THE BUS HAS GONE TO NASHVILLE FOR REPAIRS SO WE SIT AND WAIT. 24 HOURS LATER WE FINALLY GET TO CLEVELAND FLYING THE ROUNDABOUT ROUTE.

THIS GUY CALLED LARRY MCINTYRE LOST BOTH HIS LEGS IN VIETNAM AND WHEN HE WENT FOR A SWIM ONE DAY IN THE POOL NEAR HIS FLAT ALL THE OTHER RESIDENTS BANNED HIM FROM THE POOL ON THE GROUNDS THAT IT WAS TOO DISGUSTING . SO WE AGREE TO PLAY A SHOW FOR HIM, HELPING HIS LEGAL

■ *Continues over*

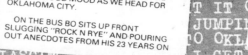

A GARBLED ACCOUNT OF THE CLASH U.S. TOUR BY JOE STRUMMER

Pix: BOB GRUEN.

■ From previous page

COSTS BUT WE DONT GET TO MEET HIM, I THINK BECAUSE, HAVING FORGOT HIS NAME, I REFERED TO HIM OVER THE P.A. AS "THE GUY WITH NO LEGS."

INCIDENTLY, TO GIVE YOU SOME IDEA OF THE SIZE OF THE COUNTRY, WE MEET SOME PEOPLE WHO HAD TRAVELLED '800 MILES TO SEE THE SHOW.

NEXT STOP IS WASHINGTON D.C. THE BUS HAS CAUGHT UP WITH US SO ITS ALL ABOARD. ON THIS DRIVE BO GIVES UP HIS BUNK TO HIS GUITAR AND HE SLEEPS SITTING UP. SO DOES MICK BECAUSE NOTHING ON EARTH WILL TEMPT HIM TO GET BACK IN ONE OF THE BUNKS.

MEANWHILE OUTSIDE ITS 32 BELOW ZERO AND AS WE ARE FILLING UP SOME PLACE THE BRAKES FREEZE UP AND ARE LOCKED SOLID. SO WE HAVE TO SIT AND WAIT A FEW HOURS FOR THEM TO THAW.

THOSE OF YOU WHO STAYED AWAKE IN SCHOOL WILL KNOW THIS IS THE US CAPITAL. STRANGELY ENOUGH MOST OF THE POPULATION IS BLACK, WHICH MAKES ALL THE WHITE POLITICIANS A LITTLE NERVOUS. WE WAS GONNA PAY A CALL ON JIMMY CARTER BUT HE WAS DOWN IN MEXICO, HAVING A MASSAGE. SO WE PLAYED D.C. AND HEADED OUT FOR BOSTON. EVEN THOUGH THIS WAS ONLY LAST WEEK MY MEMORY HAS GONE AGAIN SO LETS SAY IT WAS OKAY AND GET ON WITH IT, WHICH MEANS NEW YORK! NEW YORK! (SO GOOD THEY NAMED IT TWICE ETC.).

NEW YORK IS DEFINATELY AN O.K. TOWN. ALL THE STREETS ARE STRAIGHT AND ITS LAID OUT LIKE A CHESS BOARD. SOME PARTS ARE DEAD FLASH LIKE MANHATTAN AND SOME PARTS ARE BURNT OUT SLUMS LIKE THE SOUTH BRONX.

WE WAS PLAYING THE PALLADIUM, A BIT LIKE THE RAINBOW. THIS WAS THE THIRD GIG IN THREE DAYS, AND WITH ALL THE TRAVELLING WE WAS PRETTY KNACKERED. DURING THE SOUND CHECK I OVER HEARD A YANK TALKING TO HIS MATE "WOW THESE GUYS HAVE HAD IT, THEY CAN HARDLY STAND UP, NEVER MIND PLAY!"

THEN BO TOLD ME THE WORST AUDIENCES IN THE US WERE DETROIT AND NYC. "IF YOU CAN PLAY NEW YORK YOU CAN PLAY ANYWHERE"

BY GIG TIME THE PLACE WAS PACKED, AND ALL THE TOP LIGGERS IN TOWN WERE THERE. WE WERE PLENTY NERVOUS. HALFWAY THROUGH THE SHOW I CHECKED THE AUDIENCE AND BECAME CONVINCED THAT WE WERE GOING DOWN LIKE A TON OF BRICKS. BUT LIKE THEY SAY ITS A TOUGH TOWN AND BY THE END OF THE DAY WE MANAGED TO WHIP IT OUT AND GIVE 'EM SOME OF OUR BEST.

WE STUCK AROUND FOR A DAY OR SO TO SEE THE SIGHTS LIKE STUDIO 54 WHICH IS OKAY BUT NOTHING TO WRITE HOME ABOUT. TO GET IN WITHOUT PAYING YOU HAVE TO TURN UP WITH ANDY WARHOL.

ONE MORE SHOW TO GO, IN TORONTO. WE FLY THERE TO DO THE GIG WHICH IS IN A CINEMA. THE DRESSING ROOM ACTUALLY IS A TOILET AND THE P.A. SOUNDS AS IF ITS FILLED WITH HAMSTERS ON COKE. EVEN THOUGH IT SOUNDS ROUGH WE REALLY ENJOY IT AND SO DO

THEY, STORMING THE STAGE AT THE END ENGLISH STYLE. ONE OF THE FUNNIEST THINGS I EVER SAW WAS THESE TWO BOUNCERS TRYING TO HOLD THE WHOLE AUDIENCE BACK. JUST THE TWO OF THEM! AFTER THE FIRST NUMBER THEY WERE SWAMPED SO THEY GAVE UP AND WENT HOME.

AND THE NEXT DAY SO DID WE.

TO BREAK, CRACK, STORM OR BLITZ AMERICA YOU HAVE TO WORK AS HARD AS ELVIS COSTELLO, SHAKE HANDS AND SMILE LIKE THE BOOMTOWN RATS, AND SOUND LIKE DIRE STRAIGHTS. OF THE THREE, WE COULD MAKE THE FIRST BUT NOT THE REST SO WE ARE GOING TO GO BACK TO PLAY THE US AGAIN BUT WE MUST ALSO PLAY BRITAIN, JAPAN, EUROPE, AUSTRALIA, AND ITS FAIR SHARES ALL ROUND. HEY! I HEAR THEYRE REALLY ROCKING IN RUSSIA . . .

ABOVE AND LEFT: The *NME* published Joe's US tour diary in full, and as he asked – all in upper case – two weeks after the Pearl Harbour Tour had ended. Joe's original typed sheets are laid behind the display copy.

RIGHT: Topper sent postcards to his family when he played gigs outside the UK. This one was sent just as the Pearl Harbour Tour ended.

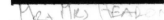

Dear Mum + Dad.
Last gig over
what a relief.
be home to
England soon.
Thank God. Very homesick
Love
Topper
+Ree

TravelTime PRODUCT

Air Mail   Par avion

Mr & Mrs HEALON

DOVER

KENT.

ENGLAND

KM-1
H. R. MacMILLAN PLANETARIUM, Vancouver, B.C., Canada
Centennial Museum of Natural and Human History
The unique cone shaped structure of the Planetarium lends an exciting setting to the Vancouver skyline. Situated at Vanier Park, in the Kitsilano area, on the south shore of English Bay. This attraction is an amazing adventure into the world of the stars.

C.P. Air Photo by W. J. L. Gibbons, AMPA

KS-2922B

LEFT: Backstage before a gig, L-R: Mick, Joe, Bo Diddley, Paul, Topper (standing on a box). Bo loved Topper's drumming and often got him on stage for an encore during the Pearl Harbour Tour.

RIGHT: To help pass the endless miles of American highway on the bus, Paul and Mick made compilation cassettes which would be played in rotation on the bus. A collection of Paul's tapes is shown here, all with hand-made covers.

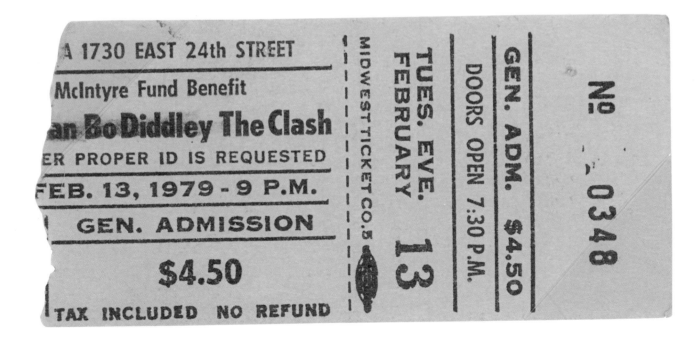

LEFT: An original ticket stub from the Cleveland date of the tour, now on display in the Rock and Roll hall of Fame in that city.

FOLLOWING PAGE: The band hadn't taken the enormous backdrop photos that they had been using on stage to the States with them (see previous chapter), but instead hung huge flags of different nations behind the stage.

A-side: English Civil War (Johnny Comes Marching Home) (2.36)

[Traditional/Jones/Strummer] Produced by
Sandy Pearlman

B-SIDE: PRESSURE DROP (3:25)

[Frederick Hibbert] Produced by The Clash

RELEASED 23 FEBRUARY 1979
UK CHART PEAK: #25

JOE: It takes the piss out of the people who say, 'Oh yeah, it's gonna happen'. Cos It goes: 'Aha, haha, I told you so, hurrah tra la la', and then it goes on to ask, 'who did anything about it?' A week after the RAR rally, some white guys in Wolverhampton opened a car window and fired a shotgun at a bunch of West Indians.

MICK: That happened the night we were playing there. We went out the next morning and read about it in the paper.

Strummer shows delight at
thumbs up for Clash newie.

GP tips the wink to DB after
complimentary remarks.

THE CLASH: English Civil War (CBS).

A wise enough if a miscued and rock'n'rolly warning about all things uniformed and sinister that this chap can flow to easier than any tuppenny ha'penny "Olivers Army". But then it was a CBS choice we hear. The flip is the old Toots "Pressure Drop" from the set of yore but done more professionally, less manic. Now is this a good thing? It sounds OK anyway and they at least *feel* the stuff

— which is more than can be said for the disgusting rubbish "ol' Keef" pays his bills with. (By the way, Richards' junk was released this week too). Despite myself, The Clash are still the only rock group I would cross the road for.

CHERYL LYNN: To Be Real (CBS).
GLORIA GAYNOR: I Will Survive (Polydor).

I grant you, not two of the newest 45s about, but two of the best certainly. Lynn, who survived to win the US talent show *The Gong Show* — a

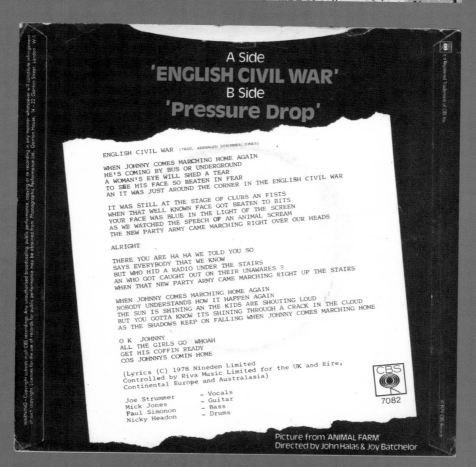

LEFT: Mick relaxes backstage as the American tour comes to an end. The band had been very well received which helped them to feel more comfortable as the tour progressed.

RIGHT: On returning from the USA the band set about finding a new manager, having sacked Bernie Rhodes. The *NME* ran a cheeky ad for them, unasked.

Punk band seeks deal
(a one off small ad special)

COULD YOU MANAGE THIS BAND? Yes, rumours about the **Clash's** imminent (and imminenter by the day, we hear) split from Renault dealer and anarchist theorist, **Bernie Rhodes**, have reached such a point that we here at *Sounds* though it was time we helped them out by printing their picture so that any prospective manager could check them out.

Don't they look dejected just lying there in the corner on the floor? Doesn't someone out there feel like opening their heart (and cheque-book) to such a downcast bunch of rock and roll stars? Some malicious rumours have it that Bernie

Rhodes is trying to get rid of his management contract to the highest bidder, so whichever one of you decides to make an offer for them better be ready with the readies.

Obviously, until they find this much needed creative person to put their affairs in order, any stories about prospective live shows should be treated with a great deal of scepticism. Apparently, the Harlesden Roxy gig will be played but no-one's yet sure when. So, come on, you managers, and stop us all believing one story we heard that Bernie only sent **Topper** and **Paul** to New York the other week so they could meet their new manager.

MEET THE NEW BOSS

PAUL: After Bernie left, Caroline Coon stepped in, but she wasn't a serious contender as far as being a manager went. She said she'd keep things going and organize stuff, like for the first tour of America that was coming up. So Joe and I said we'd really like Bo Diddley to tour with us, thinking it was the most outrageous thing we could ask, and somehow she managed to swing it.

JOE: After the Pearl Harbour Tour, where the audience had been hip enough to get us, we came back to London and had no manager. Somehow we got into Blackhill Management.

PAUL: Blackhill were a regular management company: you go on tour, you

record, you go on tour, you record, and so on. They had none of the excitement that Bernie had.

MICK: Although Bernie was always 100 per cent working for the group, he wouldn't share with us and there was always something going on that we didn't know about. I wish he'd let us in on a lot of stuff because then there wouldn't have been so much friction.

PAUL: Because we'd sacked Bernie, we had to move out of Rehearsals Rehearsals and needed somewhere new to work. Johnny Green [Clash road manager] found us a studio near Pimlico called Vanilla and it was perfect, private.

MICK: When we split from Bernie we had to get out of Rehearsals Rehearsals because it was Bernie's place. So Johnny Green found the new place in Pimlico. But in Rehearsals Rehearsals was Bernie's jukebox, which had all our favourite records on it, things like Pressure Drop and Two Sevens Clash, MPLA by Tapper Zukie, stuff that had inspired us. When we split Bernie wanted his jukebox back and kept going on about it. So eventually we put it in a van and drove it round to his house. He wasn't in, so we left it in the street outside. He did get it.

PAUL: Blackhill was a really boring management company, always smoking spliffs and wanting to have band meetings, but I said I wouldn't go to any unless they got me a rabbit outfit. One day they wanted a meeting and there was this limp rabbit outfit waiting for me, so I said 'Right you lot, I'll get you back for this'. I went and put it on and came back to the meeting, but started hitting and kicking everybody and swearing and completely disrupted the whole meeting. Mick and Joe were in hysterics.

London Calling Tour

LINE-UP: STRUMMER, JONES, SIMONON, HEADON

Support acts varied. The gigs showcased new material from the forthcoming *London Calling* album

31 MAR: Beaufort Market, London. What was to be a free gig in protest against the closure of a cheap market was cancelled by the police minutes before it was due to start.

5 JUL: Notre Dame Hall, London, secret gig

6 JUL: Notre Dame Hall, London, secret gig

14 JUL: Rainbow, London, Southall Defence Fund benefit. Also playing were Aswad, the Members and Bongo Danny & The Enchanters

4 AUG: Turku, Finland, Ruisrock Festival. Also playing were Graham Parker & The Rumours and Steel Pulse.

This very short tour comprised a cancelled show, a couple of 'secret' dates, a benefit and a couple of festivals. At the end of March The Clash agreed to appear at a benefit gig at a street market that was facing closure; when the police cancelled the gig the hundreds of punks who'd gathered to see them rioted. The band went back to writing, playing and demoing new songs for what would be their third album, at Vanilla. In July they played two warm up shows and another benefit at London's Rainbow Theatre. Then they recorded, breaking off to play a festival in Turkey in August. Less than a month later they flew to America for their Take The Fifth Tour.

TOPPER: We were working all the time then, we never had holidays. But to me it was one big holiday. Why would you want to go on holiday when you loved what you were doing? If I'd had a holiday I'd have probably only gone and played in New York or recorded an album somewhere.

PAUL: Mickey Gallagher got involved in making *London Calling*, which was fine, he did some really good stuff. But I didn't enjoy having a fifth member on tour. I thought it would have been fine as it was. I understood musically that the songs needed that extra embellishment of keyboards but I prefer to be straightforward, not have the extras.

SONGS PLAYED:

Clash City Rockers / White Man In Hammersmith Palais / Safe European Home / Jail Guitar Doors / I'm Not Down / Death Or Glory / I Fought the Law / London Calling / Rudie Can't Fail / Lovers Rock / City of the Dead / Police And Thieves / Four Horsemen / Jimmy Jazz / Hateful / Stay Free / Capital Radio / Janie Jones / Hate and War / English Civil War / Tommy Gun / London's Burning / Remote Control / Complete Control / Brand New Cadillac / What's My Name / White Riot

For the London Calling Tour the front men wore either red, white or black shirts and each had 1950s-style rocker hairstyles.

The Cost of Living EP
A-side: I Fought The Law (2.39)

[Sonny Curtis] Produced by Bill Price

GROOVY TIMES (3:29)

[Strummer/Jones/Headon/Simonon] Produced by
Bill Price

B-SIDE: GATES OF THE WEST (3:28)

[Strummer/Jones/Headon/Simonon] Produced by
The Clash/Bill Price

CAPITAL RADIO TWO (3:19)

[Strummer/Jones] Produced by The Clash/Bill Price

RELEASED 11 MAY 1979
UK CHART PEAK: #22

MICK: *The Cost Of Living EP* was the first time we worked with Bill Price. Bill had worked with all the right people, he was a really good workman and an English gentleman. Although we used to drive him over the edge.

PAUL: There was something on the TV or in the papers about the cost of living and for some reason Joe and I saw humour in those words and were down on our knees, laughing away, saying, 'Oh no! The cost of living!'

I FOUGHT THE LAW

MICK: When we were working on *Give 'Em Enough Rope* in San Francisco there was a fantastic jukebox at the studio, the Automat. It had the Bobby Fuller Four's version of I Fought The Law and Joe and I had a great time listening to it. A lot of the tunes we did by other people were tunes we liked and were listening to and playing at the same time.

TOPPER: When Mick and Joe first played it to me on an acoustic guitar I said, 'Oh no, I'm not doing that, it sounds terrible'. Of course as soon as we got some drums on it and electrified it, it sounded great.

Groovy Times

JOE: That was sparked by the fences that were being put up around the English football grounds. It looked horrible, like cages. It distressed me.

MICK: I always connected that one with the washing powder cover, which was a Daz packet. The credit for Bob Jones on harmonica is for me, it was a Bob Dylan joke.

Gates of the West

MICK: It was our reaction to being in America. I think we recorded it at the Record Plant in New York.

JOE: It was going to be called Rusted Chrome.

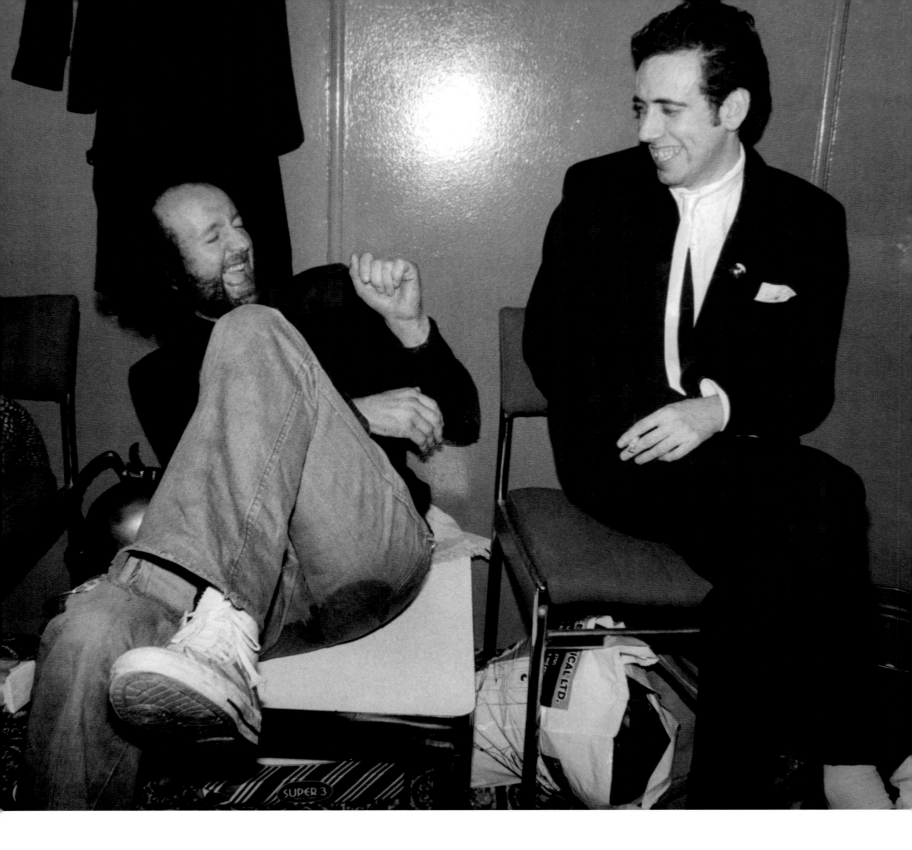

THE MAKING OF LONDON CALLING

TOPPER: Guy [Stevens] was there occasionally and when he was there he contributed a kind of madness and made us laugh, stopped us from getting too serious. So the album, although it was all written, rehearsed and then recorded, still has that unrehearsed sound to things, which was Guy's doing.

Producer Guy Stevens with Mick during the making of the *London Calling* album in London.

MICK: I probably thought of using Guy Stevens as producer. I'm not sure, but I don't remember anyone else being discussed. I knew Bill Price had worked with Guy and that he knew him well. We went to his house to meet him before we'd begun and he was really upset about a Led Zeppelin film he'd just seen, *The Song Remains The Same*, and he had the record of it in his hand and was getting more and more crazy about the fantasies that the band had filmed and he suddenly threw the record away in disgust. It hit Joe in the eye, knocking him over. Guy was really upset and fussed round Joe as he lay on the floor with a black eye coming up. It was some pre-production meeting.

JOE: At the time we were at our lowest ebb, and I think that's when we showed our mettle. We rehearsed every day down in Pimlico between May and August and came up with what would become *London Calling*.

MICK: Vanilla was very, very secluded and not many people came to see us because it wasn't easy to find the place. It was in the back of a garage and you wouldn't know there was anything there so we were cut off from everyone. You had to come by prior appointment. We were there for six months or so.

PAUL: We were pretty tight as friends when we were rehearsing the *London Calling* album. We'd work religiously for five or six hours every day in this room with no windows, just the four of us, really close at this point.

MICK: The arrangements were done before we went into the studio. We had the whole record down as demos, plus some extra tracks that didn't make it onto the finished album. But there's an instinctual feel to *London Calling* as you go along.

TOPPER: Guy came into the studio one day where there was a mountain of orchestra chairs piled up and pulled one off the top, so that the whole lot fell over. If you listen you can hear them in the background on one of the songs. The chairs falling and Guy going, 'Ouch!'

JOE: We went into Wessex Studios with Guy Stevens and knocked that album out. As soon as we finished the last chord of it, we had Bill Price mix it with Guy overseeing and went back to America to tour again.

PAUL: Guy turned up at the studio one day with some fella and I thought it was a mate of his or something. He sat there almost the whole day, listening in on the session. Later we discovered that he was Guy's taxi driver, who'd picked him up that morning.

MICK: Guy was a big Arsenal fan and used to go to Highbury before coming into the studio. He'd get a taxi and make the driver wait while he visited the hallowed turf. Every day he came in he'd be wearing his Arsenal scarf.

PAUL: One day we're playing a song and in the control booth there are two grown men fighting over the mixing desk. Guy was wrestling Bill, holding up

a record. We went in to find out what the problem was and it was Guy trying to put on this Man Utd versus Arsenal record of a game. I suppose he was trying to get some enthusiasm going, I don't know. He liked to get a mood going in the studio, but we were in the middle of a song. Bill was trying to keep the song going and Guy wanted to put his record on.

MICK: Before Guy came in, Bill would set the faders on the desk into position and we'd be playing. Then Guy would arrive and try to push every one of them up and there'd be a struggle. Guy would be going, 'Push it up!' and Bill would be pulling them back and they'd be falling over the desk, struggling. They'd even end up on the floor fighting.

TOPPER: Guy lightened the whole thing up. Halfway through a take he'd start fighting with the engineer over the desk. Or the police would turn up with him three hours late because they'd found him at some roadworks which he'd fallen into. I loved all that.

MICK: Guy had a way of coming downstairs that was all his own. In the

Issue 1 of *The Armagideon Times*, produced by The Clash, which included cut-and-paste collages by friends/roadies Robin Banks and Terry Razor, design by Jules Baum (who would work on all Clash design from then on), and photos by Pennie Smith. There was also a *Story of the Clash* written by Joe and Mick.

The Armagideon Times carried ads, as the above spread shows. The bottom left is for a release of an old 101'ers single. The photograph above it includes keyboard player Mickey Gallagher who was also a member of the Blockheads (who shared management with the Clash at the time). Bottom right is an ad for *Zigzag* magazine.

FOLLOWING PAGE: Filming the video for London Calling (the single), by the Thames.

studio there was a long staircase and Guy would kind of throw himself down them two or three at a time, and tumble all the way down. One day he came down really quickly and came into the room where we were playing and picked up a ladder and swung it around his head. When Joe was playing the piano Guy would say, 'Play it like Jerry Lee Lewis, Jerry Lee Lewis,' spitting in his ear, and banging the piano lid up and down. One day he poured a can of beer into the piano saying it would make it sound better. Which I think it did.

TOPPER: My best drumming is on *London Calling*. We used to write, rehearse and then record, and that's how we worked up the whole album. That's probably why it's our best, because it was written, rehearsed and then recorded, rather than us just going into the studio to see what turned up.

JOE: Many say that it's our finest hour, that double album. It was done with a lot of non-stop work. We weren't nightclub people and so what we did was write, rehearse and then record it.

MICK: We worked up a bunch of songs, in batches, in Vanilla. We were quite

Take The Fifth Tour of America

LINE-UP: STRUMMER, JONES, SIMONON, HEADON
Support acts were the Undertones, Bo Diddley, Sam And Dave and various other local acts

8 SEP: Monterey CA. Tribal Stomp Festival with Peter Tosh, Robert Frith, Maria Muldaur, the Mighty Diamonds and Joe Ely
12 SEP: Civic Center, Saint Paul MN, extra support David Johansen
14 SEP: Aragon Ballroom, Chicago IL, extra support Bo Diddley
17 SEP: Masonic Temple, Detroit MI, extra support Sam And Dave
18 SEP: Cleveland MA, extra support Sam And Dave
19 SEP: Orpheum Theater, Boston MA, extra support Sam And Dave
20 SEP: Palladium, New York NY, extra support Sam And Dave
21 SEP: Palladium, New York NY, extra support Sam And Dave. The famous photo of Paul by Pennie Smith, used on the front of the *London Calling* album, was taken on this night.
22 SEP: Walnut Street Theater, Philadelphia PA
25 SEP: St Denis Theater, Montreal, Canada, extra support the B Girls
26 SEP: O'Keefe Center, Toronto, Canada, extra support the B Girls
28 SEP: Clark University, Worcester MA, extra support acts the Necessaries and Gang War featuring Johnny Thunders and Wayne Kramer
29 SEP: Ritchie Colisseum, College Park MD
2 OCT: The Agora, Atlanta GA
4 OCT: Armadillo Club, Austin TX, extra support Joe Ely and the Skunks
5 OCT: Cullen Auditorium, Houston TX, extra support Joe Ely and the Skunks
6 OCT: Palladium, Dallas TX, extra support Joe Ely
7 OCT: Rocks Club [The Rox], Lubbock TX, extra support Joe Ely & the Skunks
10 OCT: San Diego CA, extra support Joe Ely
11 OCT: Hollywood Palladium, Los Angeles CA, extra support Joe Ely, the LA Boys, the Rockabilly Rebels
13 OCT: Kezar Pavilion, San Francisco CA, extra support the Cramps, Dead Kennedys, the Rockabilly Rebels
15 OCT: Paramount Theater, Seattle WA
16 OCT: Pacific National Exhibition, Vancouver, Canada, extra support DOA

SONGS PLAYED:
I'm So Bored With the USA / City Of The Dead / Complete Control / London Calling / The Prisoner / Jail Guitar Doors / White Man in Hammersmith Palais / Koka Kola / I Fought The Law / Jail Guitar Doors / Spanish Bombs / Guns Of Brixton / Clampdown / Drug Stabbing Time / Julie's In The Drug Squad / Police and Thieves / Stay Free / Safe European Home / English Civil War / Capital Radio / Wrong 'Em Boyo / Clash City Rockers / Capital Radio / Tommy Gun / What's My Name / Janie Jones / Garageland / Armagideon Time / Career Opportunities / Fingernails (Joe Ely) / Jimmy Jazz / White Riot / Brand New Cadillac / Be Bop A Lula

L-R: Topper, Joe, Greenwich Village piano-playing legend Al Field, former New York Doll David Johansen and Blondie singer Debbie Harry, backstage at the New York Palladium. Earlier that night Pennie Smith had captured the now-famous image of Paul busting his bass on stage – the cover image of the *London Calling* album.

prolific in that little room. We'd say to each other, 'Let's try this, try that,' working up a tune or a lyric. But they wouldn't be quite finished by the time we got into the studio, so we'd finish them there.

PAUL: Writing songs was a problem for me 'cos I always played reggae and played reggae and played reggae, and wasn't a complete master of the instrument. I learned a few chords on guitar from watching the others on stage, thinking that if I learned a few shapes then once I had ideas for songs I could show them how to make it more rocking, but I didn't have the musical vocabulary to do that.

MICK: By the third album we were still learning, still developing and we broadened our musical style. There was a point where Punk was getting narrower and narrower in terms of what it could achieve and where it could go. It was like painting itself into a corner and we wanted to do anything and everything. We thought you could make any kind of music.

PAUL: One day at Wessex all these coppers came in and started running around, looking for Guy. Topper legged it, Mick and Joe froze and I was coming down some stairs when I saw them. I seemed to recognize one of them – it was Wilko from Ian Dury's Blockheads. The band had come from the *Top of The Pops* studios where they'd been filming I Wanna Be Straight.

JOE: There was a real intensity of effort and our recreation was playing 5-a-side football as a way of starting our rehearsal days. We'd play football until we dropped and then we'd start playing music. It was good limbering-up exercise. We didn't do these things with thought, we just did it by accident.

MICK: One day Mickey Gallagher [keyboard player] broke his arm playing football with us, which put him out of action for most of the album. He could only play the Hammond organ with one hand, so Joe and I bluffed a lot of the piano bits.

ABOVE: An original ticket stub from the band's first night at New York's Palladium.

BELOW: Another of Topper's postcards home.

The Clash were accompanied on the tour by the *NME*'s illustrator Ray Lowry, who filed regular reports for the paper. He 'designed' the cover of the *London Calling* album and illustrated the lyric sheets which came with the album in the form of inner sleeves.

Clash USA '79
Final curtain

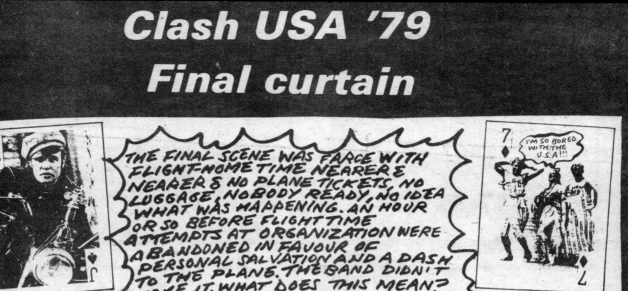

THE FINAL SCENE WAS FARCE WITH FLIGHT-HOME TIME NEARER & NEARER & NO PLANE TICKETS, NO LUGGAGE, NOBODY READY, NO IDEA WHAT WAS HAPPENING. AN HOUR OR SO BEFORE FLIGHT TIME ATTEMPTS AT ORGANIZATION WERE ABANDONED IN FAVOUR OF PERSONAL SALVATION AND A DASH TO THE PLANE. THE BAND DIDN'T MAKE IT. WHAT DOES THIS MEAN?

MY LAST DISPATCH WAS SUPPRESSED BY THE AUTHORITIES BUT CHRONICLED CLASH SHOWS IN AUSTIN TEXAS ON THE 4TH. OCTOBER — 'CLASH QUADROPEDS!' DALLAS ON THE 5TH — 'PRESIDENT KILLERS' WITH HOUSTON THE WORLD!' AND LUBBOCK ON THE 7TH AS HOLLYMANIA SWEEPS CLASH TOUR. FROM LUBBOCK, THE BAND FLEW AND THE ALCOHOLICS BUSSED (VIA ROUTE 66) TO LOS ANGELES AND THE WILDEST SHOW OF THE WHOLE TOUR. THE HOLLYWOOD PALLADIUM AUDIENCE LOOKED DIFFERENT — AS MEAN AND NASTY AND POSY LOOKING AS AN ENGLISH AUDIENCE — AND WERE DETERMINED TO GOZ ALL OVER ANYTHING ONSTAGE THAT WASN'T THE CLASH AND TO HURL A GOOD BIT ON THEM AS WELL. JOE ELY (A CONSTANT PRESENCE ON THIS TOUR) AND THE (ROCKABILLY) REBELS PLAYED THROUGH NON-STOP ABUSE AND SPIT AND THE ELY BAND MADE THE MISTAKE OF RETALIATING WITH A DUSTBIN OF WATER, WHICH UNDERSTANDABLY MADE THE FRONT ROWS EVEN

AT THE ARMADILLO WORLD HEADQUARTERS TRASH ARMOURED, BURROWING 'CLASH ASSASSINATE ON THE 6TH — 'ARSEHOLE OF THE WORLD' — 'BULLOCKS TO LUBBOCK BUS!' INTERESTING AND INFORMATIVE OF THE LAST FIVE DATES OF THE

MORE HOSTILE TO ANYTHING ON THE STAGE. A LOT OF THIS WAS THE RITUAL BELLIGERENCE THAT AUDIENCES EVERYWHERE

I KEEP MY FINGERNAILS LONG SO THEY CLICK WHEN I PLAY WHITE RIOT!!

JOE ELY — COWBOY PUNK

THINK THAT THEY HAVE TO DISPLAY, AND THE CLASH CAME ON TO GREAT CHEERS, MASS JUMPING UP AND DOWN, SURGES ON TO THE STAGE, FIGHTING, CURSING, SPITTING AND STOMPING ASS (OBSCURE AMERICANISM — SEE ALSO GITTIN' DOWN AND KICKIN' ASS). AT THE END OF THE SET WITH JOE ELY, THE REBELS, A FEW DOZEN OF THE AUDIENCE, THE CLASH AND ASSORTED ROADIES, BOUNCERS AND LIGGERS ON THE STAGE PLUS A CONSTANT STREAM OF BODIES BEING HURLED OFF INTO THE PULSATING MASS, THE HALL LOOKED LIKE ONE OF THOSE BIG CECIL B. DEMILLE BLOWOUTS JUST BEFORE SAMSON COMES OUT AND PULLS THE ROOF DOWN OR MOSES ENTERS ON A MOUNTAIN TOP WITH A MESSAGE FROM GOD FOR ALL THE FORNICATING SINNERS DOWN BELOW. GOOD SHOW

SAN FRANCISCO (13TH OCT), SEATTLE (15TH) AND VANCOUVER ALL TRIED BUT COULDN'T REALLY MATCH LOS ANGELES. SAN FRANCISCO WAS A GREAT SHOW BUT THE AUDIENCE WERE A BIT LESS BOISTEROUS THAN L.A., SEATTLE, I DIDN'T HAVE A DRINK ALL NIGHT AND DON'T REMEMBER TOO MUCH OF IT. VANCOUVER (16TH) WAS A QUIET END TO THE TOUR WITH JOE STRUMMER AGAIN RAILING AGAINST PASSIVE AUDIENCES STEALING HIS SOUL. THE PARADOX HERE, OF COURSE, IS THAT THE REWARD FOR GOING OVER THE TOP AND SHOWING ULTIMATE ENTHUSIASM BY CLAMBERING ON STAGE IS TO BE BUNDLED OFF AND OUT OF THE DOOR OR HURLED BACK INTO THE CROWD — AND ANYWAY (AS THE LONE GROOVER WAS ASKING RECENTLY) IS JUMPING UP AND DOWN ANY KIND OF INTELLIGENT RESPONSE TO MUSIC THAT ASPIRES TO DEAL WITH REALITY?

MODERN DANCE

$E = Mc^2$

KVESTIONS, KVESTIONS. **BACK HOME…** AND ALREADY SICK OF MAKING PLANS FOR NIGEL AND THE COLD AT NIGHT AND AUTHORITARIAN VIOLENCE BEING SO NEAR AND SO PERSONAL AGAIN. THE OPTIMISM AND THE NAIVE HOPE THAT THIS LAST ROCK AND ROLL UPSURGE WAS ACTUALLY GOING TO CHANGE ANYTHING HAS LONG GONE, OF COURSE, BUT IT'S A STUPID MISTAKE TO TURN INWARD AND IGNORE THE ISSUES THAT THE CLASH BROUGHT INTO THE 'POP' MUSIC FIELD OF INTEREST, OR REVILE THEM FOR FAILING TO OVERTURN THE GOVERNMENT. IF THE CLASH PACKED IT IN TOMORROW WE'D LOSE THE SOLE LIVING EVIDENCE THAT ROCK AND ROLL ASPIRES TO BE ANYTHING MORE THAN BLIND ESCAPISM AND THEY'D BE REPLACED BY SOMETHING INFINITELY LESS WORTHY WITHIN WEEKS.

I'VE HEARD OF ELVIS PRESLEY

A REBEL

HOLLYWOOD

I WAS SICK BENEATH THE HOLLYWOOD SIGN — I VOMITED ON PARTS OF AMERICA THAT OTHER LIGGERS CAN'T REACH.

I'D LIKE TO BE BACK ON THE BUS WITH THE LAST ROCK & ROLL BAND.

By Ray Lowry

London Calling

[UK LP CBS CLASH3/US LP EPIC36328]

RELEASED 14 DECEMBER 1979 UK/JANUARY 1980 US
UK CHART PEAK: #9
US CHART PEAK: #27

A double album for the price of a single, and now regarded as the band's musical masterpiece, it was voted the best album of the 1980s by *Rolling Stone* magazine (in 1999). Musically a clear departure from the punk sound still raging in the UK, most reviewers loved it. The album entered the UK charts at #9.

TOPPER: It was one of the most enjoyable times with the band, making *London Calling*.

MICK: I don't think the first American tour was the inspiration for *London Calling*. A few of the songs on the second album had talked about that. I think by this time the lyrics were actually the spur to start doing different kinds of music.

JOE: It was a really, really good time, making that album.

SIDE ONE:
London Calling
Brand New Cadillac
Jimmy Jazz
Hateful
Rudie Can't Fail

SIDE TWO:
Spanish Bombs
The Right Profile
Lost in the
  Supermarket
Clampdown
Guns of Brixton

SIDE THREE:
Wrong 'Em Boyo
Death Or Glory
Koka Kola
The Card Cheat

SIDE FOUR:
Lover's Rock
Four Horsemen
I'm Not Down
Revolution Rock
Train In Vain

Joe Strummer (rhythm guitar, piano, vocals), Mick Jones (guitar, piano, vocals), Paul Simonon (bass), Topper Headon (drums), Mickey Gallagher (organ), The Irish Horns (brass). Produced by Guy Stevens, engineered by Bill Price and Jerry Green. Recorded in Wessex Studios, London.

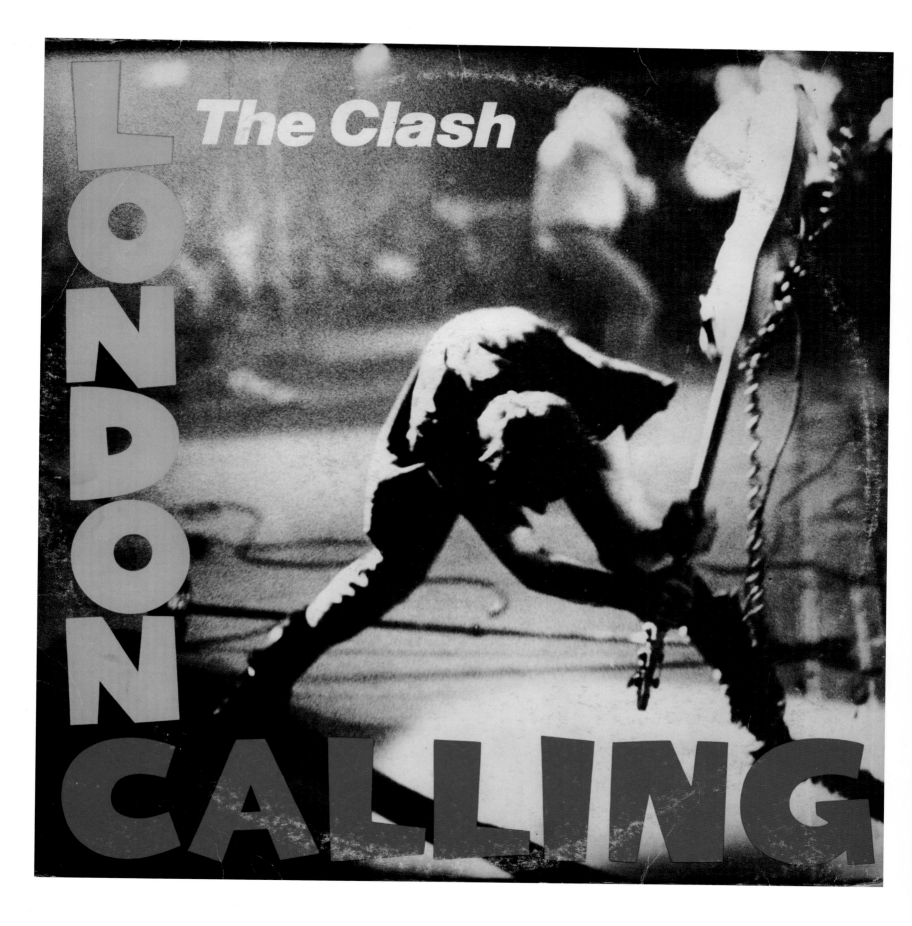

Paul rests between
numbers in Vanilla
studios, while making
London Calling.

PAUL: Across the road from Vanilla there was a football pitch that we used to play on. One day some guys from the record company came down with some Americans and we got them onto the football pitch with us. Not being the most skilful player I used to chop everybody, so whenever I had the ball they'd all run away. Mick was really swift and nimble and Joe was the work-horse who'd always be struggling to get there. Topper was pretty nifty, too. But these record company guys had no idea, we were kicking them in the shins and pushing them over, which was fun.

MICK: We didn't spare the boot the day the record company execs came down and played football with us. It was a concrete pitch, too. Anybody who came to visit us would be dragged out to play football while we were at Vanilla.

Guns of Brixton
PAUL: I realized that you get money for writing songs. I didn't get any money for doing the artwork or making the clothing and thought, 'sod that, I'm going to get more involved in making the music'. Hence I came up with 'Guns of Brixton'.

PAUL: I actually wanted Guns of Brixton to be a bit more rocking, but musical incapability on my part made it a real task to communicate that to the others.

Card Cheat
MICK: We recorded the whole track twice to get that Phil Spector Wall of Sound. We recorded it and then overdubbed it, which is why it sounds so big. Every instrument, we'd play it all together and then play it over again.

Brand New Cadillac
TOPPER: I'll always remember doing that. One take, live, Guy said, 'That's it!' and I said, 'You can't keep that, it speeds up!' and he said, 'Great! All rock 'n' roll speeds up. Take!' And from then on the sessions just cooked.

PAUL: Guy made me feel really at ease and if I played wrong notes he didn't care. After we'd played Brand New Cadillac I said I made a mistake on that and he said, 'It doesn't matter, it's great'.

Lost in the Supermarket
MICK: It was written by Joe and I always felt that he was talking about me growing up, even though I didn't grow up in the suburbs. It touched me on a personal level and everybody thought that I'd written it because I sang it. It's not always the way it seemed in terms of who wrote what, but generally I wrote the music and Joe wrote the lyrics.

TOPPER: The night before we recorded that I went to see Taj Mahal play and his drummer played a lot of snare beats on his floor tom. When I went in the next day I thought, 'Sounded good last night, I'll try that on this track'.

Death or Glory

PAUL: While we were playing 'Death or Glory' Guy lost it. He ran into the room picking up chairs and smashing them against the wall and we're thinking 'he's gone insane', while still playing the song.

Rudie Can't Fail

JOE: I didn't write it for *Rude Boy*, it was a long time after. We'd had a good summer [of 1979] going to West Indian blues dances and drinking Special Brew for breakfast – we'd had a good season.

Spanish Bombs

MICK: Joe was really into Lorca and this is the spirit of Lorca.

JOE: We were riding home from Wessex in a mini-cab at 4 in the morning and it was on the radio news. Every day at about that time they were going on about Basque bombing beaches in Spain. I turned to my girlfriend Gaby who was sitting next to me and said, 'There should be a song called Spanish Bombs.'

Clampdown

JOE: We were playing the tune for a few weeks before I got a lyric for it. When Mick wrote the tune he called it Working And Awaiting and then for some reason we changed it to Fo Fuck's Sake before it became Clampdown. The near-nuclear meltdown at Three Mile Island got me started on the lyric.

That Cover Photograph

PAUL: I'd chucked my basses around before and didn't have any respect for them in the first place. The moment I got a new bass I'd get a hammer and start bashing it around, digging bits out. I saw it as a tool, that's all. We were playing the Palladium in New York and there was a lot of tension, it felt like we were playing London. Getting near the end of the show I was feeling that nothing was complete, I didn't feel satisfied. Possibly because the audience was restricted to sitting down and couldn't get up and dance, even though we always stressed that whenever we played the audience should stand up and be close to the front. It made me feel empty and out of frustration I pulled the bass off and bashed it around – because there'd been no interaction with the audience, which is what we as a group thrived on. Pennie Smith took the photograph of that.

MICK: I caught Paul smashing his bass out of the corner of my eye. But if you look at that picture there are lots of other things going on, too. There's a bouncer running across the back of the stage, it's a real action shot.

An original poster for the 'surprise' Christmas gigs played in their own backyard, at a former youth club situated under the Westway in Portobello Road. Below is an original handbill for the Christmas day gig.

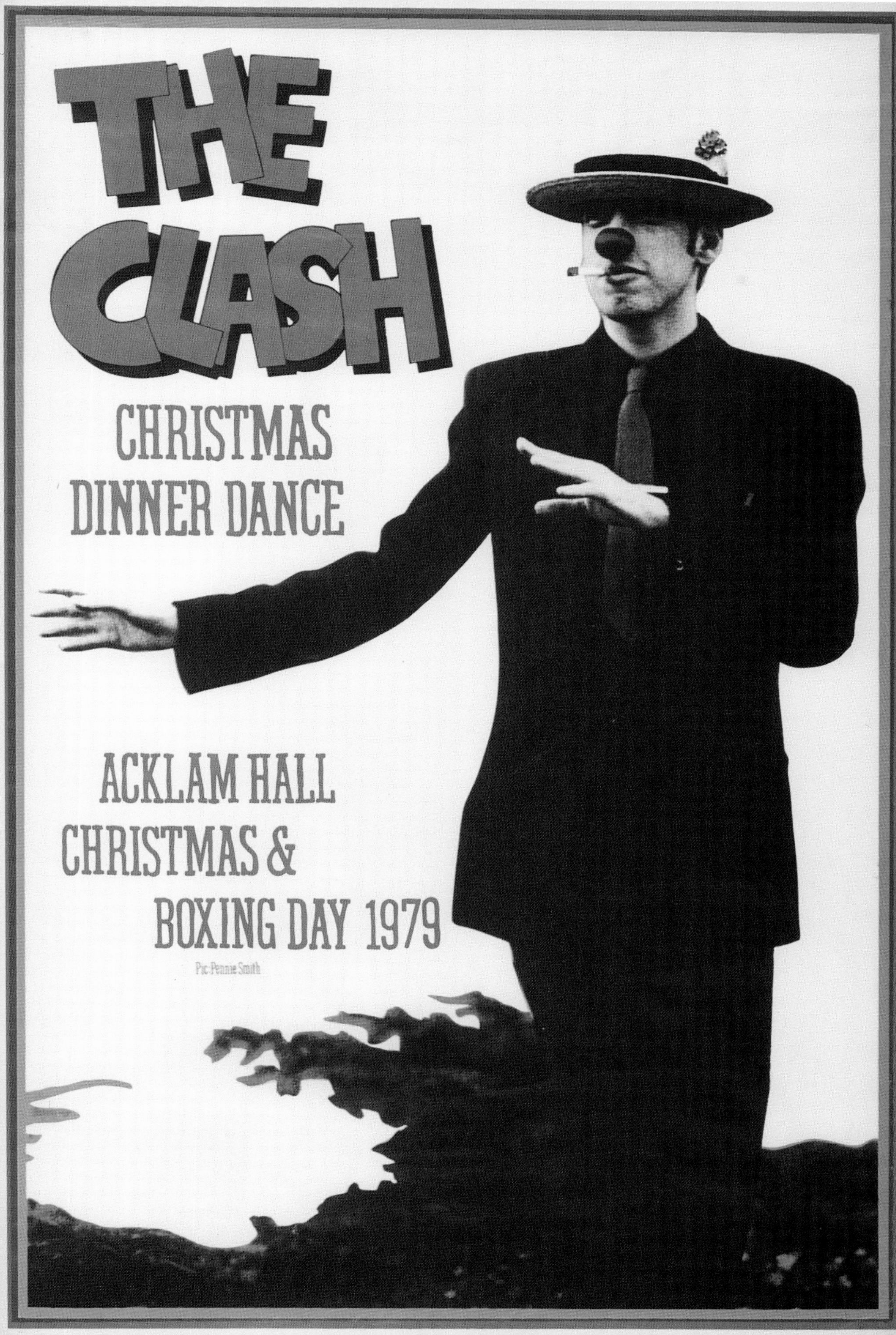

THE CLASH

CHRISTMAS
DINNER DANCE

ACKLAM HALL
CHRISTMAS &
BOXING DAY 1979

Pic: Pennie Smith

Photographed in America during the Take The Fifth Tour.

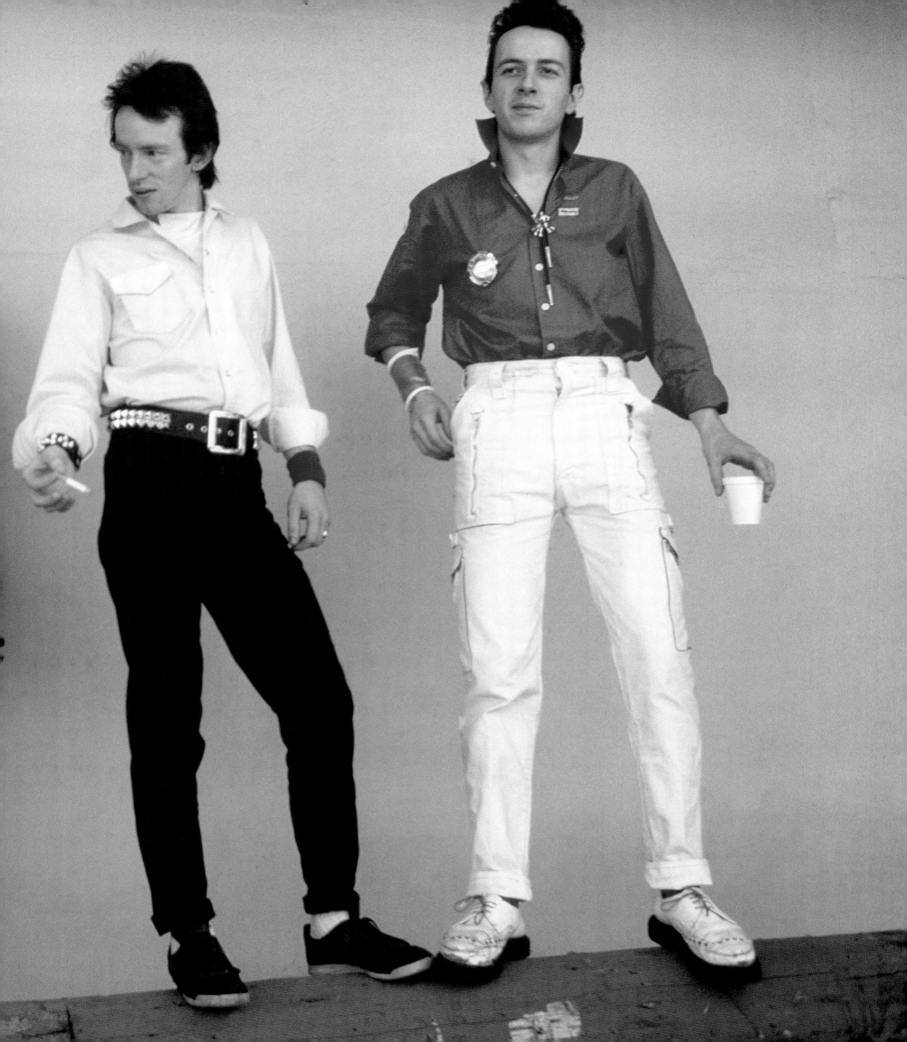

A-side: London Calling (3:19)

[Strummer/Jones] Produced by Guy Stevens

B-SIDE: ARMAGIDEON TIME (3:49)

[Jackie Mittoo/Keith Williams] Produced by The Clash

12" RELEASE B-SIDES:
JUSTICE TONIGHT (4:09)

[Jackie Mittoo/Keith Williams] Produced by The Clash

KICK IT OVER (4:44)

[Jackie Mittoo/Keith Williams] Produced by The Clash

RELEASED 7 DECEMBER 1979
UK CHART PEAK: #11

JOE: Mick made me go back and rewrite the lyric, well, the verses anyway. When there's a big football match in London, people fill the streets of Soho and there were some verses about these mobs. Mick said to me, 'In the chorus it's London Calling you're saying, [so] go back and write some more verses and see if you can come up with something better'. So I rewrote all the verses.

THE CLASH: London Calling (CBS). Hello? Hello? Operator, I think I've got a crossed line — there's someone ploughing a pre-apocalyptic furrow on my phone. Apparently the Ice Age is coming and there's been a nuclear error, but this chap seems quite happy because he lives by the river. What does it all mean?

What it means, sir, is that The Clash have released a new slice of pop-demagoguery, one which displays a greater musical maturity than before without relinquishing the essential Clash spirit, their earlier abandonment replaced this time round by a tense restraint, as if The Police were pretending to be The Angelic Upstarts.

Ah! So it's a cold-blooded attempt at a chart hit?

Well, I don't know about that, sir, though it would be nice to see them on Christmas *Top Of The Pops,* wouldn't it? 'London Calling' is actually quite a spiffy little *entree* to the album of the same name, a plea for youthful solidarity set to a strident marching rhythm.

Does this mean The Clash are the Glenn Millers of the '80s?

We'll just have to wait and see whether they cross the channel by DC10, sir. Until then, it's chest out, stomach in, toe the line and thank God

and Guy Stevens for the powerful cleanliness of the production.

Does this mean that Hapshash & The Coloured Coat are hip again?

No, sir.

1980

'I think it was a brilliant, incredible single album and a really, really good double album. But I think there's a lot of filler to make it a triple, personally.'
TOPPER

The band returned to England in mid-October 1979, following the Take The Fifth Tour of America. They took a couple of months off to promote the release of London Calling the single (7 December), which would reach number 11 in the UK singles chart, and the release of *London Calling* the album. On the band's insistence the double album was sold for the price of a single LP, and was in the shops just in time for Christmas (14 December). The release was held over until January in America. The album would make number 9 in the UK charts and number 27 in the USA.

Sixteen Tons Tour of the UK

LINE-UP: STRUMMER, JONES, SIMONON, HEADON

Support acts varied throughout the tour, but the band were joined by Mikey Dread

5 JAN: Friars, Aylesbury
6 JAN: Odeon, Canterbury
8 JAN: Top Rank, Brighton
9 JAN: Top Rank, Brighton
11 JAN: Leisure Centre, Crawley
12 JAN: Pavilion, Hastings
13 JAN: Locarno, Bristol
14 JAN: Gaumont, Ipswich
16 JAN: De Montfort Hall, Leicester
18 JAN: Caird Hall, Dundee, Scotland
19 JAN: Odeon, Edinburgh, Scotland, support acts Josef K and Mikey Dread
20 JAN: Odeon, Edinburgh, Scotland, support acts Josef K and Mikey Dread
21 JAN: Apollo, Glasgow, Scotland, support acts First Priority and Mikey Dread
22 JAN: Apollo, Glasgow, Scotland, support acts First Priority and Mikey Dread
23 JAN: University, Lancaster, support act Mikey Dread
24 JAN: Tiffany's, Blackpool, support act Mikey Dread
25 JAN: King George's, Blackburn, support acts the Not Sensibles and Mikey Dread
26 JAN: Leisure Centre, Chester, support act Mikey Dread
27 JAN: Top Rank, Sheffield, support act Mikey Dread
29 JAN: St Georges, Bradford, support acts Violation and Mikey Dread
30 JAN: Royal Spa, Bridlington, support acts the Akrylics and Mikey Dread
31 JAN: University, Leeds, support act Mikey Dread
1 FEB: Victoria Hall, Hanley, Stoke-on-Trent (cancelled)

SONGS PLAYED:

Clash City Rockers / Brand New Cadillac / Safe European Home / Jimmy Jazz / City Of The Dead / London Calling / Koka Kola / I Fought the Law / Rudie Can't Fail / Spanish Bombs / Guns of Brixton / Train In Vain / Wrong`Em Boyo / White Man in Hammersmith Palais / Bankrobber / Clampdown / Stay Free / Police & Thieves / Tommy Gun / Capital Radio / Janie Jones / Complete Control / Armagideon Time / English Civil War / Julie's Working For The Drug Squad / Garageland / London's Burning / White Riot / Hit The Road Jack / Revolution Rock / Protex Blue / Keys To Your Heart / Fingernails

Retaining some of the 1950s style from the London Calling Tour, the band wore red, white, black (and sometimes other 1950s-style coloured shirts) with black suits, quiffs and boots. Here Mick plays a vintage blacktop Gibson Les Paul guitar from the late 1950s.

3 FEB: Apollo, Manchester, support act Mikey Dread

4 FEB: Apollo, Manchester, support act Mikey Dread

5 FEB: Top Rank, Birmingham, support act Mikey Dread

6 FEB: Top Rank, Birmingham, support act Mikey Dread

7 FEB: Tiffany's, Coventry, support act Mikey Dread

8 FEB: Guildhall, Portsmouth, support act Mikey Dread

10 FEB: Wessex Hall, Poole, support act Mikey Dread

11 FEB: Sophia Gardens, Cardiff, support act Mikey Dread

12 FEB: Stateside, Bournemouth, support act Mikey Dread

13 FEB: Top Rank, Southampton, support acts Strate Jacket and Mikey Dread

15 FEB: Electric Ballroom, London, support acts Mikey Dread and Joe Ely

16 FEB: Electric Ballroom, London, support acts Mikey Dread and Joe Ely

17 FEB: Lyceum, London, support acts Mikey Dread and Joe Ely

18 FEB: Odeon, Lewisham, support acts Mikey Dread and Joe Ely

20 FEB: Victoria Hall, Hanley, Stoke-on-Trent (cancelled)

22 FEB: Liberty Theatre, Balham, London, support acts Mikey Dread and Joe Ely

27 FEB: Palais De Sports, Paris, France

The previous year had ended with The Clash on home territory when they played two secret gigs at Acklam hall, a youth club under the Westway, on Christmas Day and Boxing Day. On 27 December they played the Hammersmith Odeon as part of a four-night series of benefit gigs for Kampuchea. The headline act on the night The Clash played was Ian Dury & The Blockheads (top of the bill on the other nights were Wings, The Who and Queen), whom Mick joined on stage for a performance of Sweet Gene Vincent.

Those gigs were a warm-up for the international Sixteen Tons Tour, which would begin in January 1980 in Aylesbury and travel through the UK, America and Europe before ending in Iceland on 21 June.

Then they went into the studio to record a fourth album.

SIXTEEN TONS

PAUL: From day one we decided that when we were tuned up and it was time to go on, we'd rush out rather than amble on. But that changed over the years and we chose certain songs that we'd come on to. Sixteen Tons by Tennessee Ernie Ford was an early one, and it developed from there.

TOPPER: I felt we were on top of the world the whole time when we were touring. I loved touring, loved every minute of it.

PAUL: Mikey Dread turned up in Scotland wearing a duffle coat and he'd never seen snow before, having just come from Jamaica. He was great and we instantly clicked. I knew his records 'cos Don Letts had passed some on to me and I knew all about him.

Remarkably, given the popularity of the band at the time, The Clash still appeared at small (less than 2,000 capacity) places. The tour began in Aylesbury where Toots And the Maytals, who were billed to support, were replaced on the night at short notice by Ian Dury And the Blockheads because Toots couldn't make it. Original poster for the gig, right.

FOLLOWING PAGE: L-R Paul, Mick, Topper and Joe pose straight-faced, sharp suited and looking distinctly unlike any other band of the time.

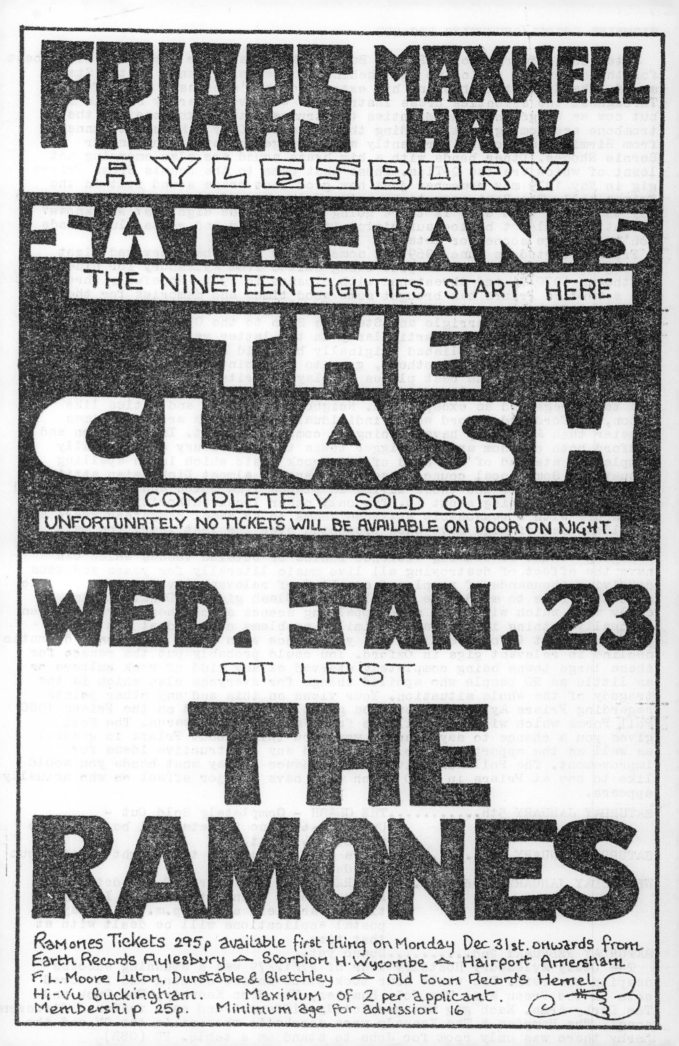

A-side: Bankrobber (4:34)

[Strummer/Jones] Produced by Mikey Dread

B-SIDE: ROCKERS GALORE. . . UK TOUR (FEATURING MIKEY DREAD) (4:41)

[Strummer/Jones/Mikey Campbell] Produced by The Clash

RELEASED 8 AUGUST 1980
UK CHART PEAK: #12
NO US RELEASE (SEE PAGE 268)

PAUL: We decided that we wanted to release a single a month and the first one we put forward was Bankrobber. But the head of the record company didn't like it. He said it sounded like David Bowie backwards, which I didn't understand. So the UK record company wouldn't release it. But the Dutch did and it was then imported, which made the UK company release it. But it stopped our flow of putting out a single a month.

make many dents on the Clash's own vision of themselves as r'n'r outlaws, a vision that this doubtless 'soulful', 'risk-taking' piece of rootless romanticism will help bolster.

Meantimes Peel and public pressure will surely result in this getting released and charting and CBS will look very stupid. But I shouldn't worry Morrie my boy, it's all money. Anyway I can't see what's bothering you, people buy PiL records after all.

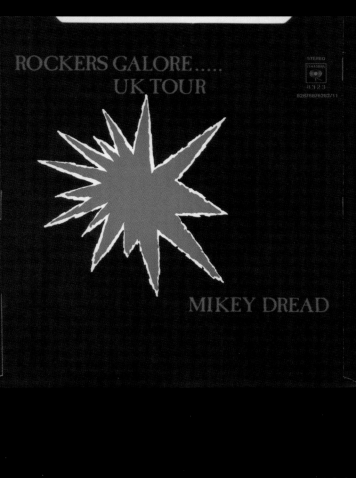

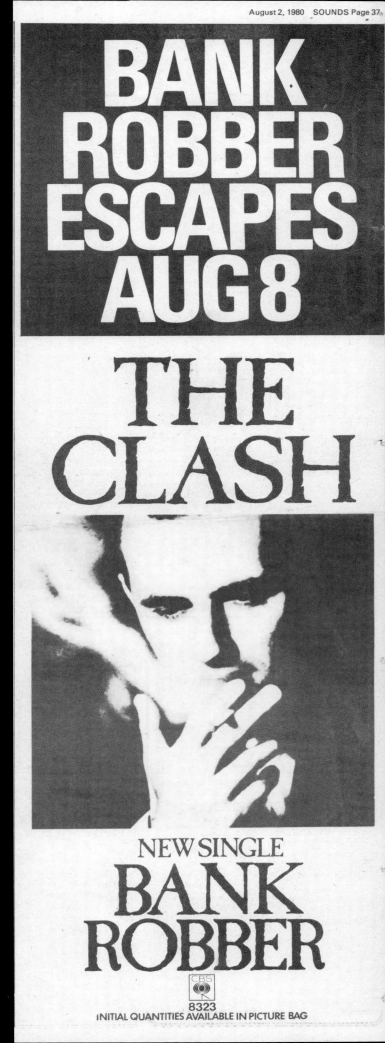

BANK ROBBER ESCAPES AUG 8

THE CLASH

NEW SINGLE
BANK ROBBER

CBS
8323
INITIAL QUANTITIES AVAILABLE IN PICTURE BAG

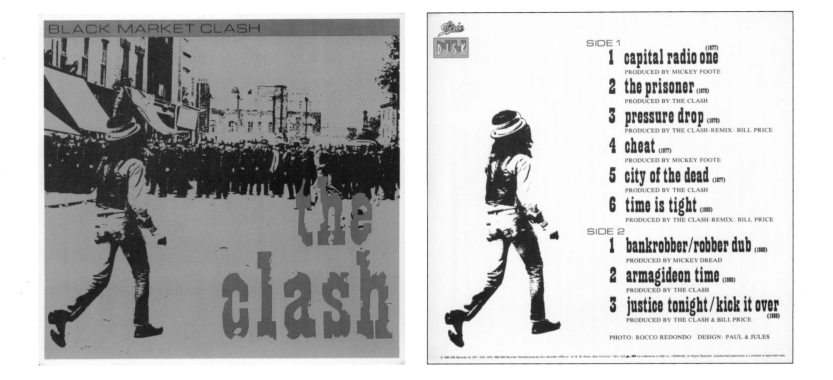

SIDE 1
1 **capital radio one** (1977)
PRODUCED BY MICKEY FOOTE
2 **the prisoner** (1978)
PRODUCED BY THE CLASH
3 **pressure drop** (1979)
PRODUCED BY THE CLASH-REMIX: BILL PRICE
4 **cheat** (1977)
PRODUCED BY MICKEY FOOTE
5 **city of the dead** (1977)
PRODUCED BY THE CLASH
6 **time is tight** (1980)
PRODUCED BY THE CLASH-REMIX: BILL PRICE

SIDE 2
1 **bankrobber/robber dub** (1980)
PRODUCED BY MICKEY DREAD
2 **armagideon time** (1980)
PRODUCED BY THE CLASH
3 **justice tonight/kick it over** (1980)
PRODUCED BY THE CLASH & BILL PRICE

PHOTO: ROCCO REDONDO   DESIGN: PAUL & JULES

BANKROBBER

MICK: We had a big row at Heathrow Airport (I can't remember where we were going) with the head of CBS, Maurice Oberstein, who was there with his dog and lady chauffeur. He didn't want us to put out 12 singles in a year. But eventually Bankrobber came out in England – so we got one single out in twelve months – and it got to number 12 in the charts. We'd never appear on *Top Of The Pops* [the only nationally aired music chart show on UK TV at the time] because it was rubbish, so they got their dance troupe, Legs & Co, to do a routine to it. They were all dressed up like bankrobbers wearing masks and hats and did a hilarious dance.

JOE: All summer long that was the only record you heard on the radio and in the Grove. One day I went up Ladbroke Grove to get a newspaper and a bunch of black schoolgirls got off a bus, and one of them went, 'There's that guy who did Bankrobber' and they surrounded me and stood looking, 'cos they couldn't believe that some weird-looking white dude had made this record. I'll never forget it, they stood there staring at me, and didn't say anything. They couldn't compute it.

MICK: We made a video to go with Bankrobber, and filmed part of it in Lewisham when we were playing there [February 1980] with Johnny and Baker. They were standing outside a bank in Lewisham High Street wearing hats, long coats and masks like gangsters from an American movie and the police pulled them because they thought they looked dodgy. As if robbers would be that stupid!

ABOVE: In September 1980 Epic in America released the *Black Market Clash* compilation containing the songs which they'd left off the first album, plus various B-sides and tracks not available in the States except on bootleg (hence the ironic title). The cover image is of Don Letts walking towards police lines during the Notting Hill riots of 1976.

RIGHT: A rare, original ad for Bankrobber from 1980 which mixes American Western and Gangster movie imagery with Brixton streets (Atlantic Road used to be one of the main drags for drug dealers in the area). The video for the single was filmed around the corner from Atlantic Road, in Lewisham High Street, on the day that the band played there.

FOLLOWING PAGE: Mick, Joe, Topper and Paul's personal information forms, created for the programme to accompany the 16 Tons Tour, *The Armagideon Times* Volume 2.

NAME: MICHAEL JONES

AGE: 24

BIRTHPLACE: SOUTH LONDON

HEIGHT: QUITE TALL

HAIR: BLACK

EYES: BROWN

INSTRUMENTS: GUITARS (several) HARMONIUM

INFLUENCES: MY HOME LIFE

FAVE COLOUR: BLUE

FAVE FOOD: NO MEAT

FAVE DRINK: TEA

FAVE ANIMAL: ZEBRAS + DOGS

LIKES: MORBID CHARACTERS. COMEDIANS. GRANDMOTHERS.

DISLIKES: CHEESY THINGS, "the stench of a lie" HAVING TO THINK ABOUT HOW DREADFULL "THINGS" ARE ALL THE TIME. T.O.T.P.

AMBITION: TO LEARN TO PLAY THE PIANO.

SAVED BY DOG

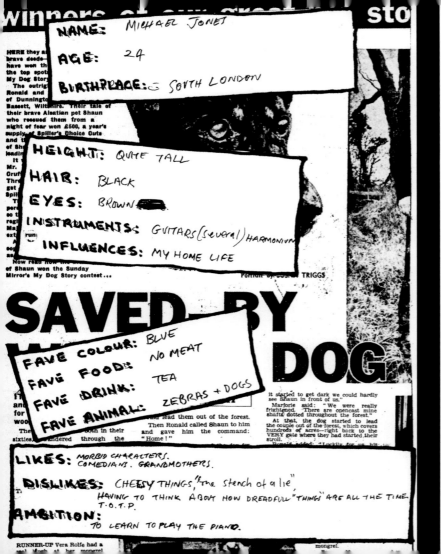

When the SPIRIT WALKED!

NAME: JOESEPH STRUMMER

AGE: 27

BIRTHPLACE: ANKARA, ANATOLIA

HEIGHT: 5-8

HAIR: BROWN

EYES: 11

INSTRUMENTS: RHYTMN,

INFLUENCES: CONCENTRATION

FAVE COLOUR: BLONDE

FAVE FOOD: RICE

FAVE DRINK: KOKA KOLA

FAVE ANIMAL: LIONS

LIKES: CIGARETTES

DISLIKES: VIOLENCE

AMBITION: TO BE BETTER

RECOGNIZE THIS, READER? THAT'S RIGHT---IT'S HADES, INFERNAL REFUGE OF LOST SOULS!

...AND THIS? WELL, WHO DOESN'T KNOW NEW YORK? BUT---WHAT'S THE CONNECTION?

EVEN NOW, I WAS ABOUT---THROUGH THE STRANGEST VISITOR THAT EVER GRACED A SLEUTH'S OFFICE!

THAT'S RIGHT---I'M A MISSING PERSONS SPECIALIST! WHOM DO YOU WANT ME TO FIND?

NOT A PERSON ---A SOUL!

JOHN WILSIN 1911-1951

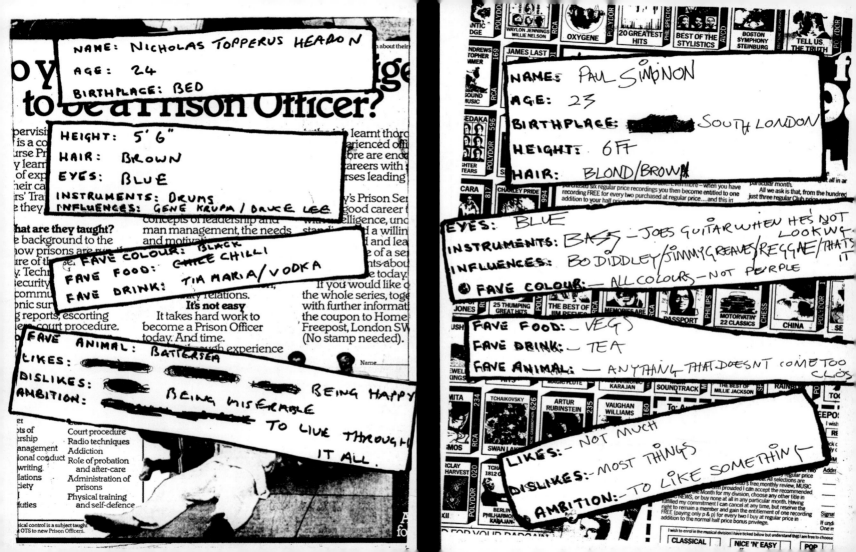

NAME: NICHOLAS TOPPERUS HEADON
AGE: 24
BIRTHPLACE: BED

HEIGHT: 5'6"
HAIR: BROWN
EYES: BLUE
INSTRUMENTS: DRUMS
INFLUENCES: GENE KRUPA / BRUCE LEE

FAVE COLOUR: BLACK
FAVE FOOD: CHILE CHILLI
FAVE DRINK: TIA MARIA / VODKA

FAVE ANIMAL: BATTERSEA
LIKES: ▓▓▓▓▓
DISLIKES: ▓▓▓▓▓ BEING HAPPY
AMBITION: ▓▓▓ BEING MISERABLE TO LIVE THROUGH IT ALL.

NAME: PAUL SIMONON
AGE: 23
BIRTHPLACE: ▓▓▓ SOUTH LONDON
HEIGHT: 6FT
HAIR: BLOND/BROWN

EYES: BLUE
INSTRUMENTS: BASS - JOES GUITAR WHEN HE'S NOT LOOKING
INFLUENCES: BO DIDDLEY/JIMMY GREAVES/REGGAE/THATS IT
FAVE COLOUR: - ALL COLOURS - NOT PURPLE

FAVE FOOD: - VEGS
FAVE DRINK: - TEA
FAVE ANIMAL: - ANYTHING THAT DOESNT COME TOO CLOSE

LIKES: - NOT MUCH
DISLIKES: - MOST THINGS
AMBITION: - TO LIKE SOMETHING

SANDINISTA!

JOE: It was three pieces of long-playing vinyl for the price of one and we took a knock on it in order to bring it out. We forwent our royalties so the company would release it. Many times I've debated with people about what should be on it, what shouldn't be on it but now, looking back, I can't separate it. It's like the layers of an onion: there are some stupid tracks, there are some brilliant tracks. The more I think about it, the happier I am that it is what it is. The fact that it was all thrown down in one go and then released like that makes it doubly outrageous – triply outrageous. I can only say I'm proud of it, warts and all. It's a magnificent thing and I wouldn't change it even if I could. And that's after some soul searching.

L-R: Paul, Mikey Campbell AKA Mikey Dread, Mick, Topper and Joe holding a 45rpm single. Mikey joined the 16 Tons Tour from Jamaica and flew into a cold, snowy winter. He'd stay with the band, toasting on stage and mixing in the studio for over a year.

MICK: We were on a roll with *Sandinista!* as far as material was concerned. There was a lot of jamming in the studio and a lot of that turned into songs.

JOE: The great thing about *Sandinista!* is that we'd just done a really long tour of Britain and the US and, rather than falling down exhausted and jetting off to opposite ends of the world or something, we were so up for it that we went straight into a studio.

TOPPER: After *London Calling* we'd go into the studio without an awful lot of material and jam, 'cos it worked so well before.

JOE: CBS didn't want to buy us any time, but there we were in New York having finished the tour and all we wanted to do was record so we forced them to pay for three weeks at Electric Ladyland.

PAUL: *Sandinista!* was the turning point when everybody got involved in the songwriting. Myself and Topper were getting more confident in our musical abilities and we were contributing more.

MICK: We were a Punk band, but that didn't mean that we had to just go, 'One Two Three Four' and start every number like that. We could do different types of things. Obviously we were developing as musicians as we went along, there was less struggling with our instruments and it had become a really good thing with the bass player and drummer, and Joe and I gelling on top.

JOE: We went in there and just churned that album out in three weeks, right there on the floor. We wrote it right there – some of those takes are the songs actually being written as they're going down.

TOPPER: I was starting to play steel drums, a bit of piano, and to contribute a bit more musically, but you know, I'm primarily a drummer, not a songwriter.

PAUL: Norman Watt-Roy of the Blockheads came in and did some bass work while I went off for a while to make a film with Steve Jones and Paul Cook (ex-Sex Pistols), and he did a lot of stuff. Then when I came back I over-dubbed some of it, did some new stuff and I think we kept some of his work on there.

JOE: We had Mikey Dread on hand, we called in Mickey Gallagher and Norman Watt-Roy from the Blockheads for a bit of musicianship, and we had New York musicians dropping in. It was a real scene going on there.

PAUL: It was great having Mikey in the studio with us. He got involved and became a member of the group, really, in a more interesting way than Mickey Gallagher, just playing keyboards.

JOE: We were in there for the whole three weeks, day and night. I never went to a bar or a nightclub or anything.

MICK: Joe made a bunker for himself in the studio, out of flight cases, and he'd go in to bang out some lyrics then he'd bring them out and I'd sort of do

FOLLOWING PAGE: Joe lights a cigarette on the sidewalk of 8th Avenue in New York. By this time The Clash were not an English band, more of an international one, and their songs began to reflect that. They recorded in America using Latin rhythms and an English sensibility.

Joe working on lyrics in the studio. *Sandinista!* was the first album that the band wrote and recorded solely in the recording studio, Electric Ladyland in New York.

the same for a tune. Then we'd start playing around with it and a lot of songs came quickly that way. That's how it ended up being a 'Three For The Price of One' album.

JOE: A spliff bunker was a great thing to have, 'cos I was keen to hang with people, otherwise you're in an isolated bubble. But it was done carefully because you cannot have people pouring wine into the mixing desk or behaving like that, so I invented the spliff bunker where you could smoke, hang out and talk in the main body of the studio, removed geographically from the control room. It was somewhere where sanity could reign and people could EQ things correctly.

MICK: By the time we were making *Sandinista!* we were really experimenting. The whole of *Sandinista!* is an experiment. It was a continuing development, we were still learning our stuff, taking in influences. In order to have output you must have input.

JOE: The spliff bunker was the place where we'd come up with the next thing. As soon as there was a rough mix down we'd say, 'Fresh tape on the reel, let's get the mics out', 'cos we were going night and day, which is why it had to be a triple album, even though it would have been better as a double album or a single album or an EP. The fact is we recorded all that music in one spot at one moment in one three-week blast. For better or for worse, that's the document of what happened.

JOE: I used to sleep under the piano. You couldn't get us out of that studio if you tried. They had to prise us out of there after three weeks.

PAUL: At one point we went to Kingston, Jamaica, which was great, 'cos I was there at last. I spent the whole time with Mikey and he'd introduce me around to guys. One day he says, 'You gotta check this bloke out, he's been shot 18 times.' I noticed he had a pistol tucked in his sock. Afterwards Mikey says, 'He's famous 'cos he caught these guys robbing a bank and made them crawl all the way to the prison from the bank.' Mikey was my passport out there. If I'd been on my own I'd have been at the mercy of Dodge City. I mean, that's what Kingston was like, Dodge City.

MICK: If it's mellow and laid back in a lot of places, that's because we were becoming mellower by that time. We were pretty cooled out.

PAUL: While in Kingston we went to Studio One to record. We started, and for some reason Topper had to leave, so we got Style Scott from Roots Radics to play drums, and got a really good groove going. A month earlier, the Rolling Stones had been in the studio and they'd dished money out all over the place to keep everybody happy, so when we're there people start asking Mikey for the money. So a weird situation occurs where Mikey comes into the studio and says, 'Better go boys, the gunmen are on their way down.' We had to get out of there really quickly, just grab our instruments and leave.

A-side: Train In Vain (3:09)

[Strummer/Jones] Produced by Guy Stevens

B-SIDE: BANKROBBER (4:34)

[Strummer/Jones] Produced by Mikey Dread

ROCKER'S GALORE ...UK TOUR (WITH MIKEY DREAD) (4:41)

[Strummer/Jones/Mikey Campbell] Produced by The Clash

RELEASED IN JUNE 1980 IN HOLLAND, GERMANY, SPAIN, BRAZIL, NEW ZEALAND AND AUSTRALIA IN THIS FORMAT, THERE WAS NO UK RELEASE. IN AMERICA TRAIN IN VAIN WAS BACKED WITH LONDON CALLING AND HAD A US CHART PEAK OF #23 IN DECEMBER 1980. BANKROBBER WAS RELEASED AS A SINGLE IN THE UK IN AUGUST 1980 (SEE PAGE 256)

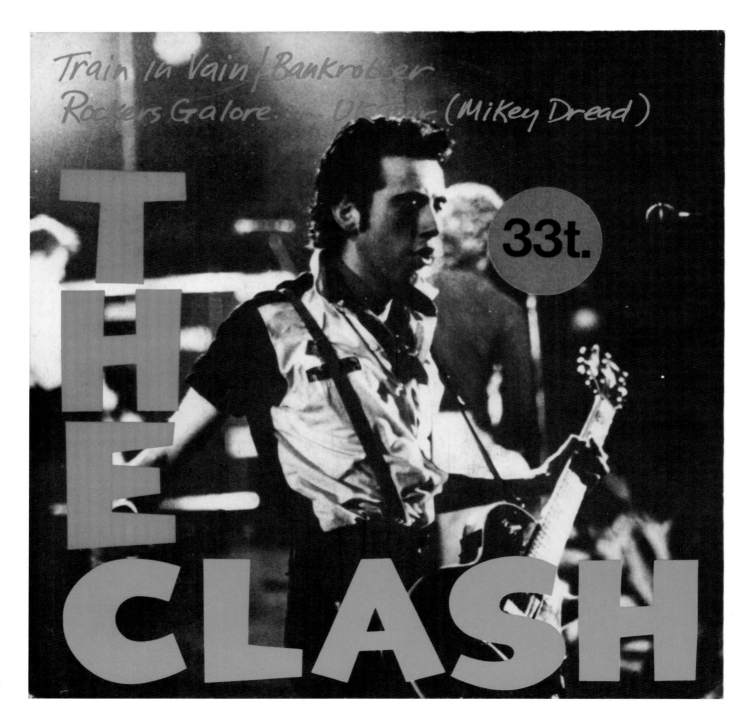

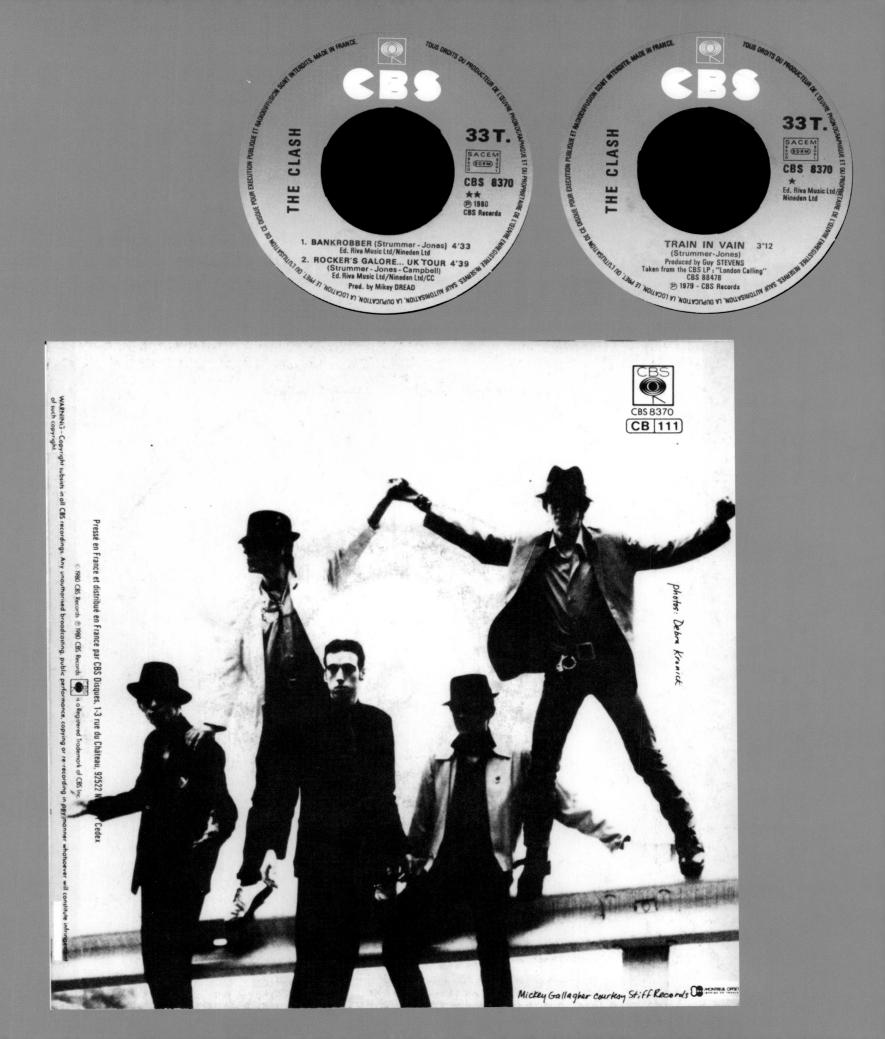

Sixteen Tons Tour of the USA

LINE-UP: STRUMMER, JONES, SIMONON, HEADON
Support acts were Mikey Dread, Lee Dorsey and the B-Girls

1 MAR: The Fox, Warfield, San Francisco CA
2 MAR: The Fox, Warfield, San Francisco CA
3 MAR: Santa Monica Civic Center, Los Angeles CA
6 MAR: Tower Theater, Philadelphia PA
7 MAR: Palladium, New York NY
8 MAR: Capitol Theater, Passaic NJ
9 MAR: Orpheum Theater, Boston MA
10 MAR: Motor City Roller Rink, Detroit MI
27 APR: Roxy Theater, Hollywood CA, 'secret' gig

SONGS PLAYED:

Clash City Rockers / Brand New Cadillac / Safe European Home / Jimmy Jazz / London Calling / The Guns Of Brixton / Train In Vain / Protex Blue / White Man In Hammersmith Palais / Koka Kola / I Fought the Law / Spanish Bombs / Rudie Can't Fail / Police & Thieves / Stay Free / Julie's Working For The Drug Squad / Wrong 'Em Boyo / Complete Control / Janie Jones / Clampdown / Armagideon Time / English Civil War / Garageland / Bankrobber / Tommy Gun / Hit The Road Jack / I'm So Bored With The USA / 48 Hours

After spending January and February touring the UK, after a rush across America from West to East in the first ten days of March, the band entered Electric Ladyland studio in New York with a few ideas but no really new songs. They virtually lived in the studio and worked up a long list of songs, the most finished of which — Somebody Got Murdered, Charlie Don't Surf, The Call Up and Stop The World among them — would feature on the next leg of the Sixteen Tons world tour in May. In between, the band flew to Jamaica to record in Channel 1 Studios, spent some time in Wessex Studios with Bill Price before returning to New York and the Power Station to finish off tracks for the remarkably low-priced triple album, *Sandinista!* (three LPs for the price of one!). Throughout the Sixteen Tons Tour the band wore either red, black or white outfits on stage, sported 1950s-style quiffs and came on stage to the sound of Tennessee Ernie Ford's 16 Tons single hit from 1955.

TOPPER: I found it really hard when we weren't touring or recording. If I got a couple of months off, say, I'd go back to Fulham and amuse myself by getting messed up with drugs. But the whole time we were working, I loved it.

Paul on stage in New York.

LEFT: **Mick at work, in the spotlight, on stage in the 16 Tons uniform.**

ABOVE: **Backstage before going on, the band prepare to play live.**

FOLLOWING PAGE: **Backstage in New York, Topper (left) has a beer while Joe (right, with cigarette) gets his photograph taken.**

JOE: When we were in Jamaica recording 'Junco Partner' with Mikey Dread there were gunfights going off all around us in Trenchtown. There was a political rally taking place and we went in like complete idiots, without knowing that we had to buy off the godfather to be allowed in. We started to record a tune called Kingston Advice which kinda made it in a botched way onto the back end of that album, but we had to finish it somewhere else. I was sitting at the piano in Studio One, which has that lovely out of tune sound which is the sound of the town, when Mikey tapped me on the shoulder and I said, 'What?' and he says, 'We have to run' and I looked into his eyes and realized that he was completely serious. He had a tiny Renault like those cars the farmers drive chickens to market in, not even a station wagon, just a tiny Renault with a bit on the back. The whole of The Clash and our party ran out of Studio One and jumped into this thing. Our guitar necks sticking out the back and I think there were people hanging on to the Renault too, and we drove right out of there. These natty Congos were running with us, 'cos the gunmen were gonna come down and slice everybody up. For, 'Who do you think you are – coming into Kingston without paying you white rassclatt'. Things like that happen and it was all good for us, grist to the mill.

A-side: The Call Up (5:25)

[Strummer/Jones] Produced by Bill Price/The Clash

B-SIDE: STOP THE WORLD (2:32)

[Strummer/Jones/Headon/Simonon] Produced by
Bill Price

RELEASED 28 NOVEMBER 1980
UK CHART PEAK: #40

MICK: For the video of Call Up we were in an army surplus store and had the run of the place. They had a few Army trucks and loads of gear and the song of course was about not joining up. There was a thing at the time in the US where you had to register for the draft, and after that you could be called up at any time. But we were left to run wild in this place which is why we look like that…

NO DRAFT

CBS

THE CALL UP
(Clash)
Produced by Bill Price and Clash
Engineered by Jeremy Green

CLASH

S CBS 9339
Side A

Nineden Ltd.
℗ 1980 CBS Records
5.25
MCPS/BIEM

Original sound recording
made by CBS Records

S CBS 9339
Side B
Nineden Ltrd.
℗ 1980 CBS Records
2.31
MCPS/BIEM

STOP THE WORLD
(Clash)
Produced by Bill Price and Clash
Engineered by Jeremy Green

CLASH

CBS

Original sound recording
made by CBS Records

CBS
9339

STOP THE WORLD

THE PANORAMA OF THE CITY IS WRONG,
IN FACT THE CITY SEEMS TO BE GONE!
BURNING RUBBER AND SMOKE IN MY EYES,
THERE'S A FLAT BURNING JUNK HEAP
FOR TWENTY SQUARE MILES!
THEY TOOK IT INTO THE NUCLEAR MINE
JUDGING BY THIS, THEY LEFT NOTHING BEHIND,
DOWN IN THE BUNKERS IN THE CRUST OF THE EARTH
NOW CROUCH THE WEALTHY AND NOBLE OF BIRTH . . .

. . . IF I COULD RIDE A TRAIN AROUND THE CITY,
THAT HOLDS THIS AS OUR FATE,
I'D RIDE FROM ELECTRO-CIRCUIT CENTRAL,
TO THE SHOCK INDUCER GATE . . .
. . . NOT FORGETTING THE BY-PASS
ACROSS THE WASHINGTON HOOKS,
THROUGH THE PHONES AND DESKS AND SCREENS,
OF THE KREMLIN'S CROOK OF CROOKS . . .

. . . THERES SOME PANEL IN A CIRCUIT BOARD,
DESTINATION OF THE OVERIDE,
SCANNING THE WILD WIND . . .
. . . BLOWING THROUGH THE BERLIN CORRIDOR,
SPOTLIT IN A PALACE, SHIELDED FROM DUST . . .

MALFUNCTION OR NOT, THE FAILSAFE IS THE CRUX,
SO FAR AWAY FROM US – SHAKING WITH THE MYSTERY TEARS.
ONE LONELY NIGHT – IN LADBROKE GROVE,
FARAWAY IN THE DESERTS OF OMAHA!
THEY GOT IT NAILED DOWN – SWISS TIGHT!
THE BANK NOTES OF EUROPE,
THE EMPERORS AND KINGS,
CURL IN THE AUTUMN – AS THE BURNING OF LEAVES,
. . . AND I'VE CLEANED MY BLACK GUITAR . . .

NINEDEN LTD

**CAMPAIGN FOR NUCLEAR DISARMAMENT
29 GREAT JAMES ST
LONDON WC1**

THE DEAD MAN'S SHADOW

THE GRANITE FRONT DOOR STEP OF THE SUMITOMO BANK, HIROSHIMA
BRANCH, HAS A MARK RESEMBLING A HUMAN SHAPE CLEARLY
DISTINGUISHED FROM THE OTHER PART, AFFECTED BY THE RADIATION HEAT
(260 METERS FROM THE CENTER OF THE EXPLOSION)

CB
LC

Sixteen Tons Tour of Europe

LINE-UP: STRUMMER, JONES, SIMONON, HEADON

Support acts are largely unrecalled and not stated on tour posters or tickets; local acts.

12 MAY: Markthalle, Hamburg, Germany
13 MAY: Metropole, Berlin, Germany
14 MAY: Schwabingerbrau, Munich
15 MAY: Oberlaa, Vienna, Austria
16 MAY: Wartburg, Wiesbaden, Germany
18 MAY: Philipshalle, Dusseldorf, Germany
20 MAY: Markethalle, Hamburg, Germany. Gig ended in a riot, Joe arrested for hitting someone with his guitar.
21 MAY: Chateau Neuf, Oslo, Norway
22 MAY: Olypen, Lund, Sweden
23 MAY: Eriksdalsballen, Stockholm, Sweden
24 MAY: The Scandinavium, Gothenburg, Sweden
26 MAY: Cambrai, France
27 MAY: Palais de Sports, Paris, France
28 MAY: Hall Tivoli, Strasbourg, France
29 MAY: Palais D'Hiver, Lyon, France
30 MAY: Théâtre De Verdure, Nice, France
1 JUN: Piazza Maggiore, Bologna, Italy
3 JUN: Parco Ruffini, Torino, Italy
9 JUN: Assembly Rooms, Derby
10 JUN: Colston Hall, Bristol
11 JUN: Colston Hall, Bristol
12 JUN: Mayfair, Newcastle
12 JUN: Victoria Hall, Hanley, Stoke-on-Trent (cancelled)
14 JUN: Reitel Festival, France
16 JUN: Hammersmith Palais, London, support act Holly & The Italians
17 JUN: Hammersmith Palais, London, support act Holly & The Italians
18 JUN: Victoria Hall, Hanley, Stoke-on-Trent
21 JUN: Laugardalshöllin Sports Hall, Reykjavik, Iceland
(**+23 AUG:** Heatwave Festival, Mosport Park, Toronto, Canada)

SONGS PLAYED:

Brand New Cadillac / Safe European Home / Clash City Rockers / Koka Kola / I Fought the Law / White Man In Hammersmith Palais / The Guns Of Brixton / Train In Vain / Spanish Bombs / City Of the Dead / 48 Hours / Somebody Got Murdered / Jail Guitar Doors / Police & Thieves / Clampdown / Jimmy Jazz / Stay Free / Bankrobber / English Civil War / Hate and War / Tommy Gun / London Calling / Janie Jones / Armagideon Time / Complete Control / London's Burning / Capital Radio / What's My Name / Revolution Rock / White Riot / Hit The Road Jack / Charlie Don't Surf / I'm So Bored With The USA / Garageland / Rockers Galore

The photograph was from a couple of years before, but the poster is for a gig at which a riot occurred in 1980.

FOLLOWING PAGE: A spread from French illustrator Serge Clerc's story of The Clash which appeared in *Metal Hurlant* magazine in July 1980.

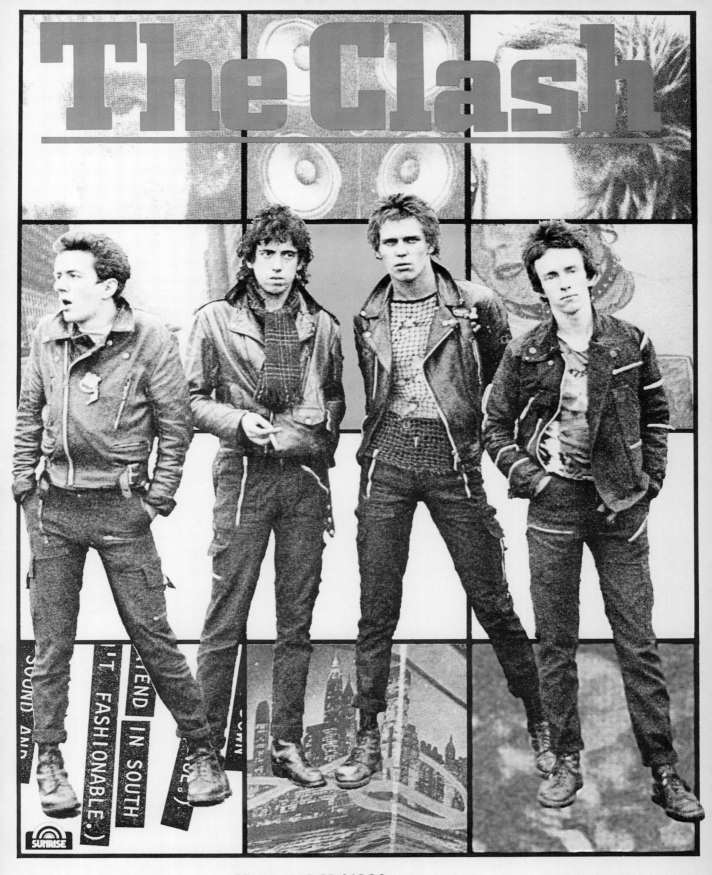

The Clash

Montag, 12. Mai 1980

12.5.

HAMBURG
Markthalle

Einlaß: 19.30 Uhr Beginn: 20.30 Uhr

Vorverkauf:
Schuhmacher, Colonnaden 37, Tel. 34 30 44
Central, Lilienstraße 24, Tel. 33 71 24
Hamburg-Tip, Gerhard-Hauptmann-Platz, Tel. 32 54 12
Wichers, Adenauerallee, Tel. 24 24 51
Collien, Eppendorfer Baum, Tel. 48 33 90
Morgenpost-Center, Speersort (Pressehaus) Tel. 33 60 61
Altona, Neue Gr. Bergstraße, Pavillon 5a, Tel. 38 62 64
Gerdes, Rothenbaumchaussee 77, Tel. 45 33 26
Eimsbüttel, Osterstraße 70, Tel. 40 73 70
Alster, Hofweg 33, Tel. 22 17 97
Hansa, Bergedorfer Straße 60, Tel. 7 21 36 34
Alt-Osdorf, Rugenbarg 8, Tel. 8 00 33 82
Verbilligte Karten im Kulturring der Jugend
Kartenverkauf über den SUNRISE SERVICE:
SUNRISE CONCERTBÜRO GmbH, Sierichstraße 54,
tel. Best. 2 79 40 50, mo.–fr. 11–18 Uhr
Kartenbestellung per Nachnahme

LE LENDEMAIN LA BATMOBILE DU DESSINATEUR-ESPION FILE LE LONG DES GRANDS BOULEVARDS...

HIII! JE VAIS VOIR LES **CLASH** EN CHAIR ET EN OS!! C'EST RUDEMENT CHIC DE M'AVOIR DONNÉ UNE INVITATION !!!

DITES, MOI AUSSI, PLUS TARD, JE PORTERAI UN MASQUE ET UN GRAND CHAPEAU COMME VOUS?! ET JE VEILLERAI QUAND LA VILLE DORT?! HEIN DITES!!

20H30. BACK-STAGE... MICK JONES DONNE UNE DERNIÈRE INTERVIEW...

OUI C'EST MOI QUI AIT ÉCRIT 'BRAND NEW CADILLAC', ET C'EST VINCE TAYLOR QUI L'A REPRIS...

C'EST À PEU PRÈS À CETTE ÉPOQUE QUE J'AI ÉCRIT 'PLEASE, PLEASE, ME'! ET AUSSI YELLOW SUBMARINE! ÉVIDEMMENT J'ÉTAIS ENCORE À L'ÉCOLE!! THAT'S ALL THANK YOU

ET JE COMBATTRAI LES FOURBES ET LES MÉCHANTS, HEIN DITES

OUI, MAIS ARRÊTE DE SAUTER COMME UNE PUCE!! N'OUBLIE PAS QUE JE SUIS EN MISSION SECRÈTE! AH, VOILÀ LE PALAIS DES SPODS !!

20H50. 'BACKSTAGE', LES CLASH S'APPRÊTENT À MONTER SUR SCÈNE...

HEM! LE SPECTACLE NE DEVRAIT PAS TARDER À COMMENCER...

Sandinista!

[UK CBS FSLN1/US EPIC 37037]

RELEASE DATE: UK 12 DECEMBER 1980/US JANUARY 1981
UK CHART PEAK: #19
US CHART PEAK: #24

JOE: By this time we'd travelled around the world and we wanted to do something that covered every sphere, every place and issue we'd seen. We were beaten with red hot sticks for singing about 7/11 stores [in the UK press], but we weren't parochial, we weren't little Englanders, we had the suss to embrace the world in all its weird varieties.

PAUL: Mick had his influences, I had mine, Joe had his and they'd be thrown in the bucket and stirred up. It was Mick who really tapped into the hip-hop thing and brought that in, some of which was technically difficult for me to master.

MICK: I always thought of it as being a record for people who were on oil rigs or Arctic stations, and not able to get to record shops regularly. It gave them something to listen to, and you didn't have to listen to it all in one go, you could dip in and out. Like a big book.

SIDE ONE:
The Magnificent 7
Hitsville UK
Junco Partner
Ivan Meets GI Joe
The Leader
Something About
  England

SIDE TWO:
Rebel Waltz
Look Here
The Crooked Beat
Somebody Got
  Murdered
One More Time
One More Dub

SIDE THREE:
Lightning Strikes
Up In Heaven
Corner Soul
Let's Go Crazy
If Music Could Talk
Sound of The
  Sinners

SIDE FOUR:
Police On My Back
Midnight Log
The Equaliser
The Call Up
Washington Bullets

SIDE FIVE:
Lose this Skin
Charlie Don't Surf
Mensforth Hill
Junkie Slip
Kingston Advice
The Street Parade

SIDE SIX:
Version City
Living In Fame
Silicone On
  Sapphire
Version Pardner
Career
  Opportunities
Shepherd's Delight

Joe Strummer (rhythm guitar, vocals), Mick Jones (guitar, vocals), Paul Simonon (bass, vocals), Topper Headon (drums, vocals), Mickey Gallagher (keyboards), Tymon Dogg (violin). Produced by The Clash, recorded and mixed by Bill Price, version mix by Mikey Dread. Engineered by Jerry Green at Wessex Studios, London, J.P. Nicholson at Electric Ladyland Studio, New York, Lancelot Maxie McKenzie at Channel One Studio, Kingston and Bill Price at Pluto Studio in Manchester and Power Station Studio, New York

Photographer Pennie Smith only took about six frames for what would become the cover image of *Sandinista!* This is one of them.

MICK: The lyrics had a lot of wit, there was a lot of different stuff going on with the lyrics, which lent itself to different musical styles. We were actually trying to reach out in different directions, trying to not be painted into a narrow corner, musically.

JOE: Mick Jones, he's the king arranger. He was always looking to do the new thing and in 1980 in New York that was rap. It was going off big time, coming out of Kurtis Blow's Sugar Hill Gang, WBLS [radio station] was busting out all over the city and we hooked into some of that vibe and made our own version of it.

MICK: I was so gone with the rap and hip-hop thing going on in New York that the others used to call me 'Whack-attack'. I'd walk around with a beatbox, wearing a baseball cap backwards and they used to constantly take the mick out of me. But they were open to all the musical suggestions I made and it wasn't only me making suggestions.

MICK: I can't remember what was going on in the studio. A lot of people having a party, I think.

PAUL: There are certain songs on there that I wouldn't have put on it, but I'm one of many members, you know. Silicone on Sapphire I don't understand, don't see the point of. To me it was just taking up space, but maybe puff-smoking people might find something to like about it.

TOPPER: I didn't enjoy doing *Sandinista!* so much, but only because I thought it should have been a double album.

PAUL: Joe and I would have settled for it being a double album but we had the scope for it to be whatever it would be.

MICK: The record company hadn't wanted us to do the 'Two For The Price of One' on *London Calling* and must have been exasperated when we suggested three for *Sandinista!*. So we stole the master tapes and held them in a safe place until negotiations were finished. They agreed it could be a triple album, but we had to take a cut in the royalties on the first couple of hundred thousand copies sold or something. I don't think it got there for ten years or so, but that was the way it went.

MICK: Then of course people thought there must be something wrong with it to be so cheap! You just can't win sometimes.

MICK: Later, a lot of people cited *Sandinista!* as an influence. I guess that was because it was so spread out and experimented with a lot of musical styles, had a lot of new ideas.

Sound of the Sinners

MICK: That was one of Joe's things. He built it up and said, 'Let's have a Gospel kind of thing', and we were able to do that by that time.

Somebody Got Murdered

JOE: The car park attendant in the World's End housing estate where I was living was murdered for five pounds. We had a phone call from Jack Nitzsche saying he needed a heavy rock number for a movie with Al Pacino, so I said OK. I hung up and went home and there was this guy in a pool of blood out by the parking kiosk. That night I wrote the lyric, gave it to Mick and he wrote the tune. We recorded it and Jack Nitzsche never called back.

TOPPER: We wanted a police dog or guard dog sound. My dog Battersea wouldn't let anyone hit me, so we went into the studio and I held onto him tight, and every time we wanted him to bark Joe would thump me. Each time Joe hit me, Battersea would go for him, so I had to hold on tight to the lead.

Charlie Don't Surf

JOE: Film was a big part of our cultural life. Somehow film seemed more important at that time. 'Charlie don't surf' was a line I pulled right off that film [Apocalypse Now]. It was like holding one end of a piece of string which had a song attached to it.

Stop The World (b-side of Call Up)

JOE: I was in the studio, it was down time, or the band weren't there and I was messing about on the organ, trying to play Green Onions, but couldn't figure out how it went. I got Topper to play along and just put down this thing because it sounded interesting, even though it wasn't Green Onions. I put the lyric to it back in England, just before it became a b-side.

Robert De Niro, left, with Joe. The Clash made a brief appearance as 'street punks' in Martin Scorcese's *King Of Comedy*, starring De Niro and Jerry Lewis, in 1980. Afterwards, the director talked about the band appearing in a project he was working on about the gangs of New York, but by the time he got around to making it – 2002 – the band were no more.

1981

'I don't remember having any holidays for the whole time we were a band. It was just one thing after another.' MICK

Sandinista! was released on 12 December 1980 in the UK as a triple album sold at the price of a single LP (reaching number 19 in the album chart) . It was released in America in January 1981 (reaching number 24 in the album chart). The triple-for-single deal that they had negotiated with CBS did them no favours, and they lost any chance of earning decent royalties. With debts mounting and the band becoming bored and disillusioned by Blackhill, the management contract was cancelled. Joe in particular wanted someone in charge who he could spark off. So it was welcome back, Bernie.

The wealth of new material written, recorded and released on *Sandinista!* meant that the band had an even longer set list to choose from on any one night.

Dear Batty,
    How are you?
Don't worry the bloke on the front is nothing to do with me. I just thought you'd like to see what a typical scottish dog looks like. Not much eh? See you soon
Lotsa luv Your Master

"BATTERSEA MUTFORD"

DOVER

KENT.

SCOTLAND contains a variety of scenery and interest unsurpassed anywhere in the British Isles. It is a land famous for its rolling hills and beautiful fishing rivers, colourful little towns and villages, long sea lochs and picturesque harbours. Between the Firths of Clyde and Forth lie Scotland's splendid capital, Edinburgh, and its commercial capital, Glasgow. Many towns such as Linlithgow and Stirling are reminders of Scotland's stormy history for centuries.
Published by John Hinde (Distributors) Ltd., Printed in Ireland

Good Luck from Scotland.

PAUL: After a couple of years working with Blackhill, Joe thankfully realized that something had to change, so he put his foot down and said I'm not going to do anything else [with them]. I'm glad he did.

PAUL: Joe wanted Bernie back because there was no excitement in the situation with Blackhill and Joe needed to have someone like Bernie around to give him confidence. At least there were ideas coming from another angle, which was what Bernie thrived on.

PAUL: I'd grown up a bit by then. So didn't play as many jokes on Bernie as I used to. Although once when we were on an aeroplane I sneaked under his seat and stole his shoes. When we got off the plane we had to meet some record company people, and Bernie went into the meeting without any shoes. After they'd started I went and threw them in to him, though.

JOE: When Bernie came back it was his idea to do a tour of big gigs.

PAUL: On a tour of big venues in Europe, we were in Germany on our way to a show when Mick says, 'I'm not going to do the show, and I want to go to New York.' Gerry the driver says, 'OK, we're going to New York' and carried on driving. We didn't, of course, but it cooled the row down that was going on with Mick.

MICK: Bernie came back on the scene because people thought that we'd gotten out of control and the first thing he wanted to do was book us for seven nights in New York.

ABOVE: As well as sending his parents postcards from abroad, Topper sent the above to his much-missed dog back home in the UK, named Battersea Mutford (he'd adopted him from the famous dogs' home).

RIGHT: One of Joe's favourite photographs of himself, taken by Pennie Smith, graced the front cover of the first edition of the *NME* for 1981. The magazine might not have enjoyed all of *Sandinista!*, but it knew the value of the band's appeal to its readership.

3 January 1981   **US $1.95 (by air)**   **25p**

ISSN 0028 6362

Aus 55c NZ 60c Den Kr 9.50 Fr NF 8.50
Ger Dm 3.80 Malaysia $2.25 Spn 125pts

NME
NEW MUSICAL EXPRESS

FEET FIRST INTO '81!
Neue Deutsche Musik
B 52s · Fire Engines
Screen Special

Joe Strummer refuses to get typecast/Pic: Pennie Smith

Despatches from the Clash zone; Strummer talks from the hip.

A RAP WITH JOE REPUBLIC ~ CENTRE PAGES

A-side: Hitsville UK (4:21)

[The Clash] Produced by The Clash

B-SIDE: RADIO ONE (6:17)

[Mikey Dread] Produced by Mikey Dread

US RELEASE B-SIDE: POLICE ON MY BACK (3:15)

[Eddy Grant] Produced by The Clash

RELEASED 16 JANUARY 1981
UK CHART PEAK: #56

MICK: I don't think we were ever bothered about what anybody said about anything we did. We started making 12-inch singles because that's what was happening in New York at the time, they were the kind of records people were making. That was what interested us.

Ready for business...

Impossible Mission Tour

LINE-UP: STRUMMER, JONES, SIMONON, HEADON

Support acts are not stated on tour posters or tickets; there were various local acts at different venues in different countries.

27 APR: Barcelona, Spain [venue unknown]
28 APR: Real Madrid basketball stadium, Madrid, Spain
30 APR: Cascais, Portugal [venue unknown]
1 MAY: Lisbon, Portugal [venue unknown]
2 MAY: Velodromo de Anoeta, San Sebastian, Spain
4 MAY: Bordeaux, France
5 MAY: Palais des Sports, Lyon, France .
6 MAY: Palais de Beaulieu, Lausanne, Switzerland
7 MAY: Zurich, Switzerland [venue unknown]
8 MAY: Hippodrome de Pantin, Paris, France
9 MAY: Palais St Sauveur, Lille, France
10 MAY: Japp Edenhall, Amsterdam, Holland
11 MAY: Forest National, Brussels, Belgium. Support acts included The Belle Stars and Vic Goddard & Subway Sect.
MAY 12: Musikhalle, Hamburg, Germany
MAY 14: Idrottshuset, Copenhagen, Denmark
MAY 15: The Scandinavium, Gothenburg, Sweden
MAY 16: Isstadion, Stockholm, Sweden
MAY 18: Eissporthalle, (West) Berlin, Germany
MAY 19: Circus Krone, Munich, Germany
MAY 21: Velodromo Vigorelli, Milan, Italy
MAY 22: San Remo, Italy [venue unknown]
MAY 23: Stadio Comunale, Florence, Italy

SONGS PLAYED:

London Calling / Safe European Home / This Is Radio Clash / Train In Vain / Washington Bullets / The Leader / Ivan Meets GI Joe / White Man In Hammersmith Palais / Clampdown / The Guns Of Brixton / Lightning Strikes / Corner Soul / Bankrobber / Somebody Got Murdered / The Magnificent Seven / One More Time / Spanish Bombs / Brand New Cadillac / The Street Parade / Charlie Don't Surf / Janie Jones / London's Burning / White Riot / Armagideon Time / Let's Go Crazy / Career Opportunities / Wrong 'Em Boyo / Junco Partner / I Fought The Law / Complete Control / The Call Up

An original poster for The Clash show in Gothenburg which actually took place a week later than shown here – on May 15. The Tour was so named because the band thought that they had an impossible job on their hands to play all the songs that they had available to them.

FOLLOWING PAGE: An original poster for the Spanish and Portuguese leg of the Impossible Mission Tour.

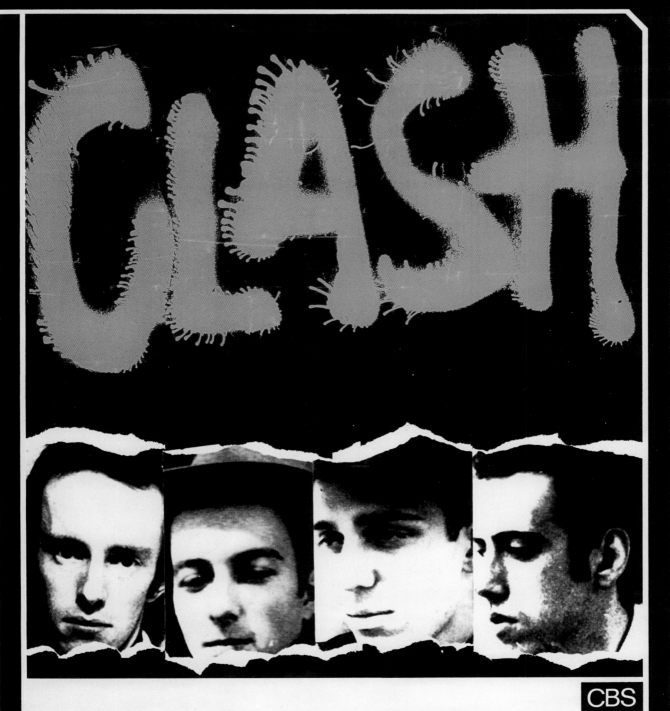

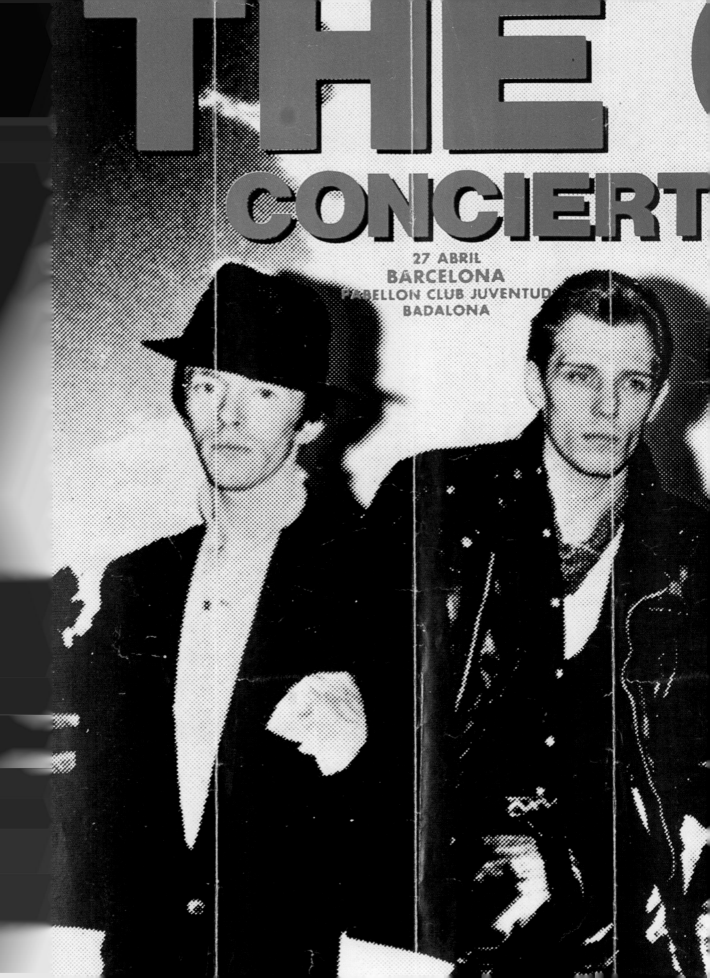

When the band played Guns Of Brixton, Paul sang the song (as he did on the recorded version, from *London Calling*) and Joe would play the bass. Paul would then play the second, rhythm guitar for the song and get to stand stage centre. He didn't often play like Pete Townshend as he'd said he'd always wanted, but he didn't exactly play like John Entwistle (who famously never moved onstage), either.

Topper's postcards home were often very dry and witty. Usually written while in a bus, plane or a car and on the move, his handwriting suffered from the motion of the vehicle in question. In this one (opposite) he finishes by writing a PS that says, 'If you can't read this, you're not the only one.'

Dear Everyone,
    We've missed
our flight and we've
got a three hour wait
Tomorrow we play Germany
Last night when we
played there was a
riot but we played on.
On German T.V. tomorrow to
20 million people. See you
soon. Lots of love
                    Nick
                    xxx
P.S. If you can't read this
your not the only ones.

MEXICHROME

Edit. Thill, S.A.
76, rue de la Senne - Bruxelles

Mr & Mrs. HEADON

DOVER.

ENGLAND.

LEFT: The Clash land in New York, ready to take the city, dressed in sombre black suits. The idea of playing the large, if scruffy, Bond's in New York's Times Square was a great PR idea that got even better when the authorities tried to cancel all the shows under health and safety regulations. When they arrived at their hotel, The Clash were on TV and radio in the city almost constantly.

RIGHT: Backstage at Bonds, L-R: Paul, Joe and Joe Ely, the Texan singer-songwriter who'd toured with the band several times in the USA and UK (on the 16 Tons Tour). When the gigs were announced as cancelled because too many tickets had been sold, there was a near riot in Times Square, which was covered by all the major and local news network TV and radio stations.

CLASH TAKE NEW YORK

JOE: When we played the residency at Bonds nightclub in Times Square, New York, I began to realize how the world really works. You can't go to a city like New York and take away the night life.

PAUL: The first night at Bonds we were closed down by the Fire Chief who believed that there would be too many people in the audience. But they'd sold the same number of tickets for a gig that happened the night before with a group called The Plasmatics, who blew a car up on stage!

JOE: We were booked for seven nights originally and, I have no proof of this, but I think some people called up the Fire Department, the Zoning Department, the This Department the That Department; there's an incredible amount of bureaucracy in a civilized country like America to prevent people from dancing or having fun, or even congregating. There had been such a heavy demand for tickets that the club box office had oversold the nights.

The Fire Department were tipped off and closed the whole thing down.

PAUL: There was a lot of politics going down in New York and a lot of club owners were pissed off that we were taking their business away. There was some weird stuff going on.

JOE: We decided to play out however many tickets had been sold for those gigs and we ended up doing 15 shows in a row, including a Saturday matinee for people under the age of the licensing laws.

PAUL: We stayed at the Iroquois Hotel, which is where James Dean used to stay when he was in New York. Just off the lobby was a barber who claimed to remember cutting Dean's hair and that he always used to sit on his doorstep and get in the way of customers. Joe and I used to get our hair cut there, of course.

Paul leaning on a Fender amplifier in a stairwell backstage at Bonds.

A-side: The Magnificent Seven (edit) (3:27)

[The Clash] Produced by The Clash

B-SIDE: THE MAGNIFICENT DANCE (EDIT) (3:25)

[The Clash] Produced by The Clash, re-mixed by Pepe Unidos

RELEASED 10 APRIL 1981
UK CHART PEAK: #34

JOE: We made an instrumental version of Magnificent Seven and WBLS radio played it to death, you couldn't go anywhere in New York that summer without hearing it. And that was us, weirdo white guys.

MICK: It was originally called The Magnificent Seven Rapper Clappers because we all clapped along to the track in overdub.

JOE: 'Vacuum cleaner sucks up budgie' was a *News Of The World* headline. I saw it when we were finishing the mix in England and stuck it on the end. The budgie came out alive, too.

A-side: The Magnificent Dance (12″ version) (5:36)

[The Clash] Produced by The Clash, re-mixed by
Pepe Unidos

B-SIDE: THE MAGNIFICENT SEVEN (12″ VERSION) (4:27)

[The Clash] Produced by The Clash

US RELEASE B-SIDE
THE COOL OUT (US 12″) (3:53)

[Strummer/Jones/Headon] Produced by The Clash,
re-mixed by Pepe Unidos

RELEASED 10 APRIL 1981
NO CHART POSITION

MICK: Hip-hop was just starting and was the dance music of the day. Magnificent Dance was another signpost to the direction we were going in. We always took on board the music that was happening around us, made it part of our thing.

The CLASH

THE TOMORROW SHOW

The CLASH

THE TOMORROW SHOW 5/6/1981

— A —

THE MAGNIFICENT SEVEN

The CLASH

THE TOMORROW SHOW 5/6/1981

— B —

THIS IS RADIO CLASH

THE CLASH
THE TOMORROW SHOW

Recorded on 5th June 1981 for 'The Tomorrow TV Show' with Tom Snyder

SIDE A:
The Magnificent Seven

SIDE B:
This Is Radio Clash

LEFT: And on the eighth day, The Clash conquered the whole of America via the TV's NBC network. On the afternoon of 5 June, the band took the short trip to the RCA building where they performed Magnificent Seven (the bootleg single shown opposite's 'A' side) and This Is Radio Clash ('B' side) while graffiti artist Futura 2000 sprayed Clash on a specially erected backdrop of the set. Then they went to play at Bonds.

RIGHT: Playing the Bonds residency meant fifteen shows in a row for almost half a month. The monotony was offset only slightly by being asked to appear on TV shows and at radio stations in and around the city.

JOE: We took a stand and it nearly killed us. There's something strangely monotonous about getting up in the same hall, playing a gig, 15 nights in a row. It's just not rock 'n' roll. You should be getting on a bus, driving a thousand miles and playing; somehow you get energy from the travelling or the newness of each place.

MICK: We were really together, our playing was pretty hot and we were confident. We were enjoying it most nights. Things were pretty good at the time.

JOE: Topper had the most physical job of the unit, to beat the drumkit. He had no help from beatboxes, it was just him on the skins. His job was by far the hardest and he did it brilliantly, 'cos mental strength was needed as well. It was hard run that one, but there was no way out of it. We were presented with a situation that had escalated out of control, we were on the News. It was great checking into New York and finding yourself on the News.

PAUL: One night after a gig I went out with one of our security guys, Gerry, to drink Sake. We drank so much Sake that there were hundreds of those little Sake bottles all around us and I was so sloshed I had to say, 'Gerry, I've got to get back to the hotel'. So he drove me back and I crawled up the stairs. The next day I saw him and asked how he was, and he said 'Terrible'. He'd gone

back to drink more Sake, met some people who invited him to a party and said, 'OK, I'll follow you' – and drove after them. He followed them for hours, until the car in front pulled over and someone he'd never seen before got out and asked him why he was following them. He'd been following the wrong car. Then he didn't remember anything else but fell asleep on a freeway somewhere. His car was all bashed up, but he was fine.

MICK: It was the start of the rap thing happening in New York and we fell in with some graffiti artists who made us a big banner with 'The Clash' on it, which we unveiled from the top of the building we were playing at.

JOE: Some nights I suppose we were good. I can't think that we were good every night.

MICK: We had lots of different support acts for the Bonds residency: one night Grandmaster Flash played and the crowd were booing them and we

were really upset by it. We always tried to bring what was going on as well as what had gone before into what we were doing. But I guess they were all there to see The Clash.

PAUL: We did some filming for Martin Scorsese who was making *King Of Comedy*. It was nice to be asked. But I couldn't see the point of it really, all we did was stand around on a street corner for an hour, drinking beer. Then someone walked past, we howled at him and he put his hand up. That was it.

MICK: We got to see some of New York and feel a part of it for the first time. I quite wanted to stay.

JOE: Because we were in New York for so long we tried to use the days, too. Don Letts was there and we made a film, *Clash On Broadway*, which eventually, by some insane twist, got burned in an argument about rental debts in a negative warehouse. Don also filmed our video for *This Is Radio Clash* while we were there and all kinds of great stuff.

PAUL: Scorsese had some ideas about making a film with us. He suggested making a film about gangs of New York that he wanted us to be involved in, but by the time he'd got any further with it, we'd split up.

JOE: At the time Scorsese was shooting *King Of Comedy* and he wanted a street gang to stand in the street and abuse Jerry Lewis and De Niro. We didn't really cotton on to what was wanted, 'cos he was too busy to *say* what he wanted, but it was a long tracking shot down the streets of New York, with thousands of people moving along the pavements. I realize now that if it were to happen today, I'd have jumped on De Niro's back or something, or tripped Lewis. Camera hogging, it's called. You gotta learn it, but at that time we were just standing around like we didn't know what to do. Only the back of my head is in that film even though I get a credit. Anyway, Scorsese wanted to hook up with us 'cos he was working on a film called *Gangs Of New York*...

MICK: I think we'd started to work on the next album while we were there because I remember playing Know Your Rights at Bonds. I guess we must have started a couple of songs for *Combat Rock* by then.

PAUL: I met Andy Warhol while we were there and he was just some bloke ambling around, really. He was kind of like David Bowie in a Warhol film.

JOE: We didn't have limos everywhere or stuff like that, we just never got into that stuff. We were happy with what we had, a bag of weed and a few beers and we were sorted.

LEFT: The sleevenotes for Ellen Foley's second album, *Spirit of St Louis*, list the producer as 'My boyfriend'. Mick Jones produced and co-wrote six of the songs with Joe. Paul and Topper also contributed their time and skills to the recording sessions. Joe's old pal Tymon Dogg wrote three of the songs and old Clash soundmen Bill Price and Jeremy Green also worked on the sessions. it was almost a regular Clash album, but with Foley – who rose to fame in 1977 duetting with Meatloaf on Paradise By The Dashboard Light – as singer in place of Joe.

RIGHT: Producer Mick Jones takes a break with singer Ellen Foley.

LEFT: Foley's debut album *Nightout* had been produced by former Mott singer Ian Hunter and guitarist Mick Ronson. Mick Jones also co-produced Hunter's *Short Back 'N Sides* album this year (though no other Clash members contributed to the recording).L-R: Mick Ronson, Mick Jones, Ian Hunter.

Clash in Paris

LINE-UP: STRUMMER, JONES, SIMONON, HEADON

Support acts: Wah!, The Beat

23 SEPT: Théâtre Mogador
24 SEPT: Théâtre Mogador
25 SEPT: Théâtre Mogador
26 SEPT: Théâtre Mogador
27 SEPT: Théâtre Mogador
28 SEPT: Théâtre Mogador
29 SEPT: Théâtre Mogador
30 SEPT: Théâtre Mogador

Not content with 'taking' New York, The Clash decided that a residency in another great, foreign city would be a good thing to do. And so Paris had the pleasure of The Clash for a week of gigs at an old theatre. The band used the dates to plan the next UK tour in support of the release of This is Radio Clash, which began in early October and the set lists for these dates and those are almost identical.

SONGS PLAYED:

Broadway / One More Time / This Is Radio Clash / Know your Rights / Should I Stay Or Should I Go? / Charlie Don't Surf / The Guns Of Brixton / White Man In Hammersmith Palais / The Magnificent Seven / Train In Vain / Ivan Meets GI Joe / Clash City Rockers / Koka Kola / Bankrobber / The Leader / Junco Partner / Graffiti Rap / Washington Bullets / Ghetto Defendent / Complete Control / Clampdown / I Fought The Law / Somebody Got Murdered / London Calling / Police & Thieves / Jimmy Jazz / Lightning Strikes / Overpowered By Funk / Armagideon Time / Safe European Home / Innoculated City / Brand New Cadillac / Spanish Bombs / Janie Jones / White Riot / Street Parade / Hit The Road Jack

RIGHT: Joe backstage with Ranking Roger, the lead singer of support band The Beat.

LEFT: Joe's backstage pass for the Paris residency.

FOLLOWING PAGE: One night from the residency at the Théâtre Mogador.

A-side: This is Radio Clash (4:10)

[The Clash] Produced by The Clash

B-SIDE: RADIO CLASH (4:10)

[The Clash] Produced by The Clash

UK 12" RELEASE B-SIDE:
OUTSIDE BROADCAST (7:22)

[The Clash] Produced by The Clash

RADIO 5 (3:38)

[The Clash] produced by The Clash

RELEASED 20 NOVEMBER 1981
UK CHART PEAK: #47

MICK: There were two versions, one on either side and a different set of lyrics to each. It's all about information; we had too many boxes everywhere!

MICK: For the video we filmed ourselves dancing on the roof of Bonds, dancing around with Futura 2000.

A1797

82876876282/15

Radio Clash Tour

LINE-UP: STRUMMER, JONES, SIMONON, HEADON

Support acts were Theatre of Hate plus local acts

5 OCT: Apollo, Manchester
6 OCT: Apollo, Manchester
7 OCT: Apollo, Glasgow, Scotland, extra support act Plastic Files
8 OCT: Apollo, Glasgow, Scotland
10 OCT: Royal Hall, Bridlington Spa
11 OCT: Lyceum, Sheffield
12 OCT: Royal Court, Liverpool
15 OCT: Coliseum, Saint Austell
18 OCT: Lyceum Ballroom, London, extra support Stimulin
19 OCT: Lyceum Ballroom, London
20 OCT: Lyceum Ballroom, London
21 OCT: Lyceum Ballroom, London
22 OCT: Lyceum Ballroom, London
25 OCT: Lyceum Ballroom, London
26 OCT: Lyceum Ballroom, London

SONGS PLAYED:
Broadway / One More Time / Radio Clash / Know Your Rights / The Guns Of Brixton / Protex Blue / Train In Vain / The Magnificent Seven / White Man In Hammersmith Palais / Ivan Meets GI Joe / Clash City Rockers / Koka Kola / Junco Partner / The Leader / Spanish Bombs / Complete Control / Ghetto Defendant / Somebody Got Murdered / Clampdown / London Calling / Charlie Don't Surf / Police & Thieves / Safe European Home / Janie Jones / Street Parade / Armagideon Time / Washington Bullets / I Fought The Law / Should I Stay Or Should I Go? / Stay Free / Brand New Cadillac / Innoculated City / Career Opportunities / Bankrobber / London's Burning / White Riot / Graffiti Rap / Julie's In The Drug Squad (4th Lyceum gig only)

Back in the UK, the band played large venues culminating in another residency, this time at London's Lyceum near The Strand.
Backstage pass, seen left.

1982

'I lost it, really, on the tour of the Far East. I was standing in a lift with Joe and he's saying, "How can I sing all these anti-drug songs with you stoned out of your head behind me?" There was a lot of friction building up.' TOPPER

At the beginning of 1982 The Clash flew to Japan to begin a two-month tour of the Far East and Pacific Rim. After spending March and April writing, rehearsing and recording a new album, they played a festival in Holland on 20 May, and nine days later began an American tour with a new drummer, having sacked Topper. The band toured America for a month and then returned to tour the UK for a month, before heading back to the States once more for almost two months of more live dates. They hadn't taken a break from writing, recording or touring in over five years and the strain was beginning to show.

At the end of the Far East Tour, in February 1982, photographer Pennie Smith flew to Thailand and conducted a shoot with the band in the countryside. One of the frames became the cover for the *Combat Rock* LP.

Far East Tour

LINE-UP: STRUMMER, JONES, SIMONON, HEADON
Support acts not detailed

24 JAN: Shibuya Kohkaido, Tokyo, Japan
25 JAN: Festival Hall, Osaka, Japan
27 JAN: Sun Plaza Tokyo, Japan
28 JAN: Sun Plaza Tokyo, Japan
29 JAN: Sun Plaza Tokyo, Japan
30 JAN: Kosein-Kaiken Hall, Tokyo, Japan
1 FEB: Sun Plaza Hall, Tokyo, Japan
2 FEB: Festival Hall, Osaka, Japan
5 FEB: Logan Campbell Centre, Auckland, New Zealand
6 FEB: Logan Campbell Centre, Auckland, New Zealand
7 FEB: Wellington Town Hall, New Zealand
8 FEB: Town Hall, Christchurch, New Zealand
11 FEB: Capitol Theatre, Sydney, Australia
12 FEB: Capitol Theatre, Sydney, Australia
13 FEB: Capitol Theatre, Sydney, Australia
14 FEB: Capitol Theatre, Sydney, Australia
16 FEB: Capitol Theatre, Sydney, Australia
17 FEB: Capitol Theatre, Sydney, Australia
18 FEB: Capitol Theatre, Sydney, Australia
20 FEB: Cloudland Ballroom, Brisbane, Australia
22 FEB: The Barton Town Hall, Adelaide, Australia
23 FEB: Festival Hall, Melbourne
25 FEB: AC Hall, Hong Kong
27 FEB: Thammasat University, Bangkok, Thailand

SONGS PLAYED:
Should I Stay or Should I Go? / One More Time / Safe European Home / Know Your Rights / Train In Vain / White Man in Hammersmith Palais / The Magnificent Seven / The Guns Of Brixton / Charlie Don't Surf / The Leader / Ivan Meets GI Joe / Junco Partner / Broadway / Stay Free / London Calling / Janie Jones / Somebody Got Murdered / Clampdown / This Is Radio Clash / Brand New Cadillac / Armagideon Time / London's Burning / Clash City Rockers / Koka Kola / Career Opportunities / Complete Control / White Riot / Brand New Cadillac / Jimmy Jazz / Tommy Gun / Police On My Back / Fujiyama Mama / I'm So Bored With The USA / I Fought The Law / Garageland / Washington Bullets / The Call Up

On the Far East tour, the band played 25 dates in a little over a month, more than 6,000 miles from home.

Sumo or wrestling of ancient form is regarded as the national sports of Japan. A ritual ceremony consisting of hand-clapping and stamping of feet precedes each sumo bout.
Sumo
Lucha japonesa llamada Sumo

Postcard, handwritten:

Dear Mum & Dad,
Having great time and playing better than ever before. I now weigh 9st everyone says I look like a teenager again. Really miss you alot. Hope Battys o.k. This moment I'm in transit from TOKYO to NEW ZEALAND doing a press conference in Sydney. The lack of phone calls is due to the exact opposite times over. Ie 5 in the morning is ~~the~~ 5pm there. Love you always don't work too hard. can when I come back. You wont have to at all

Mr + Mrs HEADON
DOVER
KENT
ENGLAND

相撲──相撲は日本の国技である。巨大な体と体がぶつかり会い、勝負をきそい合う。写真左上は土俵入りの風景。その他は激突した勝負の瞬間。

LEFT: Topper gets some wardrobe assistance from Kosmo Vinyl in Japan. The drummer was the official representative of Pearl drums, which is why there are Pearl logos on his kimono-style jacket.

ABOVE: On landing in Japan the band insisted that Topper clean up his act, or else leave. This postcard was one of four sent to his family on the same day, just after landing in the Far East.

JOE: I can't remember what happened… I think we went to Australia, played seven nights in Sydney, and also played two or three nights in New Zealand. We played Brisbane, Perth, Hong Kong, Bangkok and then we came home. [they also played Adelaide, Melbourne and Perth in Australia].

PAUL: The Far East Tour was great, especially going to Japan for the first time. It really was like landing on another planet. In Australia we stayed at the Sheraton in the dodgy Kings Cross area of Sydney – Mick told me The Beatles had stayed there – and when we arrived I went straight to my room to catch up on some sleep and there were cockroaches everywhere. I managed to get some sleep anyway, but was woken up by a knock at the door. Three aborigines were standing there wanting a chat. They asked if they could come up on our stage to talk about their situation. So I got Joe and we had a meeting and of course said yes. We realized the power that we had 'cos we could let these guys talk to people who wouldn't normally pay any attention to them. But when we played New South Wales, while one of the guys was on stage giving his talk, the police were at his house, beating up his wife. I didn't really enjoy Australia, probably because of that.

On arrival in Tokyo, Japanese fans bombarded the band with letters, messages, presents, flowers and polite applause. Mick recalled that it was kind of like being in The Beatles in the 1960s, a fantastic reception from polite but adoring fans. Joe kept a diary of set lists (bottom), because ones for gigs had to be written on larger pieces of paper (right); the number of songs they played was often more than thirty.

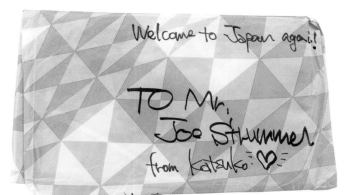

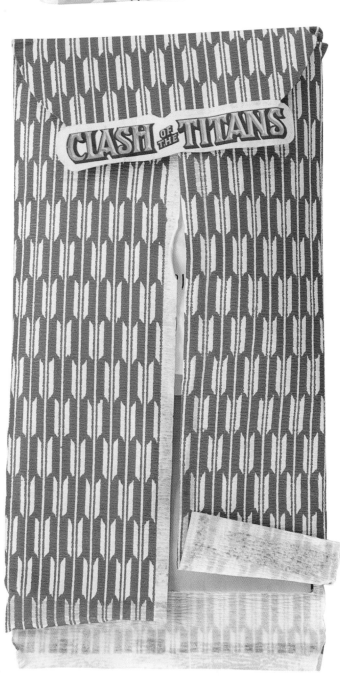

JOE: Topper's health by this time was going downhill. He'd got addicted to heroin. In the jazz days the saxophonist would be addicted to heroin, like Charlie Parker. The nature of the instrument means it's much better to be floating over the music, doing your thing, but it doesn't suit drumming, which is like nailing a nail into the floor. It's a precise thing. The beats have to be there and when Topper got addicted, he couldn't play anymore. It doesn't work with drums.

MICK: It was pretty crazy when we arrived in Japan. I'd flown there from New York, having stopped off in Alaska, and when I got there Paul was wandering around the foyer, Joe was upset and something had gone on with Topper in the elevator. It felt very strange — we were chased around like we were The Beatles or something, with lots of screaming and people throwing presents to us. It was beautiful.

TOPPER: I was out of control. I remember being sick on Buddy Holly's grave, which didn't go down too well [on the previous US tour]. I was a Keith Moon fan, you know, live fast, die young, and I lost the plot completely.

MICK: On our way to New Zealand after Japan we stopped for an afternoon in Australia and were all thrown out of the hotel for playing our music too loud. We'd only stopped off there for a couple of hours yet we managed to get banned from the best hotel in Sydney.

JOE: While we were in Thailand Paul picked up some kind of illness that knocked him out. But that was after the gig at Thammasat University, which has a very heavy history of student riots. Quite a few people had been killed there in the past while protesting.

PAUL: I had a weird time in Thailand because after the show I met my old history teacher from school — he'd written the answers to our 'O' Level questions on the blackboard because he'd felt sorry for us. He was living in Thailand, so he drove me around Bangkok while I was there and showed me the place. I jumped into a puddle at one point and a swarm of flies covered me, then I got sick and had to lie in a hospital for a week. Joe would turn up with these monks, which was odd.

One of Pennie Smith's images from the Thailand shoot, hand-tinted by Paul.

A-side: Know Your Rights (3:40)

[The Clash] Produced by The Clash, mixed by Glyn Johns

B-SIDE: FIRST NIGHT BACK IN LONDON (2:59)

[Strummer/Jones/Simonon] Produced by The Clash

RELEASED 23 APRIL 1982
UK CHART PEAK: #43
NOT RELEASED IN THE USA

MICK: Know Your Rights was one of the earliest songs we wrote for that album. It came together as we were touring the Far East, as did a few others.

JOE: Know Your Rights was a great tune from Mick that could have been a lot better. I mean the lyrics and all that stuff; it was supposed to be ironic but nobody understood that, which still makes me angry. But I think the backing track, the tune, the playing on it, are great, just not the lyrics or the singing. I love the swinging, rockabilly sound on it.

A **KNOW YOUR RIGHTS**
MIXED BY GLYN JOHNS

B **FIRST NIGHT BACK IN LONDON**
MIXED BY MICK JONES

PHOTO BY PENNIE SMITH
TINTING BY PAUL SIMONON
SLEEVE BY ARTISTS OF FORTUNE

CBS
A 2309

LEFT: Joe and Mick in the summer of 1982 in Los Angeles. Joe's ukelele suggests a return to his protest song-playing, busking days – which he'd return to in earnest a couple of years later. The final, non-Mick and non-Topper line-up undertook an acoustic, busking tour of the UK, playing in the streets of English towns in 1985. It was to be the final Clash tour ever.

ABOVE: Five years after their song about the former call girl Madam Janie Jones was released on their debut album, Janie released a single produced by Joe, of a song written by Joe and Mick and on which Mick, Joe and Paul played. Recorded at the end of 1982, Blockheads drummer Charley Charles played instead of Topper, and the band were credited as The Lash. It was later included in *The Clash On Broadway* box set.

MICK: In Thailand we only did one gig, but ended up staying for two weeks after Paul got ill. It was on the photo shoot for the *Combat Rock* cover, and Paul jumped in what he thought was a puddle but was actually some kind of black mud with loads of flies in it. He was in an old colonial-style hospital with a tropical disease. Joe and I got friendly with some monks who wore orange robes and we took them to see Paul in hospital, and they were really excited because he had a shower in his hospital room. Then the monks started coming to the hospital to have showers, loads of them queuing up to get in the shower. We had a nice couple of weeks' holiday in Thailand and then went home.

JOE: When we got back to England we went to a studio in West London and began working on the material that would become *Combat Rock*. Then we went back to New York to record it, at Electric Ladyland studio. But by this time we were all getting pretty tired because all this stuff had gone down in the space of four or five years and we'd released hours and hours of long-playing material at a rate that doesn't bear thinking about in this day and age.

MICK: We rehearsed in a kind of squat hall in West London and hired the Rolling Stones' mobile studio to park outside. We ran leads out to it and recorded the demos there.

JOE: I think we should have taken a year off, but we didn't think in those terms then. If we'd recharged our batteries the band would have still been going today, perhaps.

'Mick, Joe and Paul didn't like touring because they behaved as if they were businessmen. I loved it because I'd misbehave and do all the mad stuff, usually with the road crew. The band ended up banning me from hanging out with the road crew because whenever they'd get a damages bill they'd talk to the crew who'd say, "Well, Topper was with us. . ."'
TOPPER

A-side: Rock the Casbah (3:41)

[Headon] Produced by The Clash, re-mixed by
Mick Jones

B-SIDE: LONG TIME JERK (5:08)
[Strummer/Jones/Simonon] Produced by Mick Jones

UK 12" RELEASE B-SIDE:
MUSTAPHA DANCE (4:26)
[Strummer/Jones/ Headon] Produced by Mick Jones

RELEASED 11 JUNE 1982
UK CHART PEAK: #30
US CHART PEAK: #8

TOPPER: I wrote Rock the Casbah – the music, not the lyrics. One day I
went into the studio on my own because I don't actually know what
notes I'm playing, so rather than try to tell everyone what to play I went
and recorded piano, and then the drums and then the bass. I was thinking that it would just, you know, show them the way it could go but they
all said 'great, let's keep it'. Mick put guitar on it, Joe put the vocals on
and it was done.

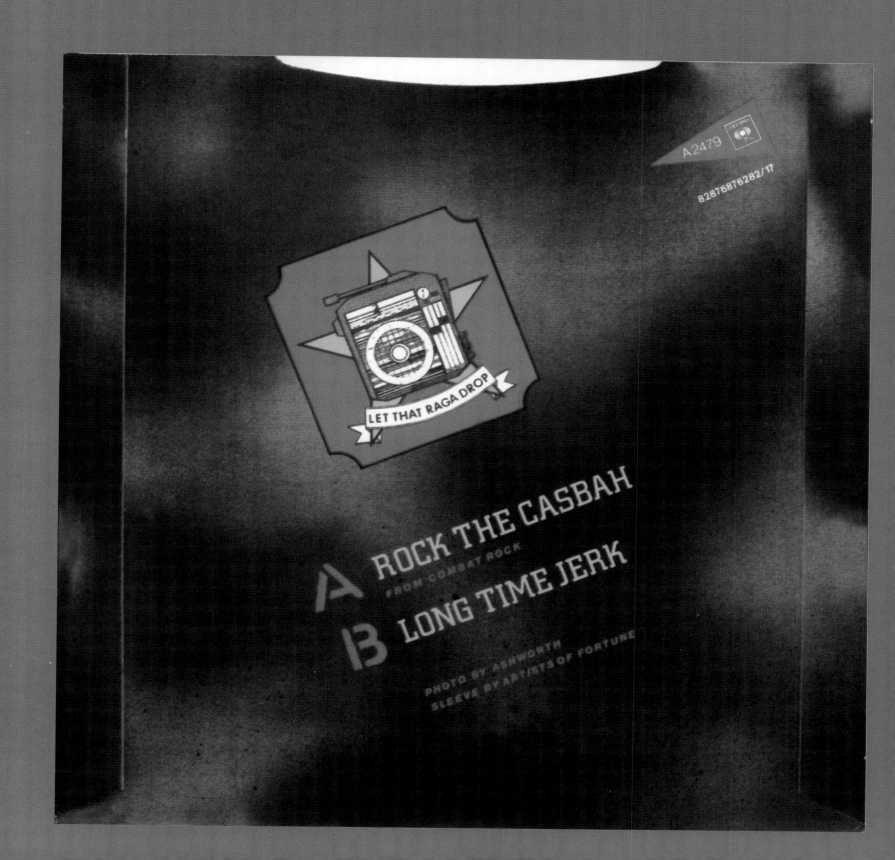

LET THAT RAGA DROP

A2479

82876876282/17

A ROCK THE CASBAH
FROM COMBAT ROCK

B LONG TIME JERK

PHOTO BY ASHWORTH
SLEEVE BY ARTISTS OF FORTUNE

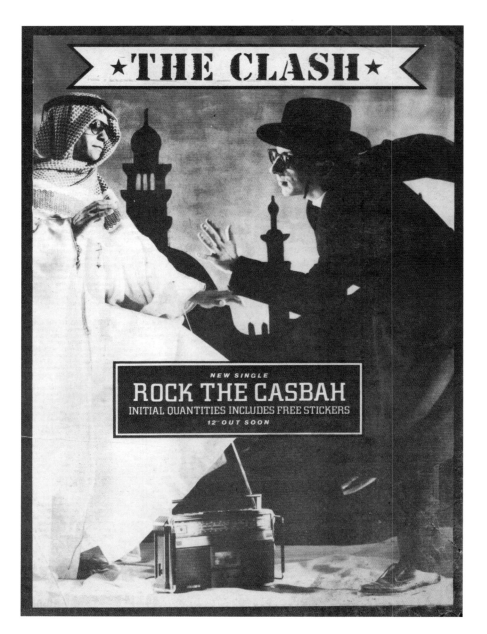

An original magazine advert for the single release of Rock the Casbah. A different photo was used on the single sleeve.

MAKING COMBAT ROCK

JOE: I think we made *Combat Rock* really quickly. I don't remember being in the studio for too long, maybe because they weren't joyful sessions and we couldn't see a way forward. Maybe we'd run out of operative juices at the time but I think it was all over pretty quickly. The mind closes off things, right? And I don't have too much of a memory of those sessions.

MICK: Things were starting to get a bit silly around then. Bernie was saying, 'Make a New Orleans record' and I was saying, 'Huh? I want it to be a rock 'n' roll album'. It kind of threw me, but we all tried to do some New Orleans rhythms at first. None of us seemed to really be communicating and it was all driving us a bit crazy, I think. Nobody seemed to be enjoying it any more.

PAUL: Mick did some mixing on the tapes but I don't think any of us were particularly pleased with it. I think at that stage Mick's guitar turned into a bassoon or something. I don't know, it just wasn't a guitar any more and that was sort of odd. Maybe he got bored of playing guitar – so he had various bits of equipment which would make his guitar sound like a harpsichord or whatever he wanted it to sound like. It was almost an orchestra but I don't know that he completely understood how to use it.

MICK: Well, the others said it; they said, 'You can mix it', and I was like, 'Oh shit!' And it was this big, sprawling mess at the time so I was in a bit of a mood for a while about it, but I think it worked out right for everybody in the end.

TOPPER: After recording *Combat Rock* and having played on it, written the song and been involved from beginning to end – that's when I felt that I was really part of the band.

MICK: We finished off recording *Combat Rock* and tried to mix it as we were going along on that Far Eastern tour. We booked studios in Australia and after the gigs we were totally dehydrated and taking salt tablets and trying to record, but it ground to a halt. We hadn't stopped since after *Sandinista*. We had too much material and it was a sprawling mess but Glyn Johns took hold of it and made it into something presentable.

PAUL: The thing with Mick is, he's an evening person, so we'd be hanging around outside the hotel waiting for Mick to get up, and it did wear you down. But then again, he'd always been like that; nothing had changed. I suppose as we got older we got more impatient with it.

MICK: It wasn't as focused or as well put together as it might have been, but in the end, who cares? What I'm saying is, we have a better life now because of the way it was.

JOE: *Combat Rock* has some of the best tunes that we ever made on it. Straight To Hell was one of our absolute masterpieces. But the band had to shatter after that record.

PAUL: All I really remember from recording *Combat Rock* is having a two-hour argument with Mick about the level of the bass on Know Your Rights. I wanted it to be a bit louder and deeper like a reggae sort of sound, so it would match up to the guitar, but Mick had his own idea and so we had a stand-up argument for two hours. Everyone else was just walking around, waiting for us to finish.

MICK: While we were in Australia we tried to record a few songs after the shows, so we'd be downing salt tablets 'cos we were so sweaty and then trying to play and mix tracks. But I began to realize that I couldn't mix at all, then.

Combat Rock

[UK CBS FMLN2/US EPIC FE 37689]

RELEASED UK 14 MAY 1982/US 28 MAY 1982
UK CHART PEAK: #2
US CHART PEAK: #7

Writing and recording of demos for the songs that would eventually be released as *Combat Rock* had begun in late 1981, at EAR studios in Latimer Road, West London, using a mobile unit. While in the Far East the band tried to record after gigs at various studios, but the conditions proved impossible. Mick was given the fifteen tracks that had been 'finished' to mix and after failing to come up with anything he liked, called the band to New York to re-do the numbers in their favourite studio, Electric Ladyland. It was Bernie who called in Glyn Johns to finish the mixes. Originally the album had a working title of Rat Patrol From Fort Bragg. Beat poet Allan Ginsberg contributed a voice-over to Ghetto Defendant, which he wrote in the studio with the band as they recorded.

SIDE ONE:
Know Your Rights
Car Jamming
Should I Stay or
  Should I Go
Rock the Casbah
Red Angel Dragnet
Straight To Hell

SIDE TWO:
Overpowered By
  Funk
Atom Tan
Sean Flynn
Ghetto Defendant
Inoculated City
Death Is A Star

Joe Strummer (guitar, vocals), Mick Jones (guitar, vocals), Paul Simonon (bass), Topper Headon (drums). Produced by The Clash. Recorded at EAR Studios, London, and Electric Ladyland Studio, New York. Mixed by Glyn Johns

Rock the Casbah

JOE: We found that whenever we'd play a tune on the *Combat Rock* sessions, it would be six minutes, minimum. After a few days of this, Bernie came down the studio and I think he heard 'Sean Flynn' and he said, 'Does everything have to be as long as a raga?' From then on everything we did we called a raga. I got back to the Iroquois Hotel [in New York] that night and wrote on the typewriter, 'The King told the boogie men You gotta let that raga drop.' I looked at it and for some reason I started to think about what someone had told me earlier, that you got lashed for owning a disco album in Iran. So I transferred that line from Bernie, to these religious leaders who tried to stop people from listening to music.

PAUL: When Casbah came out I think Mick might have been a bit annoyed 'cos it was Topper's song. I might be wrong.

Another Pennie Smith shot from the *Combat Rock* cover session in Thailand.

Should I Stay or Should I Go

MICK: It wasn't about anybody specific and it wasn't pre-empting my leaving The Clash. It was just a good rockin' song, our attempt at writing a classic. When we were just playing, that was the sort of stuff we'd play.

Red Angel Dragnet

JOE: It was in the papers at the time, the shooting of Frankie Melvin — it was a big scene. For some reason, back at the hotel I'd run out of writing paper and only had Iroquois envelopes. I wrote the lyric down the middle of the envelope and it started to flow, so I continued writing round the edge of the envelope in a spiral. I ended up writing round the edge three times. I asked Paul, 'What do you think of this?' and he moved the envelope round and round to read it. He was looking at me out of the corner of his eye, thinking, 'Joe's flipped'.

Ghetto Defendant

JOE: I asked Ginsberg for a word once, but it was just one word. He wrote his own bit for Ghetto Defendant but he had to ask us what the names of punk dances were and I said, 'Well, you've got your slam dance'. He did it on the spot; it was good.

Straight to Hell

TOPPER: Mick came up with that guitar line and you couldn't put a rock beat to it, so I started messing around with the snare. Basically it's a bossa nova.

JOE: It was New Year's Eve the day after we'd recorded the backing track. I'd written the lyric staying up all night at the Iroquois. I went down to Electric Ladyland and put the vocal down on tape — we finished at about twenty to midnight. We took the E train from the Village up to Times Square, because the Iroquois is off Times Square. I'll never forget coming out of the Times Square subway exit, just before midnight, into a hundred billion people, and I knew we'd just done something great.

Casbah Club USA + UK Tours

LINE-UP: STRUMMER, JONES, SIMONON, CHIMES

With Topper sacked, the band recruited Terry Chimes once more as drummer. Support acts in the USA on some dates were The (English) Beat, and in the UK Southern Death Cult, Under Two Flags and Pearl Harbour

29 MAY: Convention Hall, Asbury Park NJ
30 MAY: Convention Hall, Asbury Park NJ
31 MAY: Convention Hall, Asbury Park NJ
2 JUN: Fox Theater, Atlanta GA
4 JUN: The Warehouse, New Orleans LA
5 JUN: Hofheinz Pavilion, Houston TX
6 JUN: The Bronco Bowl, Dallas TX
8 JUN: City Coliseum, Austin TX
9 JUN: City Coliseum, Austin TX
10 JUN: Civic Auditorium, San Francisco CA
12 JUN: Golden Hall, San Diego, CA
13 JUN: Mesa Community Center, Phoenix AR
14 JUN: Hollywood Palladium, Los Angeles CA
15 JUN: Hollywood Palladium, Los Angeles CA
17 JUN: Hollywood Palladium, Los Angeles CA
18 JUN: Hollywood Palladium, Los Angeles CA
19 JUN: Hollywood Palladium, Los Angeles CA
20 JUN: County Bowl, Santa Barbara CA
22 JUN: Civic Auditorium, San Francisco CA
23 JUN: Civic Auditorium, San Francisco CA
26 JUN: Kerrisdale Arena, Vancouver, Canada
28 JUN: Maxbell Arena, Calgary, Canada
29 JUN: Kinsmon Fieldhouse, Edmonton, Canada

CASBAH CLUB UK TOUR

10 JUL: Fair Deal, Brixton, London
11 JUL: Fair Deal, Brixton, London
12 JUL: Stoke Mandeville Hospital Sports Stadium, Aylesbury, Buckinghamshire. A 'charity' gig for the spinal injuries unit.

SONGS PLAYED:

London Calling / Car Jamming / Career Opportunities / Know Your Rights / The Magnificent Seven / Ghetto Defendant / Clash City Rockers / Should I Stay or Should I Go? / Brand New Cadillac / Bankrobber / Somebody Got Murdered / Rock the Casbah / Complete Control / Clampdown / The Guns Of Brixton / I Fought the Law / Police On My Back / Armagideon Time / Jimmy Jazz / Janie Jones / Safe European Home / Train In Vain / Police & Thieves / Garageland / Clash City Rockers / Spanish Bombs / Radio Clash / Wrong 'Em Boyo / Charlie Don't Surf (UK only) / Pressure Drop (UK only) / I'm So Bored With The USA (UK only)

An original poster for the sixth date of the US leg of the Casbah Club Tour.

13 JUL: Victoria Hall, Hanley, Stoke-on-Trent
14 JUL: City Hall, Newcastle
15 JUL: City Hall, Newcastle
17 JUL: St Georges Hall, Bradford
18 JUL: Bingley Hall, Birmingham
19 JUL: Assembly Rooms, Derby
20 JUL: De Montfort Hall, Leicester
22 JUL: Leisure Centre, Irvine
23 JUL: Playhouse, Edinburgh
24 JUL: Ice Rink, Inverness,
25 JUL: Playhouse, Edinburgh
26 JUL: University, Leeds
27 JUL: Arts Centre, Poole
28 JUL: Guildhall, Portsmouth
30 JUL: Fair Deal, Brixton, London
31 JUL: Brighton Centre, Brighton
2 AUG: Locarno, Bristol
3 AUG: Locarno, Bristol

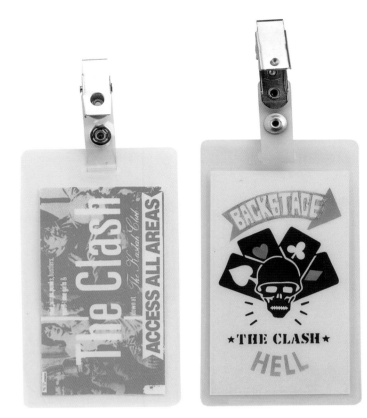

**Original backstage
passes for the tour.**

LIFE AFTER TOPPER

JOE: Without Topper Headon we'd have died with Punk, no doubt about it. You have to have people who can adapt, and we'd say, 'Right, we're playing Armagideon Time' and he'd be able to play it. Drumming, to me, is one of the more difficult aspects of the art, the full limb co-ordination. Drummers are a race apart, they're not normal men.

TOPPER: I lost it, really, on the tour of the Far East. I was standing in a lift with Joe and he's saying, 'How can I sing all these anti-drug songs with you stoned out of your head behind me?' There was a lot of friction building up over a period of time, which culminated in me being sacked.

PAUL: Topper's habits and what he was up to made a mockery of what the group was about and what Joe was writing about – and the two didn't go together. We did what we could with Topper, but it just got too much, really.

JOE: You need to have everyone firing on all cylinders, in new directions. You can't have any passengers on board because it slows the whole thing down. You lose spirit and come to a shuddering halt.

TOPPER: When the band sacked me I promised them that I'd stop misbehaving and taking substances. They said, 'OK, we'll go and do this tour and when we come back, if you've got yourself together you can rejoin.' But while they were away Joe did an interview and blew the whole story, said that I'd been sacked, and I went further downhill from there.

JOE: If your drummer is falling apart then no matter what you're putting on

A poster given away with a UK weekly music magazine. For the first time, the publicity photos included Terry Chimes (standing, right), who had been drafted in to replace Topper on the basis that the band knew him and he knew at least some of the songs already.

The CLASH

top, it's going to fall apart, like a house without any foundations.

TOPPER: Joe went to Paris as an indirect way of getting me sacked from the band. His attitude was: I've proved you can't do it without me, and now I want Topper out of the group. I'm pretty sure that's how it worked.

JOE: That was the beginning of the end, really. Whatever a group is, it's the chemical mixture of those four people that makes a group work. You can take one away and replace him with whoever you like, or ten men: it's never gonna work. It will not work and you should be grateful if even once in your life you get into a situation where there are groups like Booker T and the MGs, the Meters, Creedence Clearwater Revival, the Doors or the Stones – or any great group. It's some weird thing that no scientist could ever quantify or measure, and thank God for that.

The view from the top of the RCA building in New York.

PAUL: I didn't know where Joe had gone, or what had happened. He did turn up on a radio station saying that I could have his Bo Diddley albums if he came back, but when he came back I didn't get the albums.

MICK: We were going to do a British tour and Bernie told Joe he should do a runner and I don't know what the reason was. Joe did do that, but then he obviously couldn't stand it and actually vanished from everyone. It was another case of Paul and I being kept in the dark and it was like that a lot of the time. We didn't know what was going on and were as concerned as everyone else.

JOE: Perhaps when you're struggling it holds you together, because you're all heading towards the same point, 'Come on boys, hang in there!' But then Rock the Casbah went Top Five and *Combat Rock* went Top Five in America, which was unheard of for us, 'cos our records usually placed around 198 or something, and suddenly it all blew up. Everybody wanted control, wanted to steer the boat, and you couldn't fit us in the control room any more, everybody had their own agenda.

MICK: Bernie never let on that it was a scam and we were going, 'Shall we hire a private detective to find him?' And after Joe eventually came back from Paris the next thing that happened was that Topper left. That was the beginning of the end, really. We shouldn't have done it, but that's how things go, sometimes.

JOE: This is a stupid thing, really. Bernie said to me as the tour was about to start, 'the tickets are not selling in Scotland.' But he didn't understand the nature of The Clash fan, who is used to doing what's called a walk-up. Bernie and any promoter should have known that Clash fans wouldn't send in for tickets three weeks ahead. They like to walk up on the night. But Bernie said, 'Look, you need to disappear or something, 'cos if we go on tour. . .' And I was too stupid to say, 'Look Bernie, shut up, there's going to be a walk-up.' In the UK we weren't as highly regarded as in other parts of the globe, so Bernie said, 'Disappear. I need an excuse to cancel the tour.' Like a fool, I said 'Alright' and he said, go to Austin, Texas, so I went to France and just dicked around for a while. I ran the Paris Marathon and stood around in bars. I should never have listened to that, but you have to have some regrets.

TOPPER: I don't hold any grudges, you know, because I was out of control. I was a liability to the band.

JOE: The last show we did with Topper was at a fantastic festival in Holland where the audience beat up the bouncers and invaded the stage. They sat all around the stage and let us finish our set, which was great.

TOPPER: I was given an ultimatum and I couldn't live up to it.

JOE: It was the end of it when Topper got sacked, it was never any good after that. We messed with the original four, it was limping to its death from the minute Topper got sacked. Hopeless.

A sheet of doodles drawn by Joe while on the Casbah Club Tour.

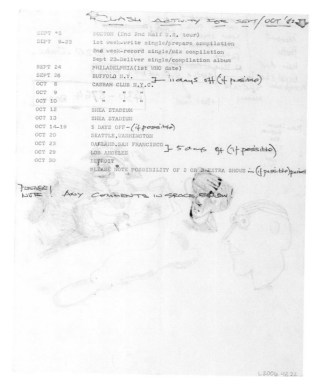

CLASH ACTIVITY FOR SEPT/OCT '82

SEPT *5   BOSTON (End 2nd Half U.S. tour)
SEPT 9-23 1st week-write single/prepare compilation
           2nd week-record single/mix compilation
           Sept 23-Deliver single/compilation album
SEPT 24   PHILADELPHIA(1st WHO date)
SEPT 26   BUFFOLO N.Y.   ] 11 days off (if possible)
OCT 8   CASBAH CLUB N.Y.C.
OCT 9   "   "   "   "
OCT 10   "   "   "   "
OCT 12   SHEA STADIUM
OCT 13   SHEA STADIUM
OCT 14-19 5 DAYS OFF - (if possible)
OCT 20   SEATTLE,WASHINGTON
OCT 23   OAKLAND,SAN FRANCISCO   ] 5 days off (if possible)
OCT 29   LOS ANGELES
OCT 30   DETROIT
           PLEASE NOTE POSSIBILITY OF 2 OR 3 EXTRA SHOWS - (if possible) period

PLEASE! NOTE! ANY COMMENTS IN SPACE BELOW!

L.2006.48.22

An original itinerary sheet for the Combat Rock Tour USA which included support to The Who at Shea Stadium in New York.

MICK: I think we started going wrong when Topper left. We lost our backbone in a way.

JOE: We called up Terry Chimes and, no disrespect to him, but it was the four people who made all those records and played all those gigs that made the group. It doesn't work if you start messing with it.

MICK: When Terry [Chimes] came back in we started doing a lot of the first album numbers again and we hadn't done them for a while, so that was weird. He stayed with us for a bit; we did the American tour with him and then went to Jamaica to play the Jamaica World Festival.

JOE: The lesson that everyone should learn is you don't mess with things if they work. If it works, do whatever you can to bring it forward but don't mess with it. We learned that bitterly.

TOPPER: The four of us gelled into something that became The Clash. Individually, none of us was as good as we had been as a four-piece band. I don't think any of us has done anything since that comes near The Clash.

JOE: We played Shea Stadium with The Who and it was fun to play Career Opportunities in a place like that, when six years earlier we'd written it in Camden Town. It's things like that, though, which make the world so interesting. Playing Shea Stadium was weird because there are some ninety thousand people in there but at least ten thousand of them are constantly on the move, getting burgers or taking a leak, so it's like you're playing to loads of people milling around. But fun, all the same.

PAUL: During the Shea Stadium gig and on the other dates of that tour, Pete Townshend would come into our dressing room and we'd have a game of football. At Shea he said come back to our dressing room, so we did and there was Daltrey and all these miserable gits sitting around who wouldn't talk to us. So Pete came back to our dressing room with us.

MICK: Playing Shea Stadium was great. Even though we were the support act, it was still exciting, and we always prided ourselves on being able to play anywhere, from the smallest to the largest place. We shot the video there (for Should I Stay or Should I Go) and there was a big thing about having a helicopter shot, but we could only have the helicopter up in the air for a certain number of minutes, so they had to get the shot in one pass.

JOE: I think it was the unexpected success of Rock the Casbah combined with the fact that we were so tired; tired of each other, tired of the road, tired of the studio. We were burned out. It just blew us apart.

TOPPER: It sounds pretty arrogant, but I think that when I was sacked, although I understood entirely why I was sacked, I don't think they were ever the same again. I could feel guilty about that because if I'd kept my act together I could still see the band being together, but I lost the plot.

A-side: Straight To Hell (Edit) (3:51)

[The Clash] Produced by The Clash, mixed by Glyn Johns

A-SIDE: SHOULD I STAY OR SHOULD I GO? (3:07)

[The Clash] Produced by The Clash, mixed by Glyn Johns

US 7" RELEASE B-SIDE: INOCULATED CITY (2:41)

[The Clash] Produced by The Clash, mixed by Glyn Johns

COOL CONFUSION (3:14)

[Strummer/Jones/Headon] Produced by The Clash

RELEASED 17 SEPTEMBER 1982
UK CHART PEAK: #17

MICK: When we appeared on *Saturday Night Live* we played Straight To Hell and Should I Stay Or Should I Go and at the end of the show I was standing next to Eddie Murphy and he goes, 'Why didn't you play Casbah?'

JOE: Just before the take, Topper said to me, 'I want you to play this' and handed me a glass lemonade bottle wrapped in a towel. He said, 'I want you to beat the front of the bass drum with it'. On the record you can hear me standing in front of this bass drum swinging this towel, with this lemonade bottle in it, whacking the front of the bass drum while the others record the backing track.

Should I Stay .... or .... Should I Go? ....

*Taken From The Epic Lp: "COMBAT ROCK" FE 37689
Produced by The Clash

SPECIAL LIMITED EDITION

★ THE ★ CLASH

THE CLASH : Straight To Hell (CBS) My feelings about the Clash change as regularly as my underpants, but my feelings about this double-'A' side are much clearer. It's fab, and although the garage-punk thrust of "Should I Stay Or Should I Go?" seems to be picking up radio play, both sides demonstrate that there's life in the old codgers yet. Even if nobody in the band can sing two notes, their anger, passion and sincerity lift them above such humble considerations.

SHOULD I STAY OR SHOULD I GO

STRAIGHT TO HELL (EDIT)

TAKEN FROM THE EPIC LP "COMBAT ROCK" FE 2/37689/EE 2

82876876282/18

Combat Rock USA Tour

LINE-UP: STRUMMER, JONES, SIMONON, CHIMES
Support acts were local bands.

9 AUG: Red Rock Amphitheater, Morrison CO
11 AUG: Civic Center, Saint Paul MN
12 AUG: Aragon Ballroom, Chicago IL
13 AUG: Aragon Ballroom, Chicago IL
14 AUG: Civic Center, Grand Rapids MI
16 AUG: Grand Theater, Detroit MI
17 AUG: Civic Theater, Akron OH
18 AUG: Stanley Theater, Pittsburgh PA
19 AUG: Carnegie Mellon University, Pittsburgh PA
20 AUG: Cape Cod Coliseum, Hyannis, support act 007
21 AUG: Cape Cod Coliseum, Hyannis, support act Gang Green
23 AUG: Cape Cod Coliseum, Hyannis, support act Jerry's Kids
26 AUG: Penn Rink, Philadelphia PA, support act Burning Spear
27 AUG: Penn Rink, Philadelphia PA, support act Burning Spear
28 AUG: Providence Civic Center, Providence RI
31 AUG: Pier 84, New York NY, support acts Gregory Isaacs, Kurtis Blow
1 SEP: Pier 84, New York NY, support acts Gregory Isaacs, Kurtis Blow
2 SEP: Pier 84, New York NY, support acts Gregory Isaacs, Kurtis Blow
4 SEP: Verdun Auditorium, Montreal, Canada, support act Black Uhuru
5 SEP: CNE Grandstand at the old Exhibition (Grounds) Stadium, Toronto, Canada, support act Black Uhuru
7 SEP: Orpheum Theater, Boston MA, support act The (English) Beat
8 SEP: Orpheum Theater, Boston MA, support act The (English) Beat
25 SEP: JFK Stadium, Philadelphia PA, supporting The Who, Santana third on bill
26 SEP: Rich Stadium, Buffalo NY, supporting The Who
30 SEP: Pontiac Silverdome, Detroit, supporting The Who
2 OCT: State University of New York (SUNY), Binghamton NY, support act Kurtis Blow

SONGS PLAYED:
London Calling / White Man In Hammersmith Palais / Know Your Rights / Spanish Bombs / The Guns Of Brixton / Somebody Got Murdered / Rock the Casbah / Ghetto Defendant / The Magnificent Seven / Wrong 'Em Boyo / Police On My Back / Charlie Don't Surf / Police & Thieves / The Leader / Brand New Cadillac / Car Jamming / Train In Vain / The Call Up / English Civil War / Garageland / Armagideon Times / Should I Stay or Should I Go? / I Fought the Law / Straight to Hell / Pressure Drop / Janie Jones / I'm So Bored With The USA / Career Opportunities / Junco Partner / Radio Clash / Clampdown / Clash City Rockers / One More Time / Safe European Home / Bankrobber / Complete Control / Stay Free / White Riot / Tommy Gun / London's Burning

L-R: Terry Chimes,
Joe, Mick and Paul
backstage at a stadium
gig on the Combat Rock
Tour USA.

3 OCT: R.P.I. Fieldhouse, Troy NY, support acts Khmer Rouge, Kurtis Blow

4 OCT: University of Vermont in Burlington, Vermont, support act Pinhead

6 OCT: SMU, North Dartmouth MA

12 OCT: Shea Stadium, New York, supporting The Who

13 OCT: Shea Stadium, New York, supporting The Who

15 OCT: William and Mary Hall, Williamsburg, Va.

16 OCT: Carnegie-Mellon University, Pittsburgh PA

17 OCT: Memorial Gym, Kent State University OH

19 OCT: Folsum Field, University of Colorado, Boulder, Colorado, supporting The Who

20 OCT: Seattle Kingdom, supporting The Who

22 OCT: Memorial Auditorium, Sacramento CA

23 OCT: Coliseum, Oakland CA supporting The Who

25 OCT: Coliseum, Oakland CA, supporting The Who

29 OCT: Coliseum, Los Angeles CA, supporting The Who

27 NOV: Bob Marley Centre Montego Bay, Kingston, Jamaica. World Music Festival with Rick James, Jimmy Buffet, The (English) Beat, Yellowman, Rita Marley and the Melody Makers

FOLLOWING PAGE: Mick
with his boombox.

1983

'There's something quite good about coming, saying your bit and then going. I quite like that.' JOE

Combat Rock had given The Clash the biggest selling album of their career, and had been a Top Ten hit around the world. In America they had played stadiums as support for The Who; they were booked to headline the US Festival in California in May 1983 (an event which had been ambitiously promoted as a 'Woodstock for the Computer Generation' by its organizer – and Apple co-founder – Steve Jobs); and the single Rock the Casbah had been a Top Ten hit. The Clash were finally on the verge of mega-rock-stardom… And yet they were in personal disarray. Topper's sacking was the beginning of their end.

US Festival Tour

A short tour to warm up before playing in front of 254,000 people at the first US Festival, organized by Apple computers and held in San Bernadino, California – Mick's last gig with The Clash. Terry Chimes was replaced by Pete Howard.

18 MAY: Civic Center Auditorium, Amarillo TX
19 MAY: Memorial Auditorium, Wichita Falls TX, support act Joe Ely
22 MAY: Majestic Theater, San Antonio TX
26 MAY: Tucson Activity Center, Tucson AZ
28 MAY: Glen Helen Regional Park, San Bernandino CA, support acts Men At Work, Flock Of Seagulls, INXS, Wall of Voodoo, Divinyls, The (English) Beat, Oingo Boingo, Stray Cats

JOE: The US Festival was 250,000 people in a dustbowl in California and I don't recall playing too well that night. There was too much going on and going off on that tour. I had stayed on the bus from Phoenix to L.A., trying to collect my thoughts about all the brouhaha going on between the band.

MICK: The US Festival was a huge gig [put on by the founders of Apple computers] which Bernie created a lot of friction about. He kept saying we had to do a press conference and we were really wound up and didn't want to do it. We were standing in front of a table with hundreds of press pushing towards us and Joe wouldn't say a word, he just turned his back. In the end Bernie was forced to answer questions while we were on stage. It was my last gig, but we were still close on stage. We didn't have any communication off-stage, though.

SONGS PLAYED:

Garageland / This is Radio Clash / Train In Vain / Rock the Casbah / White Man in Hammersmith Palais / Lost In the Supermarket / Spanish Bombs / Death Or Glory / The Guns Of Brixton / Clampdown / Know Your Rights / Somebody Got Murdered / Sound Of the Sinners / Brand New Cadillac / Police On My Back / I Fought the Law / London Calling / Straight to Hell / Should I Stay or Should I Go? / The Magnificent Seven / Police and Thieves / Hate and War / Bored with the USA / Tommy Gun / Fingernails / Armagideon Time / Koka Kola / Car Jamming / Safe European Home / Clampdown / Charlie Don't Surf

Joe stands alone in the spotlight on tour.

ABOVE: Shooting Joe's silent movie *Hell W10,* in which the band and various mates act as 1930s-style gangsters in suits, hats and shades. A gang of crooks led by Mick take protection money from the poor folk of W10 until they rise up under the guidance of Earl, played by Paul, and kick out the bad guys.

LEFT: The notebook containing Joe's original script for the film.

US

PAUL: At that point, how we appeared on stage matched how we were back-stage. Mick was all the way over there and I was over here, with Joe in the middle. Mick and I didn't talk and Joe was stuck in between. At the US gig, however, some row had broken out and some bouncer started hitting Mick and that pissed me off, so I went over and started laying into this guy's head 'cos I thought it was unfair. Mick's not Mr Muscles. And after that it was strange, but Mick and I became close again, which confused Joe.

JOE: I've heard people say that there are some nice tapes of us playing that gig, and we were OK, but I think it was an anti-climax because there were too many expectations of what it was gonna feel like to play to a quarter of a million people in one go. Perhaps whatever happened couldn't possibly match that expectation.

STAY OR GO

PAUL: Mick and I were moving further and further apart, hence the two-hour argument over Know Your Rights. We seemed to be going in different directions.

MICK: We lost communication with each other, even though we were in the same room. We were looking at the floor and that was it.

JOE: I would say that punctuality wasn't one of Mick's talents. But then talent's worth waiting for, I think, when all's said and done.

PAUL: I think we were supposed to be going on a tour, but Mick wanted a rest. I think we should have carried on touring, finished the job we'd started because we were on the verge of making a serious dent [in the charts]. But Mick wanted to go home. That probably caused a lot of frustration for Joe and me.

JOE: There was a power struggle between Bernie and Mick and I was foolish enough to let Bernie have his way. If I had any defence I'd say that Mick was intolerable to work with by this time. I mean no fun at all. He wouldn't show up and when he did it was like Elizabeth Taylor in a filthy mood. Any man would have sacked him, but I still regret that I was party to it.

MICK: I came into rehearsal just like any other day and, funnily enough, Topper had turned up to see how we were.

PAUL: We were in the rehearsal room and it was kind of 'gunfight at the OK Coral'. Joe and I had been talking and it was a matter of, 'We're grown men, I can't take anymore of this'. And we agreed that we wanted to get on with the job rather than waiting for Mick, so we asked him to leave. Joe said to him, 'We want you to leave', and Mick asked me, 'What do you say?' and I said, 'Well, yeah…' I didn't need to say any more.

MICK: I really think it was musical differences. Although there was a set-up to *cause* musical differences. Bernie's suggestion that we all try to play New Orleans music could have been setting things up so that he could say it was musical differences.

PAUL: I think Mick felt let down because I'd said to him from Day One, 'Don't worry Mick, I'll always look after you.'

MICK: These things happen, groups split up all the time. I didn't seriously think they should've carried on using the name The Clash, but that was fine. I'm surprised they put up with me for as long as they did, really.

PAUL: We'd go to the lawyer's office and it was odd, sitting in that room. One time Mick didn't turn up so Joe and I were in the strange situation of dealing with a lawyer who was representing Mick, but couldn't play guitar.

ABOVE: Paul as Earl in *Hell W10*. The film used title cards for the script and Clash songs as the soundtrack. Some of the film was used in the promo film for *Rudie Can't Fail*.

RIGHT: Mick dressed as Mr Socrates, the self-styled Landlord of Ladbroke Grove in the film.

CUT THE CRAP

JOE: Afterwards we had some fun, maybe, on a busking tour of England in the north of England, playing acoustics in the streets and bumming around. We did it to flip people's minds really. But This Is England was a nice tune, which was used by Dortmund football fans as a chant, with the words changed, obviously.

PAUL: Bernie suggested getting two guitarists for Clash Mk II, just to change the look, and 'cos it would have been too much for one person to be charged with replacing Mick. I think there are some really good songs on *Cut The Crap* and, after the experience we'd just had with Mick, I told Joe that I wouldn't get in the way. I said , 'You have control of it, mix it, everything'. But before I knew it, Bernie was all over it, it was out of Joe's hands and into Bernie's. When I finally heard it, the record bore no relation to the songs Joe had written. They were buried under a load of stuff Bernie had dug up.

TOPPER: If I could do it all again, or not do it all again, the only thing I would change is that I wouldn't take cocaine or heroin. Until I took cocaine and heroin my life was brilliant, but since then it's been hard work.

MICK: It's almost like the song 1977 in that it ends in 1984. It was always probably meant to, you know?

JOE: There's something quite good about coming, saying your bit and then going. I quite like that.

TOPPER: It was absolutely the best time of my life and I'd like to apologise for letting the side down, for going off the rails. But I think if it happened again, I'd probably do the same thing. I'm just that sort of person, you know?

PAUL: If I could do it all again I wouldn't change anything, I think it's fine as it is. We did our job, that's the story, now we're gone and that's it. Suits me fine.

MICK: The whole thing was fantastic. Who *wouldn't* write great tunes with such great lyrics and fantastic drumming – and with Paul. He was already totally there, probably from when I first met him. Bastard.

The last gang in town. . .

Index

Figures in italics indicate captions; those in bold type indicate main references to songs.

'1-2 Crush On You' 65, 72, *92*, **194**, 196

'48 Hours' 72, 94, 120, **126**, 134, 138, 268, 276

100 Club, Oxford Street, London 54, 72, *72*, *79*, 80-81, 83

101'ers *16*, *23*, *24*, 45, *54*, 56-60, 62

999 23, *62*

'1977' 6, 65, *71*, 94, **114**, **129**, 138, 146

Abba 54

ABC 204

Acklam Hall, Ladbroke Grove, London 72, *240*, 250

Action, The 32

Akrylics, The 248

Albertine, Viv 34, 87

'All The Young Punks (New Boots And Contrasts)' 178, 188

American Abstract movement 45

Amsterdam 148

Andrew C (Andrew Czezowski) 108

Anti-Nazi League 164, *164*

Apocalypse Now (film) 284

Apple computers 368, 370

'Armagideon Time' 230, **244**, 248, 268, 276, 296, 322, 328, 332, 354, 356, 364, 370

Armagideon Times, The 10, *10*, *226*, *227*, *256*

Arsenal Football Club 225, 226

Aswad 15, 218

Atlantic Road, Lewisham High Street, London *256*

'Atom Tan' 350

Australia 335, 337, 349

B Girls, The 230, 268

Baker (roadie) 51, 256

Bangs, Lester 32

'Bankrobber' 248, **254**, *256*, **256-7**, **266**, 268, 276, 296, 322, 328, 354, 364

Banks (Crocker), Robin 32, 160, 183, 184, *226*

Barcelona, Spain 296

Barnacle, Bill 50

Barnacle brothers 184

Basing Street studios, West London 183

Battle of the Midway (film) 108

Baum, Jules *226*

BBC 132, 164

    Radio One 170

'Be Bop A Lula' 230

'Be-Jing Central Committee' *92*

Beaconsfield Art School 108

Beat, The (English) 322, *322*, 354, 364, 365, 370

Beatles, the 6, 19, 42, 45, 50, *128*, 335, *336*

Beaufort Market, London 218

Bee Gees, The 15, 157

Belle Stars, The 296

Berry, Chuck 19, 23

Bessemer Grange School, London 42

Bevan, Alex 202

Birmingham 83, 164

    Barbarellas 72, 134, 138, 160

    Bingley Hall 356

    Odeon 196

    Rag Market (Punk Festival) (1977) *9*, 138

    Top Rank 172, 188, 250

Black Ark Studios, Jamaica 11

Black Market Clash 67, *100*, 105, *256*

Black Sabbath 168

Black Swan, Sheffield 72, 75

Black Uhuru 364

Blackburn

    band arrested (1978) 192

    King George's 248

Blackhill Enterprises/Management 32, 215-16, 288, 290

'Blitzkrieg Bop' 188, 196

Blockheads, the *see* Ian Dury and the Blockheads

Blondie *233*

Blossom Toes 32

Blow, Kurtis 283, 364, 365

Blue Oyster Cult 160, 181

blues 166

blues parties 41, 100, 240

Bobby Fuller Four 13, 223

Bongo Danny & The Enchanters 218

Booker T And The MGs *138*, 357

bootlegging *81*, *92*, *128*, *256*

Bordeaux, France 296

Boshier, Derek *185*

Boston MA 12

    Orpheum Theater 230, 268, 364

Boulder, Colorado: Folsom Field, University of Colorado 365

Bournemouth

    Stateside 250

    Village Bowl 94, 196

    Winter Gardens 146

Bowie, David *30*, 122, 254, 319

Boys, The 138

'Brand New Cadillac' 218, 230,

236, **239**, 248, 268, 276, 296, 322, 328, 332, 354, 364, 370

Bremen, Germany 12

Brigade Rossi 164

Brighton 199

    Brighton Centre 356

    Top Rank 198, 248

    University of Sussex 134

Brisbane: Cloudland Ballroom 332

Bristol 24

    Colston Hall 94, 134, 276

    Exhibition Centre 146

    Locarno Ballroom 188, 196, 248, 356

Brixton, London 10, 28, 31, 38, 40-41, *41*, 43

    Astoria 41

    Effra Junior and Infants school 38

    Empress Theatre 41

    Fair Deal 354, 356

Brixton Prison 167, 185

'Broadway' 322, 328, 332

Brockwell Park Funfair, Herne Hill, London 42

Bromley 48

Brussels 138

    Ancienne Belgique 196

    Forest National 296

Buffet, Jimmy 365

Burchill, Julie 113

Burgher Masters 20

Burning Spear 364

Buzzcocks, the 11, 54, 72, 134, 169

Byam Shaw School of Art, The, Notting Hill Gate, London 45

Caerphilly Cinema 94, 99

'Call Up, The' 268, **274-5**, 280, 296, 332, 364

Camberwell Art College, London 45

Camden Town, London 10, 11, 12, 184

Campbell, Mikey *see* Dread, Mikey

Capital Radio 129, 132

Capital Radio EP *92*

'Capital Radio One' *92*, **118**, **129**, 134, 138, 146, 160, 164, 188, 196, 202, 218, 230, 248, 276

'Capital Radio Two' **220**

'Car Jamming' 350, 354, 364, 370

Carbon Silicon 34

'Card Cheat, The' 236, **239**

Cardiff

    Art School 23

Sophia Gardens 250

Top Rank 94, 134, 188, 198

'Career Opportunities' 10, 34, 72, 92, 94, 112, 120, 124, 134, 138, 146, 160, 202, 230, 280, 296, 328, 332, 354, 361, 364

Cassell, 'Big John' *23*

CBS (Columbia Records) 142, 169, 170, 183

    signs The Clash 11, 108, 112-13, 122, 124, 125

    refuses to release the first album in America 178

    London Calling double album 283

    Sandinista! triple album 283, 288

Central School of Art, London 20-21, 23

Charles, Charley *343*

'Charlie Don't Surf' 268, 276, 280, **284**, 296, 322, 328, 332, 354, 364, 370

Chippenham pub, London *24*, 57

'Cheapskates' 178, 188, 196

'Cheat' 94, 120, **128**, 134, 138, 146

Chicago IL 15

    Aragon Ballroom 230, 364

Chimes, Terry

    as 'Tory Crimes' 9

    joins The Clash 10, 45, *88*, 90

    leaves The Clash 11, *90*, 96

    returns to the band 354, *357*, 361

    replaced by Pete Howard 370

City of London Freemen's School, Ashtead, Surrey 16, 18, *20*

'City Of The Dead' 138, 146, **150**, 196, 202, 218, 230, 248, 276

'Clampdown' 230, 236, **240**, 248, 268, 276, 296, 322, 328, 332, 354, 364, 370

Clapton, Eric 164

Clash, The

    the name 87

    anti-authoritarian 9

    influences 9

    uniquely political 9

    first few gigs as a trio 9

    becomes a quartet (1977) 9, 51

    early rehearsals 10-11

    Rhodes creates gigs 11

    Headon replaces Chimes 11

    live debut (1976) 54

    the look 9, 67, 71, 78, *218*, *248*, *250*, 268

first dates (July to November 1976) 72-83

first recording session 92

    bootlegged *81*, *92*, *128*

first LP *see* Clash, The

CBS signing 11, 108, 112-13

bomb threat on Europe '77 tour *138*

new musical phase 157

passionate anti-racists *164*

first visits America 183-4

band arrests 167, 184-5, 192-3, *192*

first US tour 12, 13, 200-211

    'Album of the Year' award 204

Rhodes departs 12, 171, 215, *215*, 216

Blackhill Management 215-16, 288, 290

return of Rhodes 288, 290

Bonds Casino residency, New York 302-7, 315-16, *315*, 319, 326

sacking of Topper Headon (1982) 9, 330, 354, 356-7, 360-61, 368

biggest selling album (*Combat Rock*) 368

disarray in the midst of success 368

Mick leaves 9, 373-4

last album (*Cut The Crap*) 377

Clash, The (debut album) 11, *67*, *104*, 106, *106*, **120-29**, 154, 157, 178, 202

'Clash City Rockers' 120, 138, 146, 154, **158-9**, 160, 164, 188, 196, 202, 218, 230, 248, 268, 276, 322, 328, 332, 354, 364

Clash On Broadway, The (box set) *343*

Clash On Broadway, The (film) 319

Clash Songbook

    first *112*, *129*, *144*, *188*

    second *185*

Classic cinema (now the Ritzy), Brixton, London 31

Clerc, Serge *276*

Cleveland OH 12

    Agora 202, *208*

    Rock and Roll Hall of Fame *208*

'Cloud 9' 51

Cobham, Billy 132

Coke, Janey *112*

Columbia Records *see* CBS

Combat Rock 319, *330*, *343*, 348-

53, 360, 368
'Come On' 19
'Complete Control' 11, *63*, 120, **132**, 138, 146, **150-51**, 160, 164, 172, 188, 196, 202, 218, 230, 248, 268, 276, 296, 322, 328, 332, 354, 364
Conran, Sebastian *45*
Cook, Paul *99*, 261
'Cool Confusion' **362**
'Cool Out, The' **312**
Coon, Caroline 75, *112*, 113, 185, 215
'Corner Soul' 280, 296
Cost of Living EP, The 13, **220-21**, *223*
Costello, Elvis 138
Count Bishops, The 146
Cramps, The 15, 202, 230
Cream 31
Cream magazine 32
Creedence Clearwater Revival 357
Crocker, Robin *see* Banks, Robin
'Crooked Beat, The' 280
Crosby, Bing 122
Culture Club 88
Curtis, Sonny 13
Cut the Crap 377
Czezowski, Andrew *see* Andrew C

D-Ceats 202
Dadomo, Giovanni *75, 134*
Daltrey, Roger 361
Damned, the 72, 94, 96, 120, 138, *138*
Damned Damned Damned 120
'Dancing Shoes' 126
Davies, Doreen 170
Davis Road, Shepherd's Bush 60, 61, 87, 129
Day, Roger *112*
De Niro, Robert *284*, 319
Dead Kennedys 230
'Deadly Serious' 72
Dean, James 304
'Death Is A Star' 350
'Death Or Glory' 218, 236, **240**, 370
Dekker, Desmond *43*
'Deny' 72, 120, **125**, 134, 138
Desmond's Hipcity record shop, Brixton 41
Diddley, Bo 12, 202, 204, *208*, 215, 230, 360
disco 54, 352
Dishrags, The 202
Disraeli Gears 31
Divinyls 370
DOA 230
Dogg, Tymon 23, *23*, 280, *320*
Doors, the 357
Dorsey, Lee 268
Dortmund football fans 377
Dover 48
Dr Feelgood 57, 138
Drake, Alan *33*, 34
Dread, Mikey (Mikey Campbell)

169, 248, 250, 254, *260*, 261, 265, 268, 271, 280, 292
'Drug Stabbing Time' 163, 178, 188, 196, 202, 230
dub 11, 24, 81, 166
Dury, Ian *see* Ian Dury and the Blockheads
Dylan, Bob 169, 170, 223

EAR Studios, London 350
Eddie & The Hot Rods 57, 138
Egan, Rusty 88
Electric Ballroom, London 250
Electric Ladyland Studios, New York 261, *265*, 268, 280, 343, 350, 353
Elgin Arms, Ladbroke Grove, London *23*, 57, *302*
Ely, Joe 15, 230, 250
Embassy Five 32
EMI 113
'English Civil War (Johnny Comes Marching Home)' 160, 164, 172, 178, 188, 196, 202, **212-13**, 218, 230, 248, 268, 276, 364
English National Opera 61-2
Entwistle, John *300*
Epic 202, *256*
'Equaliser, The' 280
Evans, Gil 126
'Every Little Bit Hurts' 34

fans
 allowed backstage to meet and talk 9, 99
 Japanese *336*
 Mick Jones on 96, 99
 walk-up 360
fanzines 113
Field, Al *233*
'Fingernails' 230, 248, 370
Finland 15
'First Night Back in London' **340**
First Priority 248
Flamin' Groovies 32
Flash, Grandmaster 316
Flea *65*
Flock Of Seagulls 370

Flowers of Romance *65*
Foley, Ellen *320*
Foote, Mickey 24, 114, 118, 120, 124, 125, 142, 150, 158
Ford, Tennessee Ernie 9, 19, 250, 268
Forster, Arianna (Ari-Up) *45*
'48 Hours' 72, 94, 120, **126**, 134, 138, 146, 268, 276
'Four Horsemen' 218, 236
Free 92
Fresh Air 72
Fridays (TV series) 204
Frith, Robert 230
'Fujiyama Mama' 332
Fuller, Bobby 13, 223
funk 132, 137
Futura 2000 *315*, 326

Gadd, Steve 50
Gallagher, Mickey 218, *227*, 234, 236, 261, 280
Gang Green 364
Gang War 230
Ganges, Ray 172, 174, *175*
Gangs Of New York (film) 319
garage 128
'Garageland' 120, **128-9**, 134, 138, 146, 160, 172, 188, 196, 202, 230, 248, 268, 276, 332, 354, 364, 370
'Gates of the West' **220**, **223**
Generation X 34, *90*, 108
Gerry (security) 315-16
'Ghetto Defendant' 322, 328, 350, 353, **353**, 354, 364
Gibbs, Joe *114*
Ginsberg, Allan 350, 353
Give 'Em Enough Rope (second album) 10, 12, 160, *160*, 162, 163, **178-87**, 200, 202, 223
Gladiators, The *58*
Glasgow
 Apollo 94, 146, 172, 188, 193, 248, 328
 band arrested (1978) 192, 193
 University of Strathclyde 198
GLC (Greater London Council) 196
'Gloria' 57
Goddard, Vic 296
Goldman, Vivien 108
Goodman, Dave 81
Gothenburg, Sweden: The Scandinavium 276, 296, *296*
'Graffiti Rap' 322, 328
Graham Parker & The Rumours 218
Grammy Award 10
Granada TV 146
Grand Funk Railroad 75
Grant, Eddy 292
Great Rock N Roll Swindle, The ('mockumentary') 63
Green, Jerry 236, 280, *320*
Green, Johnny *181*, 216
'Green Onions' 284
'Groovy Times' **220**, **223**
Grosvenor Square demonstration, London (1968) 20, *21*
Grundy, Bill *96*
'Guns Of Brixton' 230, 236, **239**, 248, 268, 276, 296, *300*, 322, 328, 332, 354, 364, 370
'Guns On The Roof' 160, 164, 178, 188, 196, 202
Guthrie, Woody 23

Hamburg 138
 Markthalle 276
 Musikhalle 296
Hammersmith, London
 Art School 10, 33, 34, 45
 Odeon 250
 Palais 276
Hancock, Herbie 50
Harder They Come, The (film) 68

Harlesden
 Coliseum *45*, 72, *90*, 108
 Roxy Theatre 94, 106, 168, 171, 196
Harper, Rob 96
Harry, Debbie *233*
'Hate and War' 94, 120, **125**, 134, 138, 146, 202, 218, 276, 370
'Hateful' 218, 236
Hawkins, Screamin' Jay 15
Hazan, Jack 172
Headon, Nicky 'Topper'
 background 48
 education 48, 50
 in Dover 48, 50, 51
 addiction to playing drums 50
 gigs as a teenager 50
 in London SS 51, *88*
 joins The Clash 11, 92, 132
 Joe on 137
 Guns On The Roof Episode 184-5
 fined 193
 and drugs 268, 337, 356, 377
 misbehaviour on tour *345*
 sacked (1982) 9, 330, 354, 356-7, 360-61, 368
Heartbreakers, The 94, 96
Hell, Richard 11-12, 148, 199
Hell W10 (short movie) 9, *372, 374*
Hendrix, Jimi 20, 31
Hibbert, Frederick 212
hip-hop 280, 283, 312
hippie movement 42, 166
'Hit The Road, Jack' 248, 268, 276, 322
'Hitsville UK' 280, **292-3**
Holly, Buddy 337
Holly & The Italians 276
Hollywood CA 15
 Roxy Theater 268
Howard, Pete 370
Humphries, Simon 124
Hunter, Ian *30, 320*
Hyde Park, London 20, 32
Hynde, Chrissie 34, 125

'I Can't Stand The Flies' 63, 65, 72
'I Don't Wanna be the Prisoner' 12
'I Fought the Law' 13, 120, 172, 196, 218, **220**, **223**, 230, 248, 268, 276, 296, 322, 328, 332, 354, 364, 370
'I Know What To Think Of You' 72
'I Never Did It' 72
'I Wanna Be Straight' 234
I Wanna Hold Your Hand 19
Ian Dury and the Blockheads 15, *227*, 234, 250, *250*, 261, *343*
'If Music Could Talk' 280
'If The Kids Are United' 157
Iggy Pop and the Stooges 122
IGs 51
'I'm Not Down' 218, 236
'I'm So Bored With You (+ USA)' 10, 62-3, 72, 94, 120, 134, 138, 146, 160, 172, 188, 202, 230,

268, 276, 332, 354, 364, 370
Imperial War Museum, London 183, *199*
Ingham, John 75, 113
'Inoculated City' 322, 328, 350, **362**
Institute of Contemporary Arts, London 71, 72, 83, *83, 90*
INXS 370
IRA (Irish Republican Army) 34, 81, 185
Irish Horns, The 236
Isaac Newton Boys School, London 43
Isaacs, Gregory 364
'Israelites, The' *43*
'Ivan Meets GI Joe' 280, 296, 322, 328, 332

Jagger, Mick *19, 21*
'Jail Guitar Doors' 120, 138, 146, 154, **158**, 160, 164, 188, 196, 202, 218, 230, 276
Jam, The *24*, 72, 134, 138, 181
Jamaica 162-3
Jamaica World Festival 361
James, Rick 365
James, Tony 34, 57, 92
'Janie Jones' 72, 92, 94, 120, 134, 138, 146, 160, 172, 188, 196, 202, 218, 230, 248, 268, 276, 296, 322, 328, 332, *343*, 354, 364
Japan 330, *335, 336*, 337
Jerry's Kids 364
'Jimmy Jazz' 218, 230, 236, 248, 268, 276, 322, 332, 354
Jobs, Steve 368
Joe Ely & The Skunks 230
Johanssen, David 15, 230, *233*
Johns, Glyn 340, 349, 350, 362
Johnson, Wilko 234
Jones, Allan 57
Jones, Janie 65, *343*
Jones, Mick
 early life 28, 30-31
 on his mother 28, 30
 Jewish background 30-31
 education 10, 31, 32-3, 34, 45
 roadies for a school band 31
 learns the guitar 32
 meets Keith and Bernie 34
 meets Paul 45, 51
 in London SS 51
 and Paul's bass playing 57, 61
 concerned with how a thing looked 67
 on the fans 96, 99
 joins The Clash 10
 as an arranger 126, 128, 283
 personality 144
 arrested 192, *192*
 co-produces Ellen Foley *320*
 leaves The Clash 9, 373-4
Jones, Steve 59, 66-7, 99, *99*, 188, 199, 261
Josef K 248

journalists 75, *80*, *134*, *181*, *184*
'Julie's Been Working For the Drug
    Squad' 178, **184**, 196, 202, 230,
    248, 268, 328
'Junco Partner' 271, 280, 296, 322,
    328, 332, 364
'Junkie Slip' 280
'Justice Tonight' **244**

Kampuchea benefits 250
'Keys To Your Heart' 63, 248
Khmer Rouge 365
'Kick It Over' **244**
Kilburn and the High Roads 57
King Of Comedy (film) *284*, 319
Kings Road, London 84, *85*
Kingston, Jamaica 11, 163, 265
        Channel 1 Studios 268, 280
        Studio One 265, 271
        Trenchtown 271
'Kingston Advice' 271, 280
Kinks, the 19, 20, 63, 65, 92, 129
'Know Your Rights' 319, 322, 328,
    332, **340-41**, 349, 350, 354,
    364, 370, 373
'Koka Kola' 230, 236, 248, 268,
    276, 322, 328, 332, 370
Kramer, Wayne 230
Krupa, Gene 50
Kursal Flyers & Crazy Cavan 72, 81
Kurtis Blow's Sugar Hill Gang 283

LA Boys, The 230
LaBritain, Pablo *20*, 23, *62*, 88
Ladbroke Girls School, London 43
Lansdowne, Johnny *20*
Larry McIntyre Fund Benefit 202
'Last Gang In Town' 157, 160, 164,
    178
'Leader, The' 280, 296, 322, 328,
    332, 364
Led Zeppelin *182*, 225

Legs & Co 256
Let It Rock, King's Road, Chelsea
    (later Sex, then Seditionaries) 34
'Let's Go Crazy' 280, 296
Letts, Don 10, *100*, 105, 108, 250,
    256, 319
Levene, Keith
        meets Mick 34
        meets Paul 45
        joins The Clash 10
        drug-taking 78
        leaves The Clash 10, *65*, 72, 81
        forms Flowers of Romance *65*
        forms Public Image Ltd *65*
        Murder Global *65*
Lewis, Jerry *284*, 319
Lewis, Jerry Lee 227
'Lightning Strikes' 280, 296, 322
Lisson Grove Labour Exchange,
    London 60
'Listen' 72, 75, *92*, **118-19**
Liverpool 32
        Erics 134, 146, 188
        Royal Court 328

Stadium 94
'Living In Fame' 280
London Calling 9, 15, 218, **224-9**,
    230, *233*, 234, *234*, **236-40**,
    246, 261, 268, 283, *300*, 328
'London Calling' 157, 218, 230,
    236, **244-5**, 246, 248, 266,
    276, 296, 322, 332, 354, 364,
    370
London SS 51, *88*
London Underground 23, 56
'London's Burning' 51, 72, 92, 94,
    120, **126**, **129**, **132**, 134, 138,
    142, 146, 160, 164, 172, 188,
    196, 202, 218, 248, 276, 296,
    328, 332, 364
'Long Shot Kick De Bucket' *43*
'Long Time Jerk' **346**
'Look Here' 280
Lorca, Federico Garcìa 240
Los Angeles CA 12, 15, 183, *343*
        Coliseum 365
        Hollywood Palladium 230,
            354
        Santa Monica Civic Center 268
'Lose this Skin' 280
'Lost in the Supermarket' 236,
    239-40, 370
Lott, Tim 168
Louis Armstrong pub, Dover 50
Lous, the 11, 146
'Love Machine' 51
Lovers of Outrage 146
'Lover's Rock' 218, 236
Lowry, Ray *234*
LWT (London Weekend Television)
    96
Lyceum Ballroom, London 172,
    198, 250, 328, *328*
Lydon, John (Johnny Rotten) 59-
    60, *65*, 67, 84, *85*, 88, 96, *99*,
    163

Macally, Rocco (Redondo) *67*,
    100, *104*, 105, 125
MacGowan, Shane *79*, 83, *83*
McKenzie, Lancelot Maxie 280
McLaren, Malcolm 34, 66-7, 79,
    81, 87, *99*, 150
McManus, Mick 41
'Magnificent Dance, The' **312-13**
'Magnificent Seven, The' 280,
    296, **310-11**, **312**, *315*, 322,
    328, 332, 354, 364, 370
Manchester
        Apollo 146, 188, 196, 250,
            328
        Belle Vue 196
        Electric Circus 94, 134
        Elizabethan Ballroom, Belle
            Vue 146
        Pluto Studio 280
        Rafters Club 188
Manchester United Football Club
    226
Marchbank, Pearce *112*
'Mark Me Absent' 65, 72

Mark P (Mark Perry) 113
Marley, Bob 126
Marley, Rita 365
Marquee Club, London 10-11
Matlock, Glen 59, *65*, 78, 88, 96,
    99
Matthew, Brian 19
MC5 33
Meatloaf *320*
Melody Maker 19, *24*, 51, 57
Melody Makers, The 365
Melvin, Frankie 353
Members, The 15, 218
Men At Work 370
'Mensforth Hill' 280
Merthyr Tydfil 24
Metal Hurlant magazine *276*
Meters, The 357
Metro club, Notting Hill, London
    104
Michon, Alex 71
'Midnight Log' 280
Mighty Diamonds, The 230
Miles *112*
Mingay, David 172, 174
Minneapolis 15
Miracles, The 51
Misty 13
Mittoo, Jackie 244
Mod culture *45*
'Modette, Mad Jane' 83, *83*, 122
Monro, Matt 125
Montego Bay, Jamaica: Bob
    Marley Centre (World Music
    Festival) 365
Monterey CA 15
        Tribal Stomp Festival 230
Moon, Keith 50, 337
Moro, Aldo 164
Morrison, Jim 24
Moss, John 88
Motown 157
Mott the Hoople *30*, 32, *92*, *320*
MPLA 216
Muldaur, Maria 230
Mungo Jerry 169
Munich, Germany 12, 138
        Circus Krone 296
        Schwabingerbrau 276
Murder Global *65*
Murphy, Eddie 362
Murray, Charles Shaar 128
Murray, Pete 19
Murvin, Junior 11, 126
Music Machine, Camden, London
    172, 188, 198, *198*, 199
'Mustapha Dance' **346**

Nashville Rooms, The, West
    Kensington, London 34, 58, 59
National Front Party 164, 166, *167*
NBC TV network *315*
Necessaries, The 230
Needs, Kris *56*, *84*
Negative Trend 202
New Romantics 88
'New Rose' 96

New York City 12, 15, 163, 183,
    184, *261*, *271*
        Bonds nightclub 302-7, *315*,
            316, 319, 326
        Iroquois Hotel 304, 352, 353
        Palladium 202, 230, *234*, 240,
            268
        Pier 84 364
        Power Station Recording
            Studios 268, 280
        RCA building *315*, *358*
        Record Plant 223
        Shea Stadium 10, 361, *361*
New York Dolls 32, 33, 51, *233*
News Of The World 310
Nice, The 32
Nicholson, J.P. 280
Night of Pure Energy gig (Institute
    of Contemporary Arts, 1976) 72,
    83, *83*, 90
Night of Treason gig (Royal
    College of Art, 1976) 72, *75*, 83
Nightout 320
999 23
'1977' *6*, 65, *71*, 94, **114**, **129**, 138
Nitzsche, Jack 284
NME (*New Musical Express*) 19,
    92, 129, *132*, 137, *137*, *166*, *167*,
    192, *207*, 216, *234*, *290*
        interview (with Tony Parsons)
        92, **118**
        unsolicited ad for a new Clash
            manager *215*
'Not Fade Away' 19, *19*
Not Sensibles, The 248
Notting Hill, London 105
Notting Hill Carnival riots (1976)
    67, 100, *100*, 104-5, *104*, 125,
    129, *256*

Oberstein, Maurice 108, *112*, 256
Oingo Boingo 370
'One More Dub' 280
'One More Time' 280, 296, 322,
    328, 332, 364
'1-2 Crush On You' 65, 72, *92*,
    194, 196
100 Club, Oxford Street, London
    54, 72, *72*, 79, 80-81, 83
101'ers *16*, 23, *24*, 45, *54*
Orsett Terrace, Bayswater 63, 126
Outlaw Joey Wales, The (film) 78,
    79
'Outside Broadcast' **326**
'Overpowered By Funk' 322, 350

Pacino, Al 284
Palmolive (Paloma Romera) 126
'Paradise By The Dashboard Light'
    320
Paris 162
        Bataclan 138
        Hippodrome de Pantin 160,
            296
        Palais De Sports 250, 276
        Le Stadium 196
        student riots (1968) 20

Théâtre Mogador 322-5
Parker, Charlie 337
Parker, Graham 218
Parsons, Tony 75, 113, 118
Pearl drums *335*
Pearl Harbour 354
Pearlman, Sandy 12, 160, *160*, 171,
    178, 181, 183, 184, 194, 212
Perry, Lee ('Scratch the Upsetter')
    11, 42, 126, 132, 163
Perry, Mark (Mark P) 113
Perth, Australia 332
'Piano Song' 172
Pinhead 365
Pink Floyd 169
Pioneers, the 24
Pitney, Gene 19
Plasmatics, The 302
Pogues, The *79*
'Poison Flour On The Hour' 65
'Police and Thieves' 11, 120, 122,
    126, **128**, *129*, 134, 138, 146,
    160, 164, 172, 176, 188, 196,
    202, 218, 230, 248, 268, 276,
    322, 328, 354, 364, 370
'Police On My Back' 280, **292**,
    332, 354, 364, 370
Pollitt, Tessa *45*
Pollock, Jackson *58*, 67, 78
Polydor Studios 92, *92*, 108, 125
Pop, Iggy 122
Pop Group, The 13
Portobello Market, London 43, 57
Portobello Road, London 65, 100,
    100, *108*, *240*
Powell, Enoch 164
Prefects, The 134
Presley, Elvis 6, 58, *122*, *200*
'Pressure Drop' *92*, 134, 138, **212**,
    354, 364
Pressure Drop 216
Pretty Things, The 32
Price, Bill 220, 225, 226, 236,
    268, 274, 280, *320*
'Prisoner, The' *92*, 138, 146, 154,
    160, **176**, 188, 230
Procol Harum 92
prog rock 54
'Protex Blue' 63, 72, 94, 120, **126**,
    134, 138, 146, 196, 248, 268,
    328
Public Image Ltd 65
Punk
        the word 57
        shedding everything known
            before 61
        clothes-making *66*
        bootlegging *81*
        and Teddy Boys 84, *85*, 157
        opposition to 87
        popularity of 96, *96*, 157
        a roots movement 113
        gains credibility 113
Punk Festival (100 Club, 1976) 72,
    72, 81, 83
Pursey, Jimmy *163*, 169

Queen 250

'Radio 5' **326**
'Radio Clash' **326**, 328, 354, 364
Radio One 170, **292**
Rainbow Theatre, Finsbury Park,
London 13, 15, 51, 134, *137*, 146,
148, 154, 157, 174, 218
Ramone, Joey 61
Ramones, The 61, *61*, 120, 126
Ranking Roger *322*
rap 283, 316
RAR *see* Rock Against Racism
rastas vs. skinheads 157
Raw Power 122
Razor, Terry *226*
Ready, Susan *112*
'Rebel Waltz' 280
Rebels, The 15
Record Mirror 168-71, 181
Record Plant, New York City 12
'Red Angel Dragnet' 350, **353**
Red Hot Chilli Peppers 65
Redondo, Rocco *see* Macally,
Rocco
reggae 11, 24, 43, *43*, 45, 61, 78,
108, 137, 166, 176, 234
Rehearsals Rehearsals, Camden
Town *34*, *62*, 65, *68*, 72, 75, 78,
83, 125, 126, 137, 167, 216
'Remote Control' 120, 134, 138,
142-3, 146, 218
Rentals, The 202
'Revolution Rock' 236, 248, 276
Rhodes, Bernie *87*, 162, 181
meets Mick 34
meets Paul 45, 51
helps The Sex Pistols 45
poaching of Joe from the
101'ers 60, 61
creates The Clash gigs 11, 75,
168, 171
painting of Rehearsals
Rehearsals 78
and McLaren 79, 87
reluctant to be photographed
80
as mentor 88
and Rocco's photographs 105,
125
and CBS signing 108, 112, 113
first Clash album cover 125
'Complete Control' 132, 150
White Riot tour *137*
Paul's mural 167
strained relationship with the
band 168-71
selection of Pearlman 183
Guns On the Roof incident
167, 185
departure of 12, 171, 215, *215*,
216
returns to the band 288, 290
New Orleans music
suggestion 348, 374
making of *Combat Rock* 348,
350

and the fans 360
US Festival Tour 370
and Mick Jones 373
and Clash Mk II 377
Rich, Buddy 50, 132
Rich Kids 88
Richard Hell and the Voidoids 146,
148
'Right Profile, The' 236
Rip-Off Park Allstars 23-4
Riva Music Ltd *185*
Roadent (Clash roadie) 11, *45*, 122
Robinson, Tom 164, 169
Rock Against Racism (RAR) 13,
164-7, 168, 212
'Rock the Casbah' **346-7**, *348*,
350, **352**, 354, 360, 361, 365,
368, 370
Rock Scene magazine 32
Rockabilly Rebels, The 230
'Rockers Galore' 254, **266**, 276
Rockets, The 72
Rocksteady 41
Rod Stewart and the Faces 32
Rolling Stone magazine 204, 236
Rolling Stones, the 6, 19, *19*, 20,
32, 265, 343, 357
Rome, Italy 42
Romera, Paloma *see* Palmolive
Ronson, Mick *30*, *320*
Root Radics 265
Rotten, Johnny *see* Lydon, John
Roundhouse, Camden Town,
London *54*, *61*, 72, 81, *106*
Roxy club, The, Covent Garden,
London 108, 137
Royal College of Art, London 72,
75, 83
Rude Boy (film) 172-5, 240
Rude Boys *43*, *45*
'Rudie Can't Fail' 218, 236, **240**,
248, 268, *374*
Runaways, the 81

'Safe European Home' 163, 172,
178, 188, 196, 202, 218, 230,
248, 268, 276, 296, 322, 328,
332, 354, 364, 370
Sam & Dave 15, 230
San Francisco CA 12
The Automat 12, 178, 183, 223
Civic Auditorium 354
Geary Temple (Fillmore) 202
Kezar Pavilion 230
The Fox, Warfield 268
Sandinista! 260-61, 265, *265*,
268, **280-84**, 288, *290*, 349
Santana 364
Saturday Night Live (TV
programme) 204, 362
Scorsese, Martin *284*, 319
Scott, Style 265
Screen On The Green, Islington 72,
78-80, 128
'Sean Flynn' 350, 352
Sex Pistols, The *59*, *65*, 72, 79, 87,
157, 199, 261
Slaughter And The Dogs 108

band forms 34
and Bernie Rhodes 45, 88
at the 100 Club 54, 80, 81
at the Elgin 57
Joe on 58
Paul on John 59-60
Sid replaces Glen *65*
the look 66-7
and The Clash's debut 75
relations with The Clash 87
Anarchy in The UK tour 94, 96,
168
swears on live tea-time
television 96, *96*, 174
only album 120
signed to EMI 113
Sha-Na-Na 24
Shadows, the 20
Sham 69 146, 157, *163*, 169
Sheffield 54, 72
City Hall 94
Lyceum 328
Top Rank 146, 188, 196, 248
Shepherds Bush Green, London 10
'Shepherd's Delight' 280
Sherwood, Adrian *65*
Short Back 'N' Sides 320
'Should I Stay Or Should I Go?'
322, 328, 332, 350, **353**, 354,
361, **362**, 364, 370
Sid Vicious Defence Fund benefit
(Music Machine, Camden, 1978)
198, *198*, 199
Siena, Italy 41
Sigue Sigue Sputnik 34
'Silicone On Sapphire' 280, 283
Silverton, Peter *122*, *181*, *183*
Simon, Kate *106*
Simonon, Nick 38, 40
Simonon, Paul
early life in Brixton 10, 38, 40-
41
education 10, 38, 42, 43, 45
moves in with his father 42-3
meets Bernie and Mick 45, 51
joins The Clash 10, 51
as a bass player 57, 61, *99*,
188
choice of band name 87
on Bernie 88
style and design director 9,
125
personality *144*
Glasgow incident 148, 193
Guns On The Roof episode
167, 184-5
destroys his bass *233*, 240
ill in Thailand 337, 343
on Topper's departure 356
Siouxsie and the Banshees 72, *72*,
81, 146
'Sitting At My Party' 72
'Sixteen Tons' 9, 19, 268
Ska 40
skinheads *43*, *45*, 71, 193
vs. rastas 157

Slits, the 11, 34, *45*, *90*, 126, *132*,
134, 137, 192, 196
Smash Hits (Hendrix) 31
Smith, Patti 81, 83
Smith, Pennie 216, *226*, 230, *233*,
240, *283*, *290*, *330*, *339*, *352*
Sniffin' Glue fanzine 113, 157
Soft Machine 32
'Somebody Got Murdered' 268,
276, 280, **284**, 296, 322, 328,
332, 354, 364, 370
'Something About England' 280
Song Remains the Same, The
(film) *182*, 225
soul 137
'Sound Of The Sinners' 280, **284**,
370
Sounds magazine 75, 106, 108,
108, 120, *122*, *134*, *171*, *181*,
182
Southall anti-fascist demos 13
Southall Defence Fund benefit
(Rainbow theatre, 1979) 218
Southern Death Cult 354
'Spanish Bombs' 230, 236, **240**,
248, 268, 276, 296, 322, 328,
354, 364, 370
Specials, the 12
Spector, Phil 239
S.P.G. (Special Patrol Group) 13
Spirit of St Louis 320
Spizz 77 188
Spungeon, Nancy *198*, 199
Stasiak, Corky 178
'State of Emergency' *114*
Staton, Candi 157
'Stay Free' 178, **184**, 188, 196,
202, 218, 230, 248, 268, 276,
328, 332, 364
Steel Pulse 12
Stevens, Guy 15, 92, 125, 132,
224-7, *225*, 234, 236, 239,
240, 266
Stevens, Shakin' 72, 87
Stevenson, Ray *96*
Stewart, Rod 32, 96
Stiff label 120
Stimulin 328
Stinky Toys 72, 81
Stooges, The 32, 33
'Stop The World' 268, **274**, **284**
'Straight To Hell' 349, 350, **353**,
354, **362-3**, 364, 370
Strange, Steve 99
Stranglers, The 83, *138*, 181
Strate Jacket 250
Stray Cats 370
'Street Fighting Man' 20, *21*
'Street Parade, The' 280, 296,
322, 328
Street Porter, Janet 96
Strummer, Joe (John Graham
Mellor)
background 16, 19
born in Ankara 16
education 16, 18, 19-21, *20*,
23

relationship with his father 18
on his parents 18-19
drug-taking 21, 78, 129
first musical instrument
(ukulele) 23, *343*
busking 23, 56
known as 'Woody' 23
in the Vultures at Newport 23-
4
forms a London bar band 10
in the 101'ers 56-7
joins The Clash 10, 45, 54, 60
personality *144*
fined 148, 192-3
Guns On the Roof incident
184, 185
arrested in Hamburg 276
and Topper's sacking 357, 360
Subway Sect 11, 72, 81, *90*, *132*,
134, 137, 192, 296
Suicide 12, 148, 188, 193, 199
Sunday Times, The 11
Sutcliffe, Stuart 45
Sweden 12, 138, *138*
'Sweet Gene Vincent' 250
'Sweet Little Sixteen' 23

Taj Mahal 50, 239
Tavares 157
Teagle, Clive 42
Teddy Boys 84, *85*, 87, 157
Temple, Julien 63, 108
Temptations, The 51
Texas 15, 28
Thailand *330*, 337, *339*, 343, *352*
Thank Your Lucky Stars (TV show)
19
Theatre of Hate 328
'This Is England' 377
'This Is Radio Clash' 296, *315*, 322,
326-7, 332, 370
This Is Radio Clash (video) 319
Thunders, Johnny (John Anthony
Genzale, Jr) 33, 230
Tighten Up albums 42
'Time Is Tight' 138, *138*
Time Out magazine 57
Toilets, The 146
Tokyo, Japan *336*
Kosein-Kaiken Hall 332
Shibuya Kohkaido 332
Sun Plaza Hall 332
Tom Robinson Band 164
'Tommy Gun' 12, 146, 157, 160,
163, 164, 172, 178, 188, **194-5**,
196, 202, 218, 230, 248, 268,
276, 332, 364, 370
Tooting, London 50
Toots And the Maytals *250*
Top of the Pops 11, 234, 256
Topper (comic book) 132
Toronto, Canada 12, 15
CNE Grandstand at the old
Exhibition (Grounds)
Stadium 364
Heatwave Festival, Mosport
Park 276

O'Keefe Center 230
Rex Danforth Theater 202
Tosh, Peter 230
tours
    Anarchy in the UK (1976) 11,
        90, 94, *94*, 96, 99, *99*, 106,
        120, 137, 150, 168
    Casbah Club USA + UK (1982)
        354-61
    Combat Rock (1982) *361*,
        364-5
    Europe '77 138, *138*
    Far East (1982) 330-39, 349
    Get Out Of Control (1977) 146-
        9, 154
    Impossible Mission (1981)
        296-301
    London Calling (1979) *10*, 216,
        218, *218*
    Out on Parole (1978) 12, 168,
        188-93
    Pearl Harbour (1979) 12, 200-
        211, 215, *215*
    Radio Clash (1981) *12*, 328-9
    Sixteen Tons (1980) 9, 248-51,
        256, *260*, 268-73, 276-7,
        302

Sort It Out (1978) 12, 196-9
Take The Fifth (1979) 15, 218,
    230-33, *234*, *242*
US Festival (1983) 368, 370-73
White Riot (1977) 11, 132-7, 142
Townshend, Pete 13, 38, 81, 199,
    300, 361
'Train In Vain' 236, 248, **266-7**,
    268, 276, 296, 322, 328, 332,
    354, 364, 370
Travers, Pat 51
Two Sevens Clash 216

Uncut magazine 57
Under Two Flags 354
Undertones, The 230
Unidos, Pepe 310, 312
United States
    The Clash first visits (1978)
        183-4
    first Clash tour 12, 13, 200-211,
        215, *215*
    The Clash's Bonds residency,
        New York 302-7
    tours of 1982 330
University of London 72, 87
'Up In Heaven' 280

US Billboard chart Top Ten *43*
US Festival, California 10, 368

Van Eyck, Tess *112*
Vancouver 12, 15, 200, 204
    Commodore Ballroom 202
    Kerrisdale Arena 354
    Pacific National Exhibition 230
Vanilla studios, Pimlico 216, 218,
    225, 227, 234, 239, *239*
Vega, Alan 193
'Version City' 280
'Version Pardner' 280
Vicious, Sid (John Simon Ritchie)
    58-9, 63, *65*, *72*, 83, 87, 104,
    126, *198*, 199
Victoria Park, Hackney *164*, 168,
    172, 174
Vienna, Austria
    Oberlaa 276
    Porrhaus 138
Vietnam War 20, *21*
Vincent, Gene 34
Vinyl, Kosmo *335*
Violation 248
Visage 88
Voidoids 11-12

Vultures, the 23, 24

Wah! 322
Wall of Voodoo 3790
Warhead 138
Warhol, Andy 319
'Washington Bullets' 280, 296,
    322, 328, 332
Watt-Roy, Norman 261
Watts, Billy *33*, 60
WBLS (radio station) 283, 310
Wessex Studios, London 225,
    234, 236, 268, 280
Westway To The World
    (documentary) 10
Westwood, Vivienne 34, 67
'What's My Name' 72, 120, **125**,
    134, 138, 146, 160, 172, 188,
    196, 202, 218, 230, 276
'[White Man] in Hammersmith
    Palais' 12, 120, 138, 146, 154,
    160, 164, 172, **175**, **176-7**, 188,
    196, 202, 218, 230, 248, 268,
    276, 296, 322, 328, 332, 364,
    370
'White Riot' 72, 92, 94, 105, 114,
    114-15, 120, 132, 134, 138, 146,

160, *163*, 164, 172, 188, 196,
    202, 218, 230, 248, 276, 296,
    322, 328, 332, 364
Whitfield Studios, London 120,
    122
Who, The 50, 250, 361, *361*, 364,
    365, 368
Who Sell Out, The 65
William Penn Boys School,
    Southwark, London 42, 43
Williams, Keith 244
Wings 250
World's End housing estate,
    London 284
'Wrong 'Em Boyo' 230, 236, 248,
    268, 296, 354, 364

Yardbirds, the 19, 20
Yellowman 365
Yes 32
Yewdall, Julian *16*

Zeros, The 202
Zigzag magazine 56, *84*, 227
Zukie, Tapper (David Sinclair) 216

Photography credits

The Editors would like to thank Jules Baume of Vegas Design, Peter Silverton, Barry Miles and www.blackmarketclash.com for all their help in putting the book together